Strategy a...

Strategy and leadership are topics of perennial interest to researchers and
practitioners alike. Yet the literature stops short from fully understanding both
concepts and their interrelationship. Current academic literature tends to
treat them as synonymous, and to take an over-voluntarist view of how
strategy is formed, an over-heroic view of how organisations are led.

Treating the concepts of strategy and leadership as separate yet inter-
related, this book departs from the mainstream strategy and leadership
literature in two significant ways. It treats the leader as only one of three main
strategy-making variables. History and context are the other two. At the
heart of this empirical study is the examination of how leadership, context
and history interact over time.

The thirteen leaders featured in the study are viewed as 'tenants of time
and context' and their leadership is analysed in terms of the historic
challenges that faced them during their tenure at the top. This view of
leadership deflects attention away from the pre-occupation with personal
attributes and individual personae, to focus instead on the processes by
which strategy is formed and organisational destinies shaped.

The case-based, multi-level perspective offered by the authors will be
welcomed by strategists, students and researchers alike, both for the realism
of the cases and the fresh insights of the analysis. The conclusions from
their studies are important and controversial, encouraging further investigation of the subject. Understanding how strategic issues and individual
biographies overlap provides us with a better insight into what makes strategies
and leadership work.

Brian Leavy is Senior Lecturer in Strategic Management at Dublin City
University and **David Wilson** is Senior Lecturer in Organisational
Behaviour and Director, MBA Programme, at the University of Warwick.

Strategy and leadership

Brian Leavy and David Wilson

London and New York

First published 1994
by Routledge
11 New Fetter Lane, London EC4P 4EE

Simultaneously published in the USA and Canada
by Routledge
29 West 35th Street, New York, NY 10001
© 1994 Brian Leavy and David Wilson

Typeset in Times by LaserScript Limited, Mitcham, Surrey

Printed and bound in Great Britain by
Mackays of Chatham PLC, Chatham, Kent

British Library Cataloguing in Publication Data

A catalogue record for this book is available from the British Library.

Library of Congress Cataloging in Publication Data
Leavy, Brian, 1950–
    Strategy and leadership / Brian Leavy and David Wilson.
        p.   cm.
    Simultaneously published in the USA and Canada.
    ISBN 0–415–07091–0   ISBN 0–415–07092–9 (pbk)
1. Leadership. 2. Leadership–Case studies. 3. Strategic planning. 4. Executives. 5.
Organizational behavior. I. Wilson, David C. (David Charles), 1951–   .
II. Title.
HD57.7.L438   1993
658.4′092–dc20

                                                                93–23853
                                                                    CIP

Contents

Figures

Tables

Foreword

This book is an empirical study of strategy and leadership, as the central characterisation of leaders as tenants of time and context suggests. While aimed primarily at mainstream strategic management researchers, students and executives, the book, with its long historical view and its multi-level perspective on the leadership-context-strategy interaction, should also be of interest to business historians and biographers, organizational analysts, sociologists, industrial economists and to a wider spectrum of business students and executives alike.

We are indebted to many individuals and institutions in the production of this book. The Centre for Corporate Strategy and Change at the University of Warwick, under the direction of Andrew Pettigrew, provided a valuable intellectual home for this study particularly during the early stages of the research (indeed, the two authors met each other for the first time in Andrew's office, back in January 1986). We are indebted also to Dublin City University Research Committee and the British Council for the provision of financial support and to our own business school colleagues at DCU and Warwick for their general encouragement. Bill Murray of Dublin City University and Enda Hession of University College Dublin deserve special mention, particularly for their encouragement at the incubation stage of the research. So too does Yvon Dufour from the Ecole des Hautes Etudes Commerciales de Montreal, who was a visiting fellow at Warwick while this research was in progress, and a constant friend and supporter throughout the entire process. Enid Mumford, emeritus of the Manchester Business School, Richard Whipp of Cardiff Business School and Bala Chakravarthy of Minnesota and INSEAD, all encouraged us to see this research through to book form.

Crucial to the success of the whole project was the cooperation that we received from the four organizations featured in the study and the quality of access that they afforded to us. We would like to thank all of the personnel from these organizations who gave generously of their time during the interview stage of the project. Special acknowledgement is due to Val Reilly (AFT), Noel Maher (IDG), the late Michael Foy (CSET) and Sean Curtin (Golden Vale) in this regard. Greg Tierney of the Irish Cooperative Organization Society also deserves special mention. We are particularly indebted to the four executives who played the crucial liaison roles between us and the organizations concerned which greatly helped in the data collection phase of the project. The four were Michael Carroll (AFT), David Dillon (IDG), Marius Martin (CSET) and Gerry Curley (Golden Vale).

We have also been greatly encouraged and supported in the production of this book by our publishers. Rosemary Nixon, Rory Smith and all of the Routledge staff involved in the project with us have been a pleasure to work with, and gracious and efficient at every turn.

Finally we would like to acknowledge the support and encouragement of Ailish, Emer, Eoin, Jo, Alex and Amy. These are the special people who have lived through the project most closely with us and who always seemed to know best when to ask (and particularly when not to ask) how the book was coming along. It is to them, to our parents and to the rest of the Leavy and Wilson clans that we dedicate this book.

1 Strategy and leadership

Strategy and leadership are topics of perennial interest to researchers and practitioners alike. The importance of both to the management of society's major institutions, in the private and public sectors, is widely recognised. This was reflected in an extensive mid-1980s Conference Board survey of chief executives in which they identified the development of strategic leadership in their senior managers as their biggest management development challenge (Shaeffer 1984). It was also reflected in the more recent publication by two major research journals, the *Strategic Management Journal* (Hambrick 1989) and *Organization Studies* (Schneider 1991), of special issues devoted to the strategic leadership and organisational leadership areas.

Yet in spite of this intense interest we still seem to be a long way from fully understanding these two concepts and how they are inter-related. The essence of leadership remains as elusive as ever, as the 'vision thing' now seems to be giving way to the 'values thing' (Kanter 1990:4). The withering comment of Bennis and Nanus (1985: 4) on the state of leadership research, that 'never have so many laboured so long to say so little', remains a very sobering thought for anyone setting out to contribute to this field. In the strategy area, while Ansoff (1987: 13) optimistically declared that 'enormous progress in the theory and practical technology of strategic management' had been made since the field emerged in its own right in the early 1960s, Pennings (1985: xi), in a state of the art conference-based review, still found a field that was 'fairly dis-jointed' with 'no well-specified models', 'pertinent contributions' showing 'little cumulative character', and an 'integral theoretical and empirical literature' which was 'not well developed'. The lack of integration in both the strategy and leadership fields is a reflection, in no small way, of the very utility of both concepts and their openness to multiple interpretations as well as uses. Is leadership an attribute, a style, a capacity for visionary thinking or some slivers of all of these things (Bennis and Nanus 1985)? Is strategy a plan for the future or a pattern from the past or both (Mintzberg 1987)? Is leadership a science or a performing art (Zaleznik 1992; Vaill 1989)? Is strategy an intellectual product or a craft process (Mintzberg 1987; Mintzberg 1990; Ansoff 1991)?

OUR POINTS OF DEPARTURE

In entering into the breach, as it were, our book has a number of points of departure which will define its approach and uniqueness in the empirical literature on strategy and leadership. Firstly it treats the concepts of strategy and leadership as distinct but inter-related. This contrasts with the tendency in much of the literature to treat the two as synonymous and to see the one as the supreme exercise and expression of the other. This tendency owes much to a decision by the Harvard Business Policy group over two decades ago to use the concept of strategy as a unifying framework for the development of a 'simple practitioner's theory' (Bower *et al.* 1991: ix) of general management and the subsequent influence that this has had on the business and academic community as a whole. The Harvard model popularised the notion of strategy as a two-stage process of formulation and implementation, the first a cognitive and analytical stage and the second an administrative one. At the heart of both stages is the leader as the 'architect of organization purpose' (Bower *et al.* 1991: 22) and the personification of strategy. We have taken our first point of departure through Mintzberg's (1978, 1987) insightful distinction between strategy formulation and strategy formation. For us the leader is just one important element in our model of strategy formation. History and context are the other two. At the heart of our empirical study is the examination of how leadership, context and history interact in the formation of an organisation's strategy and how this changes over time.

Arising directly out of this choice of strategy formation, rather than formulation, as the process of interest, our second point of departure from the mainstream strategy and leadership literature is the emphasis that we give to context in the shaping of strategy. We agree with Hambrick (1989) that over the last two decades the art of leadership seems to have been misplaced from its pivotal position in the Harvard Model in favour of the technology of strategy (product life-cycles, experience curves, growth-share matrices and the like) in much of the subsequent mainstream research and that it should be returned to a more central position. However we also feel that the strategy field has suffered in the past from an over-voluntarist perspective that under-plays the role of context and history in the shaping of strategy. This is an issue that went right to the heart of the conflict between the two doyens of the strategy field, Igor Ansoff (1991) and Henry

Mintzberg (1990, 1991), which led to their recent exchange of academic 'valentines' in the *Strategic Management Journal*.

By focusing our empirical inquiry on the interaction of leaders, context and history in the formation of strategy we are able to contribute a more thorough empirical examination of the contextual forces that shape strategy than is to be found in much of strategy research to date. We are also able to provide a fresh perspective on the role of leadership in strategy formation. In contrast to Bennis (1989), the widely acclaimed leadership guru, we have not focused exclusively on leadership and chosen only outstanding successes in our sample. We have come to view the leaders in our study as 'tenants of time and context', a metaphor that we have adapted from Thomas Flanagan (1988), the historical novelist. In all thirteen different leaders are featured in this book. In our examination of leadership and its interaction with context and history in strategy formation we will indeed meet with some heroic successes. We will also meet with some heroic failures and unheroic successes. By taking the long historical view we will see strategic issues transcend leadership tenures and leadership tenures transcend strategic issues. We will see the same leader succeed in one context and fail in another. This tenure-spanning view of leadership is one that is not often to be found in the strategy literature; the recent article by Hambrick and Fukutomi (1991) comes closest to our perspective. We will gain further insight into the wellsprings of visionary leadership but also catch some glimpses of its darker side (Leavy 1992). This darker side is very rarely explored in the leadership and strategy literature, the recent article by Osborne (1991) being a notable exception.

Our third point of departure concerns the inter-relationship between content and process in the study of leadership and strategy. In each of these fields the dominant tendency to date has been to study either the what or the how of leadership or strategy in any given study rather than both at the same time. Indeed the main division of labour that has arisen in the strategy field, largely influenced by the pre-dominance of the Harvard two-stage formulation (content) and implementation (process) model, has been between content and process research. The recent publication by the Strategic Management Journal (Montgomery 1988; Chakravarthy and Doz 1992) of two separate special issues dedicated to content and process research underlines the point. The same tendency is evident in the leadership literature where Bennis (1989: 1), in describing the difference between his two major books in the 1980s, explained that whereas his first book (Bennis and Nanus 1985) had 'covered the whats' of leadership his later book was intended to cover 'the hows'. Powerful and productive as the division of content and process has been, and can be, we take this third point of departure through the work of Pettigrew (1985, 1990) who has been foremost in encouraging research that explores how process and content are related in strategy and leadership and how they both inter-link with context.

BACKGROUND TO THE STUDY AND THE ORGANISATIONS

This is not a how-to book on leadership and strategy. It is a research-based book that yields its insights primarily through empirical description and explanatory analysis. It is an intensive case-based comparative study that empirically examines the interaction of leadership, history and context in the formation of strategy over all or a substantial portion of the life histories of four organisations. The empirical analysis is based on data collected from almost 150 hours of personal interviewing with over 40 executives, and from the examination of more than 300 separate pieces of archival material including annual reports, contemporary articles and press clippings, published histories, and internal organisational documents and memoranda. The overall approach is direct, historical and largely inductive in the style of Bower (1970) and Mintzberg (1978, 1979), and contextual in the style of Pettigrew (1979, 1990). The central empirical questions that drive the inquiry are how leadership and context influence strategy formation and how the locus of this influence varies between them over time. The leaders and their organisations are Irish but the themes developed in the study are universal.

The four organisations chosen for the study represent the main types to be found in Ireland's mixed economy: a state agency, a public limited company, a state-owned enterprise and a producer cooperative. The case narratives cover all or a substantial portion of the history of each of these organisations and their industries up to the late 1980s. An Foras Taluntais (AFT), the Agricultural Institute, was a public sector agency founded in 1958 to be the national research and development support to Irish agriculture. In 1988 it was merged with the advisory service to form a new entity: Teagasc. Our study covers the entire thirty-year period of AFT's history as an independent entity. Irish Distillers Group (IDG) was a public limited company formed by the merger of three of Ireland's four main distilling companies in 1966. The fourth was merged with the group during the 1970s. In 1988 the company was the target of a takeover battle and became a wholly-owned part of its 'white knight', the French drinks giant Pernod Ricard. The case narrative on Irish Distillers traces the evolution of the Irish distilling industry from the late eighteenth century but concentrates mainly on the period from the 1966 merger to the 1988 takeover. Our third case features the state-owned enterprise Comhlucht Siuicre Eireann Teoranta (CSET), the Irish Sugar Company. CSET was founded in 1934 as a state monopoly and one of the first major state-owned enterprises in the history of Ireland since independence in 1921. The case narrative covers the entire history of the company from its foundation to its eventual privatisation, as Greencore Plc, in 1990. Our final case involves one of the leading producer cooperatives in the important dairy sector of the Irish economy, Golden Vale Cooperative Society. The case narrative traces the evolution of the dairy industry from the late nineteenth century, when it made the transition from a farm-based to a creamery-based structure, up to 1947 when Golden Vale was formed. It then concentrates mainly on the history of the company itself from its foundation until 1990 when it decided to broaden its capital base by becoming a public limited company.

Though the research themes are largely universal the rooting of the study in the context of the small, open and mixed Irish economy does offer certain particular advantages. The causal texture of a small national context on the strategies of its organisations is more easy to understand, and consequently the contextual forces that shape strategy are more easy to isolate and empirically examine, than would be the case for a similar study sited in a much larger economy such as that of Britain or the United States. Context, when viewed in the past at the organisational level of analysis, has been too often seen in terms of largely impersonal forces with little attention paid to how contextual forces actually shape organisational action (Pfeffer and Salancik 1978; Pettigrew 1985). The empirical analysis will identify five important contextual factors and examine how they influenced the strategies of the organisations in our study. We will see the effects of not only impersonal forces but also of strategic action at higher levels in the social system on the formation of strategy at the level of the firm. In Mintzberg (1978, 1987) terminology we will see the intended and the emergent influence of national context on the realised strategies of the organisations in the study more clearly than is to be found in most other empirical research in the strategy field. We have tried to be truly multi-level in our approach to describing and analysing the influence of context on strategy, an approach which is still very rare in the leadership and strategy fields (Pettigrew 1987). By making the generation of a separate narrative on the national context of the organisations an integral part of the overall research design, we have tried to understand the contextual forces which shaped the strategies of our organisations in their own terms at national level before seeing them at the industry and organisational levels through the eyes of the organisations themselves. This particular multi-level approach has, we believe, allowed us to examine these contextual forces with more breadth and depth than would otherwise have been possible and is in itself a special feature of our study.

Our study also provides a fresh perspective on the influence of leadership on strategy formation. Our view of leaders as historical figures and tenants of time and context deliberately deflects attention away from the predominant pre-occupation of the leadership literature with the personal attributes and persona of the leader. We are, of course, interested in the personas of our leaders but we are also interested in catching their performance in the arena in flight. The currency of leadership is credibility and our approach to our empirical inquiry allows us to examine the historical process of leadership and the establishment, maintenance and in some cases loss of credibility over time. We analyse and compare our leaders, not so much on personal attributes, but on the nature of the historical challenges that they faced during their tenures at the top. We develop a classification of leaders in terms of their historical roles and offer this as a potentially fruitful way to organise future research into the leadership phenomenon. Our insights on leadership and context and on their interaction in the formation of strategy are synthesised into a relational model of strategy formation which we hope will form a useful framework for better understanding the relationship and for guiding future research in this area.

THE ORGANISATION OF THE BOOK

The remainder of the book is organised as follows. In the next chapter we develop the analytical themes and the conceptual framework within which our analysis of leadership and strategy will be carried out. Chapters 3 to 7 contain the descriptive narratives on which the analysis will be based. The first of these chapters contains the historical narrative on the national context, which is a brief political, economic and social history of modern Ireland. This is followed by narratives on each of the four organisations featured in the study. The approach to the subsequent analysis takes its inspiration from Allison's (1971) classic study of the Cuban Missile Crisis. The data is first analysed in Chapter 8 using a voluntarist perspective to help isolate and examine the influence of leadership on the formation of strategy in the organisations under study and to develop our categorisation of leaders in terms of their historical challenges. The same historical data is then revisited from a more deterministic perspective in Chapter 9 to help isolate the important contextualist factors that shape strategy. Only after we have looked at the effects of leadership and context separately do we bring them together in our final chapter to examine their interaction, explore their implications and attempt some synthesis in our development of a relational model that links leadership and context with the formation of strategy.

2   The locus of influence over strategy

Are the organisation's leaders usually in control of its destiny? Or is the environment or situational context of the organisation more generally in the driving seat? This is a perennial issue that practitioners and theorists alike continually debate among themselves and rarely resolve. In the practical world of business when performance is poor the organisation's leaders more often than not blame the environment. Yet when performance is good they generally credit themselves. Rarely do organisational strategists attribute their success to external factors and their failure to themselves. In fairness to our strategists psychologists tell us, through what they refer to as attribution theory, that this tendency is quite prevalent in social life. For us, in studying the link between leadership and context and how they interact to shape an organisation's strategy, where does the balance lie?

If the 'essence' of strategy is 'relating a company to its environment', as Porter (1980: 3) declares in the opening sentence of his now classic work, then, should leadership and strategy be mainly about trying to predict and respond to an organisation's future or should it be about trying to invent it (Sculley 1987: 429)? Some organisations in the past have clearly suffered from having too little belief in their ability to invent their futures (Hamel and Prahalad 1989) but equally leading companies in fields as diverse as soft drinks, cars and information technology have also suffered at various times in their history from over-confidence in their ability to control their own destinies. Until we get more insight into how leadership and context interact in the formation of strategy we will be unable to help our organisations and their leaders with this dilemma. The question of the locus of influence over strategy formation, and how it changes over time, has rarely been empirically examined in its own right. Yet this issue goes right to the heart of the interaction between leaders, context and strategy formation. Examination of this interaction in long historical perspective is now, as Porter (1991) points out, one of the main priorities in the development of a dynamic theory of strategy, and we have made it a central theme in this study.

How are leaders linked with context and how are both of these forces linked with the actions and outcomes of the strategy formation process? To explain the framework that we have developed for subsequent analysis we begin with a review of what the literature in the strategy and organisational analysis fields has to offer as conceptual guidance in this area.

LEADERSHIP AND CONTEXT – VOLUNTARISM AND DETERMINISM

The literature across and within the strategy and organisational analysis fields is as divided as the practitioners themselves on the question of whether organisations are in control of their own strategies and destinies or whether their environments or contexts are key. So strong is this division that much of the existing research in organisational analysis generally, including the strategy area, is polarised into competing world views along the voluntarism–determinism dimension (Burrell and Morgan 1979; Pfeffer 1982; Astley and Van de Ven 1983).

Voluntarist views of leadership and strategy

Establishing clear links and patterns between leadership and organisational strategy has long been a focus of study. Ever since the publication of Stogdill's (1974) extensive review of leadership studies concerned with determining the traits of effective individual leadership the subject has both fascinated and eluded organisation theorists. Stogdill (1974) draws on over 3,000 studies, some of which date from as far back as his early work in the 1940s. While this is not the place to review the development of leadership theories in any extensive way (see Bryman 1986 for one such account), the seemingly relentless pursuit of turning just an 'ordinary' manager into a 'leader' has characterised a great deal of this research effort and much of the normative theory developed from it.

The assumption underlying much of the pursuit of understanding good leadership has been to start with rather rational theories of the firm (or of work groups and individuals) and to try to achieve a best fit between the functional demarcation of organising and the performance of the manager. As Vaill (1989: 113) points out: 'if the organization needs a plan, we "gerundize" this desired effect into some kind of behaviour called "planning"; if the organization needs goals, the corresponding action becomes "goal setting".'

Where groups and individuals are concerned, the same kind of process is assumed. Good (i.e. effective) leaders are those who can match their leadership styles to the needs of the group or individuals in their charge

(Likert 1967; Vroom and Yetton 1973; House and Mitchell 1974). Many authors have pointed to the conceptual and practical difficulties of achieving such a match. A modern version of the matching process can be found in the efforts put into defining and achieving (through training) management competencies. The competence approach assumes a portfolio of skills and orientations that when well-developed, sow the seeds for effective leadership to grow (see Wilson 1992 for a general critique of this approach; see also Leavy 1991a for an empirically-based discussion of the limitations of a generic skills approach to strategic leadership in particular).

The over-arching theoretical framework linking all such studies and approaches is that of voluntarism (Gouldner 1980) which ascribes primacy to the role of human agency. The leader makes both an important contribution to the direction of the organisation (its strategy) and also such actions can be linked directly to the economic performance of the firm. Leadership becomes the key factor in securing the assumed link between management as a process and organisational performance.

In parallel to such assumptions, a rich vein of voluntarism also runs through much of the literature concerning strategic management. As McKiernan (1992) points out, the field of organisational strategy is characterised by the purposive formulation of future strategic actions, with the architecture of decisions and their implementation firmly held in the grasp of organisational leaders. Much of the research on strategy has concentrated on the content of strategy rather than on the process by which it is formed. The extensive work on the PIMS data base, initiated by Schoeffler *et al.* (1974) to uncover the 'laws' of the market-place; the 'experience curve' and 'business portfolio matrix' concepts of Henderson (1973) and the Boston Consulting group; and more recently, Porter's (1980, 1985) concepts of 'generic' strategies and 'value chain' are all normative and addressed implicitly at the organisational leader as formulator of strategy. They suggest what the pattern of organisational action should be on the assumption that the formation of this pattern is a matter of the leader's will, intellect and administrative skill.

Linear rational models of decision making again lend support to the above content theories of strategy. The majority of work in this area can be characterised as 'intendedly rational' (Cyert and March 1992). Bounded rationality and local goals are viewed as constraints on an otherwise optimal process. The role of the leader is to reduce such unwanted 'noise' in the decision making system. Even more processual theories of decision making tend to cluster around the voluntarist–rational paradigm. In this tradition (if we accept that term to describe the analysis of decision making as a social process beginning with Cyert and March's (1963) *Behavioural Theory of the Firm*) the social process of choice reflects the structural context (organisation structure, resource allocation systems, motivation and reward systems, information systems, etc.) within which it takes place (Bower 1970).

Even in the very recent developments in network theories (or industrial networks) that concern themselves with the inter-dependent relationships between organisations a particularly strong form of the voluntarist world view can be found. The intention in this literature is to 'make possible an integrated analysis of stability and development in industry' (Hakansson and Johanson 1992: 28). Inter-related firms thus cluster together in transactions to form a larger whole. This larger whole is seen to consist of actors (organisational leaders and managers), resources and activities. Resources are required to perform activities and actors and activities combine within the rubric of goal-directed behaviour so that actors attempt to 'increase their control over the network' (Hakansson and Johanson 1992: 29). Levels of access to information and resources may vary between actors in the network, but overall the leader of his or her organisation is seen to be in control. Such control might be direct (as in the case of ownership for example) or indirect (dependent upon the strength and quality of relations between actors in different parts of the network). Primacy is, however, given to the voluntarist actions and potential of the leader as an organisational actor embedded in a series of exchange relationships with other network actors.

The development of the voluntarist perspective also extends beyond these recent developments in strategic management theory. Such areas as total quality management (TQM), now widely embraced by manufacturing and service organisations alike, also take the proactive, voluntarist view of leadership as accurate and desirable. Deming (1986), for example, argues that effective leadership acts as a substitute for structure, hierarchy and organisational controls. Strategic objectives can be met by leaders who know how they should be met, emphasising quality rather than numbers and empowering others to perform to the best of their ability. Ultimately the strategy and the performance of the organisation is seen to be in their hands.

Determinist views of organisational action

In contrast to the voluntaristic theses outlined in the previous section, much of Organisation Theory has embraced a far more deterministic view of the role of leadership in fashioning organisational strategy. Much of the pioneering work in Organisation Theory concentrated on identifying the determinants of organisation structures within which leaders were constrained in their strategic actions. Structure was deemed to set parameters around processes. Woodward (1965, 1970), Pugh *et al.* (1969) and Perrow

(1970) drew upon substantial empirical evidence to support the thesis that organisation structure is largely determined by the type and complexity of the technology. Burns and Stalker (1961) and Lawrence and Lorsch (1967) at the same time were demonstrating the importance of the link between organisation structure and the nature of the task environment.

Independently, Katz and Kahn (1966) were busy developing the Open Systems model first elaborated in the natural sciences by Von Bertalanffy (1950) to distinguish biological from physical systems. This model provided a unifying, integrated conceptual framework which, initially at least, unified the deterministic view of organisation which was rapidly emerging. This framework (Socio-Technical Theory) took the view of organisations as social and technical systems located within and in constant interaction with a supra-system (the environment) through permeable boundaries. The role of the leader was to work within such constraints, apparently taking charge of what little autonomous discretion remained.

More recent theory in organisational analysis also shows a predominantly determinist orientation. The resource-dependence theory of Pfeffer and Salancik (1978) highlights the external control of organisations and relegates the role of leadership to one which is largely symbolic. An even more extreme form of determinism virtually eradicates the role of leadership as autonomous strategy maker altogether. The population ecology perspective (Hannan and Freeman 1977; Aldrich 1979) questioned the capacity of organisations to adapt to the contingencies of their changing environments since 'inertial' pressures preclude action at the organisational level of analysis. The relationship between an organisation and its environment is viewed as akin to natural selection, in which populations of organisations are subject to a Darwinistic process of 'survival of the fittest'. From this highly deterministic perspective, it matters even less what individual leaders do. Organisational survival in the long run will be fashioned by the interactions of organisations and their environments which will either sustain them or destroy them.

CONTEXT AND THE SCOPE FOR LEADERSHIP

While mainstream leadership and strategy research and mainstream organisation theory have largely developed within polar opposite perspectives with regard to the relationship between organisations and their environments, the voluntarism–determinism debate remains alive and well not only between these fields but within them as well.

In the organisation theory field, for example, there have been a number of notable contributions that have taken its predominant determinism to task. As Thompson (1967: 99) noted: 'technology and task environment seldom completely determine how organisations act. When the immutable facts of organisational life have been faced and the contingencies spelled out, organisations have choices.' Reinforcing this argument, Child (1972: 15) reviewed the case for contingent determinants (i.e. organisation size, technology and environment) and concluded that 'strategic choice' remains a 'critical variable in a theory of organisations'. Crozier and Friedberg (1980: 76) warned against 'a unilateral conception of environmental influences' which ignores the fact that organisations 'can "play" with the "requirements" and constraints imposed by the environment, and even manipulate them in its turn'. This view has been echoed by Pettigrew (1985: 37) who sees 'aspects of structure and context' being strategically 'mobilised' by various actors and groups as they 'seek to obtain outcomes that are important to them'. Astley (1985: 239) also rejected the almost total determinism of the 'population ecology' model arguing for a more 'community ecology' perspective in which: 'chance, fortuity, opportunism and choice are the dominant factors determining the direction in which the evolution (of populations of organisations) progresses'.

Likewise even within the strategy and related fields the tension between voluntarist and determinist perspectives can be found. The industrial organisation tradition in the field of economics has tended to support the determinist perspective by emphasising the primacy of industry structure in determining organisational strategy (see Porter 1981 for a review and critique of this perspective). However, the industry analysis perspective of Caves (1980) and Porter (1980, 1981) presents a less deterministic form of power-dependence theory than that of organisation theorists Pfeffer and Salancik (1978) and is also less deterministic than the classic Bain model (1968) of industrial economics. Yet, in highlighting how contextual competitive forces shape strategy (Porter 1979, 1980) this perspective on strategy is also less voluntarist than that which predominates in the strategy and leadership fields and is more akin to the world views of organisation theorists like Crozier and Friedberg (1980) and Pettigrew (1985) mentioned earlier.

Where then does the balance lie? While industrial economics has traditionally seen the 'invisible hand' of the market economy as the prime regulator of organisation and strategy in a capitalist economic environment, Chandler (1977) has shown that over time retained earnings has come to far outstrip fresh capital as the primary source of funding for the development and expansion of large American business. He concludes that the 'visible hand' of managerial capitalists has long since replaced the 'invisible hand' of the capital markets as the basic mechanism for strategic resource allocation in Western economies. According to Williamson (1975) and the transaction cost tradition this concentration of capital and the development of self-perpetuating managerial hierarchies is a consequence of market failure, and where this happens the locus of influence over strategic action will tend to shift from environment toward organisational strategists. In the same tradition, however, Galbraith (1952, 1984) has argued that any such tendency toward the concentration of economic power within an organisation usually invokes a countervailing tendency in the environment of the organisation, suggesting that the locus of influence question is contextually dynamic, historically shifting over cycles of time. Industry analysis theorists (Caves 1980; Porter 1980, 1981) and advocates of the 'strategic windows' concept (Abell 1978) in the strategy field would seem to support this view.

HISTORY AND THE SCOPE FOR LEADERSHIP

Also subscribing to the view that the locus of influence varies in historical cycles are a number of theorists who might be classified under the label of the institutionalist school. Authors such as Di Maggio and Powell (1983), Greenwood and Hinings (1988) and Fombrun and Shanley (1990) all argue that organisations develop institutionalised patterns of strategic behaviours which inform both current and future strategic positions. Such patterns either develop independently of individual leaders, or become deeply embedded largely as a reflection of the political face of leadership. Such 'embeddedness' (Granovetter 1985) can occur through the potency of interlocking directorships (Useem and McCormack 1981), for example, whereby organisations effectively insulate themselves from too many dependence relationships by actively seeking out board members who hold positions on the boards of related companies. Other 'interlocks' can occur where the influence of the executive directors is so strong that the non-executive directors effectively 'go native', thus reinforcing the established patterns of strategic action at the level of the firm (Norburn 1984; Lorsch and MacIver 1989). Furthermore, the appointment of future chief executives has been found to be largely within the strong influence of the current cadre of directors on the board. In other words, even the succession of new chief executives can itself reflect institutional patterning (Lorsch and MacIver 1989).

The institutionalist thesis, however, does allow for the actions of individual leaders to break the established patterns of strategic behaviours thus avoiding a totally deterministic view of strategy formation. The balance is nevertheless clear. Institutionalised patterns will be the dominant influence over corporate strategy unless crises (real or manufactured) or severe fiscal problems force the hand of change (Mintzberg 1983, 1984; Pettigrew 1985). The literature on strategic change reinforces this view.

Major strategic changes tend to happen relatively infrequently and in short revolutionary bursts (Greiner 1972; Miller and Friesen 1980; Romanelli and Tushman 1983). Indeed Mintzberg (1987) has argued that the very essence of strategy depends on stability and continuity in organisational actions over some reasonable time period (the totally reactive organisation has no deliberate strategy other than perhaps a commitment to continual change). Among the forces for continuity that have to be challenged at times of major change are the 'inertial forces' (Hannan and Freeman 1977) embedded in the many tangible commitments to specialised assets, skills, physical configurations and customary or contractual constituent relationships with employees, suppliers, customers and the like. However, major strategic change efforts must also confront significant forces for continuity that are social-psychological (Staw 1976), political (Quinn 1980; Pettigrew 1985) and cultural (Brunnson 1982; Pettigrew 1985; Johnson 1992) in nature. During the short revolutionary periods when major change is possible, individual leaders can exert high levels of influence over strategic direction, although it would seem from the institutionalist and strategic change theorists that the time frame in which this process can continue is relatively short before further patterns begin to sediment and guide future strategic action (Wilson *et al.* 1986). The pattern of control, however, individual or institutional, appears to be cyclical over time.

CONTEXT AND HISTORY IN THE SHAPING OF STRATEGY

At the very macro levels of analysis authors such as Keat and Abercrombie (1990) and Adorno (1991) argue that even if there is cyclicality in the locus of influence over organisational action, this process too is set within a wider context which imbues a certain level of overall determinism. Keat and Abercrombie's (1990) description of the 'enterprise culture', the gensis of which they trace to coincide with the election of the Thatcher Government in Britain in 1979, argues that the dominant processes of privatisation, increased market competition, reduction of dependencies both upon government and upon other organisations and the normative encourage-ment of economic analyses even on personal life (opportunity costs; added value, etc.) set an overall context in which organisations and their leaders operate. No matter whether leaders appear to be influential or not, Keat and Abercrombie argue that their influence is derived for the greater part from the prevailing norms of the societal context in which they operate.

Adorno (1991) also follows a similar line of reasoning. Organisational society (and wider social contexts) are beset with the drive to seek a rationality of action in which a state of 'illusory universality' can be maintained (Adorno 1991: 9). The actions of organisations and their leaders are thus constrained by limits placed upon reflection and/or innovation by the universal context. Empirical work from the institutionalists supports Adorno's theoretical position at least in one important regard. That is, organisational and individual action appear to be driven to coincide with what Meyer and Rowan (1977) have termed the legitimation of myth and ceremony. Strategic actions occur primarily because of previously constructed institutionalised elements and practices which effectively 'protect an organisation from having its conduct questioned' (Meyer and Rowan 1977: 349). The implications of this approach are that organisations build up recipes of strategic behaviours which bear more relation to the creation of myth and ceremony than they do to the action of leaders or the elegant techniques of strategic planning. Such myth and ceremony reflects more strongly, in Adorno's view, the prevailing norms and preferred practices of wider society than the individual actions of organisational leaders.

Narrowing the conceptual focus a little from the societal to that of the business sector reveals further empirical support for the institutional thesis. Organisations engage in role-modelling behaviours whereby their strategies are modelled upon the actions of other organisations in the business sector, or, less commonly, on the strategic behaviours of organisations outside their sector (see Grinyer and Spender 1979; Di Maggio and Powell 1983; Zucker 1988; Hinings and Greenwood 1988; Fombrun and Shanley 1990). Leadership action, therefore, might be autonomous or not, but it is likely to be action which is derived from and shaped by the strategic actions of other peer organisations in the business sector. The important factors from this perspective are the characteristics of the context (societal and/or business sector) which over-arch managerial action.

Yet, strong pressures have been exerted against the institutionalist thesis by those researchers who subscribe broadly to what have been termed the interactionist or existential perspectives, arguing that understanding strategy and leadership is best served by a focus on individual interaction, meaning and symbolism. It is useful to distinguish the various constitutive elements of these approaches for they conclude rather different analyses about organisational strategy and the role of leadership. Existentialist approaches (e.g. Sudnow 1967; Garfinkel 1967; Silverman 1970; Clegg 1975) argue that the commonsense perspective of the individual or his definition of the situation represents the 'true' account of events free from the constructs of researchers and others who seek to analyse organisational phenomena. Such a perspective renders the meaning of constructs such as organisational context to be held in the eye (and in the language) of the beholder.

Accounts in this tradition lend a descriptive richness of observation rarely achieved in social science (particularly in organisation theory). Goffman's (1982) deep descriptive account of everyday social life represents the extent to which such a rich tapestry can be constructed. Nevertheless, as Isabella (1990) has hinted, there remains the problem of further analysis. What are we to make of such accounts? Are they purely descriptive or prescriptive? Since we are unable to derive or create constructs from accounts, the uniqueness of the situation and the event remains intact but precluded from comparative analysis. We can never know whether a situation is typical or replicable.

FRAMEWORK OF THE PRESENT STUDY

In this study we have eschewed an *idée fixe* of such strength as that exhibited by those at the extremes of the voluntarist–determinist debates. Yet our empirical work, detailed as it is, precludes detailed interactionist or existential analyses. Where possible we have pointed to the sense making undertaken by individual leaders, but we make no claim to throw greater light on this perspective beyond perhaps a few glimpses and insights into managerial definitions of the situation.

The view taken in this study argues that concepts of time and context are pre-eminent in the study of strategy and leadership. From our empirical data and from the diversity of approaches discussed in this chapter we argue that there are important conceptual linkages particularly between the strategic choice, institutionalist and individualistic perspectives. The common dimensions appear to focus around history and context. In viewing the leaders in our study as 'tenants of time and context' we view the processes of leadership and strategy formation to be conceptually linked over time according to variations in both the organisational and wider contexts. Our approach is depicted in Figure 2.1. Indeed in its broadest sense our framework can be rooted in what Mills (1970: 159) has called the 'Classic Tradition' in which social science is seen to be primarily concerned 'with problems of biography, of history and of their intersections with social structures'.

Strategy formation is viewed as driven and shaped sometimes by context and at other times by autonomous action at the organisational and individual levels of analysis. In addition, the role of leaders as key organisational actors is likely to vary according to organisational context and history. In some cases this will involve directly formulating the content of strategy, in others shaping the strategy more indirectly through the management of the organisational context and the strategy process (Bower 1970; Burgleman 1983; Hickson *et al.* 1986), in still others trying to

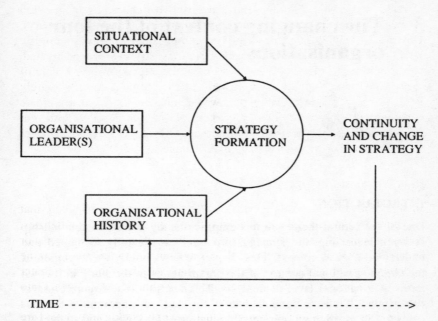

Figure 2.1 The framework

overcome the institutionalised forces for continuity in pursuit of new strategic departures (Quinn 1980; Brunsson 1982; Kanter 1983; Pettigrew 1985; Johnson 1992).

The theoretical position adopted therefore assigns a central role to the situational context in the shaping of a leader's actions and of organisational strategy. It does not implicitly assume a mode of process in the interaction between environment and organisation, nor does it ignore processes altogether. Therefore, one of the key questions addressed by the present study is how situational context influences the actions of leaders and the strategies of organisations. Situational context is also viewed as heterogeneous. A further question, therefore, is what specific features of the situational context or contextual elements impact the most upon the leadership process and on strategy formation? Since, by design, our frame of analysis is multi-level and historical we can begin to address the question of where and when leadership action comes to the fore in full relief and when it recedes into the wider tapestry of organisational context. For the remainder of this book we go on to explore empirically and analytically the historical rhythms of the interaction of leaders and contexts in the formation of strategy in an attempt to understand the nature of this interactive process.

3 The changing context of the four organisations

INTRODUCTION

One of the central themes in this empirical study is that the relationship between leadership and strategy formation can be fully examined and understood only in context. This chapter reviews briefly the evolution of the common national context of the organisations in the study in its own terms at a national level of analysis. This analysis is not merely useful background. It is an integral element of the study, as important as the four cases to follow, in this empirical examination of leadership and strategy.

The analysis begins by briefly tracing the roots of modern Irish nationalism from the late 1700s to independence in 1921. It then concentrates on the main developments in modern Ireland since independence. However, while the focus throughout the chapter is on reviewing the evolution of the national context in its own terms, the review is selective and is done with a view to understanding the origin and evolution of the main forms of organisation in the national economy in their wider political, economic, social and cultural context as the central historical theme.

THE NATIONAL QUESTION 1798–1921

The national question dominated Irish political and social life for more than a century from the 1790s onwards, and for much of the period since the Southern part of the country gained its independence in 1921 nationalism remained a dominant cultural force in the national context. It was a cultural force that played a particularly important role in forming the character, and shaping the outlook, of the revolutionary generation of Irish leaders right across the full spectrum of national political, social and economic life and in distinguishing them from the generations that were to follow.

Modern Irish nationalism has its roots in the general revolutionary ferment that swept the Western world in the late eighteenth century. Constitutional nationalists and republican extremists today both claim continuity with the republican movement in Ireland of the 1790s. This movement was heavily influenced by both the American and French revolutions of the period and was led, ironically, by an Ulster protestant, Theobald Wolfe Tone. Tone's attempt at the overthrow of British rule in Ireland by armed revolution was a military failure. Until the Tone rebellion, Ireland had been administered for many centuries as a separate kingdom under British colonial rule. Pitt, the British Prime Minister of the period, became alarmed at the revolutionary ferment in Ireland. He was moved to try to pacify the country and finally to quell her long-running separatist tendency through the radical measure of establishing the full political integration of Great Britain and Ireland by the Act of Union of 1801.

From 1801 until 1921 Irish politics was dominated in one way or another by concerted efforts to repeal the Act of Union and restore a substantial measure of self-government to the country. The main grievances that fuelled this desire for national autonomy were the religious repression of the Catholic majority and the insecurity of the mass of tenant farmers at the hands of non-resident landlords and their local agents. First the religious question, and later the land question, both dragged the national question in their trains (Lyons 1973). O'Connell's mass movement for Catholic emancipation became a mass movement for repeal of the Union once its initial objective was secured in 1829. The Young Ireland movement of the 1840s, which drew its inspiration from Garibaldi and the Risorgimento in Italy, raised the consciousness of the mass of Irish people in their historical and cultural distinctiveness. From this period onwards nationalism became a central cultural force in modern Irish social life.

The Great Famine of 1846, and the inept handling of it by a remote administration, fuelled the mass movement for land reform and ultimately for political Home Rule. Under the leadership of Parnell, Home Rule for Ireland became the single biggest issue in Irish politics with a majority of the Irish representation at the Westminster Parliament, and Davitt's mass land reform movement, aligned solidly behind the cause. The support of Prime Minister Gladstone, based as it was on principle as much as on political pragmatism, was also crucial in keeping the Irish question at centre stage in the British Parliament throughout the latter end of the century. At the same time, on the wider social canvas, the rise in cultural nationalism led to a gaelic revival which saw the foundation of the Gaelic Athletic Association in 1884 and the Gaelic League in 1893. According to Lyons (1973: 227) 'of all the factors influencing the rise of a new and urgent sense of nationality at the end of the nineteenth century' this gaelic revival 'has come to be regarded as perhaps the most significant'.

By the turn of the century Home Rule had still not been secured. Parnell died in 1892 and the defeat of Gladstone's second Home Rule Bill in 1893 led to his retirement from active politics. Within Ireland a substantial minority concentrated mainly among the Protestant people in the north-east of the country were bitterly opposed to Home Rule, which they feared would mean 'Rome Rule'. They were supported by the Conservative Party in Britain which feared that Home Rule for one part of the United Kingdom would threaten the integrity of the whole union.

In 1905 Arthur Griffith founded Sinn Fein ('Ourselves') as a movement to pursue economic nationalism and foster self-reliance in Ireland. He drew his inspiration from Franz Deak and the success of Deak's abstentionist policy in eventually securing a separate parliament for Hungary from the Imperial Government at Vienna. The political support for Griffith's party and its abstentionist policy remained small up to and during the Great War as most Irish nationalists continued to support the Home Rule party of Parnell's successors. However, in 1916 a group of young idealists took events into their own hands and staged an armed insurrection. The Easter Rising of 1916 was a military failure but the execution of the leaders, many of them poets and intellectuals, had an enormous effect on Irish public opinion. In the 1918 Westminster elections the Sinn Fein movement became the main political expression for Irish nationalism. Sinn Fein, with the overwhelming support of Irish nationalist opinion now solidly behind it, refused to participate in the Westminster Parliament and set up a provisional government in Dublin. This unilateral political action was supported by an armed guerilla struggle, the War of Independence, against the Crown forces. The country was ungovernable from Westminster without the most repressive measures. The British Government came under enormous pressure from world opinion, particularly from the United States, to find a political solution and the Anglo-Irish Treaty was negotiated in 1921 to settle the problem.

Northern Unionists remained strongly opposed to the break up of the union with Britain under the 1921 settlement. Ireland, and the province of Ulster, were partitioned under the new arrangement. This still left a large number of nationalists under Northern Ireland jurisdiction, which in time proved to be a poor basis for the development of a stable polity in that part of the island. The settlement also split the nationalist movement in the South. While it offered self-government with dominion status under the British Crown it fell short of full sovereignty for which many nationalists had risked life and limb. The establishment of the Irish Free State under the 1921 Treaty led to the outbreak of a civil war which lasted for almost a year. This split in the nationalist movement was the origin of the two major political parties which have dominated Southern Irish politics ever since.

The Irish Free State cut its final formal political connection with the British Commonwealth in 1949 and became a republic.

Industrial development up to 1921

Ireland remained primarily an agricultural country right up to the establishment of the Irish Free State in 1921. Until then the most significant development on the industrial and organisational front was the development of the Cooperative Movement in the late nineteenth century.

The Cooperative Movement in Ireland was founded by Sir Horace Plunkett in 1889 in what was to be a unique triumph of economic reason and pragmatism over political passion. Plunkett was a unionist on the Home Rule issue but he was more interested in the process of economic development than in the main political question of the day. In Plunkett's view the general failure of the Irish tenant farmer to rise above subsistence level was a basic impediment to the development of the whole Irish economy. While the efforts of Davitt and Parnell had secured the tenant farmer's position on the land, his position in the market system remained dependent and insecure. He was at the mercy of traders and middlemen for the extension of credit and for the distribution and disposal of his product. To Plunkett this situation was iniquitious for two main reasons. Firstly it was creating a fatalistic and dependent culture throughout rural Ireland which was undermining the national character, and secondly it was inhibiting the evolution of a mass market for manufactured goods which in turn was inhibiting the whole process of national industrial and economic development.

The timing of Plunkett's direct intervention in the organisation of Irish agricultural production and processing was also influenced by the advent of the mechanical cream separator into dairy processing. He 'saw the "industrialisation" of butter production as inevitable but also recognised the danger of the process falling into the grasp of middlemen' which would have made the farmer 'even more helpless than before' (Bolger 1977: 65). By 1891, after a few frustrating early attempts, Plunkett managed to help establish sixteen creameries formed along cooperative lines. Having demonstrated the feasibility and value of the cooperative organisation on the ground, Plunkett founded the Irish Agricultural Organisation Society in 1894 to promote and coordinate the development of the cooperative movement nationwide. By 1898 there were over 120 cooperative societies established around the country and by 1920 this number had grown to over 400. The impact of the cooperative movement on the image of Irish dairy products and on the economic welfare of the producers was dramatic.

Plunkett's influence on the development of Irish dairying extended to the involvement of the State. He was elected to Westminster in 1895, as the

Unionist MP for South Dublin. He persuaded fellow Irish MPs to put aside their political differences and work for the promotion of economic legislation. In 1899, due mainly to the efforts of his cross-party committee, the Department of Agriculture and Technical Instruction for Ireland was set up. Thus began the State's involvement in the provision of educational, research and advisory services in this area, which over the long run came to make a major contribution to the development of Irish agriculture.

On the more general front, conditions up to the foundation of the Irish Free State in 1921 did not favour a rapid or extensive process of industrialisation. The reasons why, many of them alluded to earlier, have been graphically summarised by Lyons (1973: 55) as follows:

> The rapid decline of the population in the decades after the Famine; the poverty of the people and the retarding effect of the land system upon their ability to accumulate savings and thus provide either the nucleus for industrial development or a market for its products; the frequently disturbed state of the country; the scarcity of coal and of raw materials; the cost and difficulty of transporting Irish goods to centres of trade;. . . the impossibility of building up manufactures in a backward country under a free trade regime which exposed it to the formidable rivalry of more highly developed competitors – all of these things together combined to make Ireland a place where, with a few important exceptions, businessmen preferred not to risk capital in the hazardous enterprise of creating new industry in so unpromising an economy.

There were, however, some notable exceptions. Outside of agriculture itself the main industries in which there was some substantial concentration of capital were brewing, distilling, biscuit-making, textiles, ship-building and engineering. Most of these industries were centred around the key ports of Dublin and Belfast. The textile, ship-building and engineering industries were concentrated in and around Belfast and the two biggest ship-building firms, Harland & Wolfe and Workman & Clark, employed over 20,000 workers between them by 1914. Biscuit-making was most highly developed in the Dublin area with the firm of W & R Jacob employing over 10,000 workers by 1907 and was a significant export activity. So also were brewing and distilling though these were more dispersed throughout the country. The largest brewer was Arthur Guinness & Sons of Dublin, which alone accounted for around two-thirds of the country's total output. The distilling industry was less concentrated with over twenty significant producers. However the industry was dominated by the firms of Power and Jameson in Dublin, Cork Distillers Company in Cork and Bushmills in Antrim. By 1907 there were around 9,000 people employed in these two industries nationwide.

In spite of these exceptions, however, 'Ireland remained at bottom an agricultural country with one industrial region and a handful of trading centres' (Lyons 1973: 69). Four-fifths of Irish exports went to Britain, most of which were agricultural, and about two-thirds of Irish imports came from Britain. Irish foreign trade, though not large in itself, was larger per head of population than that of Britain. This was the economic inheritance of the new Free State administration which took over the running of the country after the 1921 settlement.

THE NEW STATE 1922–57

While reaction in England and in the Commonwealth was generally very favourable to the Anglo-Irish Treaty (Packenham 1951) the settlement quickly led to civil strife in Ireland. Those in the Sinn Fein movement who felt that the cause for the 'Republic' had been betrayed refused to acquiesce in the new arrangement. The new Free State administration had to resolutely assert its authority over former fellow comrades-in-arms and within a year brought the civil hostilities successfully to an end. The tragedy of the Civil War was that the lives of many talented Irishmen, who had worked together in the separatist cause, were lost just when their newly emergent nation-state needed them most. Griffith, 'the greatest intellectual force stimulating the national revival' and the man that looked destined to lead the first Free State administration died prematurely of heart failure in 1922, 'worn out by past labours and privations and present anguish' (Packenham 1951: 340–342). Within a week of Griffith's death the newly independent state suffered further tragedy through the loss of Michael Collins, Commander-in-Chief of the new regular army and the military genius whom Griffith had credited with having won the War of Independence. Collins, still only in his early 30s, was shot and killed in an ambush by a group of irregulars. The bitterness and recriminations that arose from the Civil War were to dog Irish political life for as long as these events remained living memories.

The first Free State administration 1922–32

With Griffith and Collins gone the mantle of leadership in the first Free State administration fell to W. T. Cosgrave and the pro-Treaty faction of Sinn Fein, now restyled Cumann na Gael. Cosgrave's primary concern was to establish the machinery for self-government as quickly and as efficiently as possible. His administration was greatly aided in this task by having inherited 'a complete apparatus of government, both central and local' from the departing British regime (Dooney 1976: 1). The lasting legacy of this first administration was that it succeeded in quickly establishing and making effective a cabinet system of government that has largely remained the basic blueprint for the government of Ireland ever since.

One of the major difficulties that faced this first administration was the political instability that remained after the civil hostilities had been brought to an end. The anti-Treaty faction of Sinn Fein, led by Eamonn de Valera, continued to contest General Elections in the Free State. However, while they enjoyed considerable support among the electorate they refused to participate in the parliament of the new state and the Cosgrave Government governed for nearly six years without a credible opposition and alternative government-in-waiting. In 1926 de Valera broke with the more extreme elements in what remained of Sinn Fein after the Treaty to form the Fianna Fail Party. Fianna Fail entered the Dail for the first time in 1927 and faced what was, in de Valera's own words, the 'painful and humiliating step' of having to take the Oath of Allegiance to the British Monarch that had been a major stumbling block to its acceptance of the Treaty (Nowlan 1967: 12). This action by Fianna Fail represented a major step forward towards the firm establishment of constitutional politics in the new state. However, the assassination of Home Affairs Minister, Kevin O'Higgins, by a small group of anti-Treaty extremists in 1927 served as a sharp reminder to all that potentially destructive civil war tensions remained not far below the surface of Irish political life at this time.

The first administration was pre-occupied with political issues and its economic policies were 'cautious and experimental' (O'Brien 1962: 15). It used the tariff mechanism sparingly and its overall economic approach was broadly *laissez-faire*. It accepted that the main business of the country was agriculture and it made few concerted moves to develop a more diversified national economy. In relation to agriculture it concentrated its efforts at trying to improve the overall standard of Irish farm products. It introduced a succession of modest measures regulating the breeding of livestock and the quality of dairy produce that, in a country unused to direct government regulation of products and markets, 'were regarded as almost totalitarian at the time' (Meenan 1967: 71).

The one major intervention that this first administration took in the agricultural area was its rationalisation of the dairy industry in 1927 and its support for the cooperative movement in this process. The movement in Ireland had reached its nadir by 1920, primarily in the dairy sector. This sector suffered from the post-war slump that depressed the key British food market for most of the 1920s. As the decade progressed dairy processing in Ireland became characterised by serious over-capacity and by unbridled competition which threatened the future structure of the whole industry. By 1926 there were 580 creamery operations of which the cooperative movement controlled 400. The remainder were controlled by private capital. In spite of their superior numbers it was the cooperative creameries that were most threatened by the severe competition, and in the prevailing conditions the future role of the movement in the industry was under serious threat. In these circumstances, Dr Henry Kennedy, the movement's national secretary, persuaded the Minister for Agriculture to intervene in order to save the movement 'from disaster if not extinction' (Bolger 1977: 114). The Minister, using the mechanism of the state-funded Dairy Disposal Company, bought out most of the proprietary operations, closed down those that were marginal and arranged for the transfer of the rest over time to cooperative ownership.

Aside from this major intervention the Cosgrave administration's use of state resources for industrial and economic development remained cautious and piecemeal like its policy on tariffs. State funding was used to harness the Shannon river for electricity generation. Overall, however, the main contribution of this first administration was in establishing and securing the institutions and machinery of government, a major achievement given the troubled nature of the early years of statehood. Its achievements in the industrial and economic sphere have been generally viewed as lacklustre and conservative.

Economic self-sufficiency 1932–57

The Irish Free State had its first change of administration in 1932. Few at the time would have predicted that Fianna Fail could have come to power so soon, even fewer still that it would remain in office for sixteen years. The peaceful first transition of power between the former Civil War protagonists was further evidence that democratic, constitutional politics were now securely established in the new state.

The 1932 election brought to power two of the outstanding personalities in modern Irish history, Eamonn de Valera and Sean Lemass. Both men had been revolutionaries in the 1916 Rising. De Valera, as one of the leaders, had been spared execution because he was born in America. He was President of the Provisional Government during the War of Independence and during the Treaty negotiations. De Valera has been justly described as one of those individuals 'whose impact, influence and personality have set them apart from their contemporaries' and a man whose 'towering presence' presides 'over a great part of the story of modern Ireland' (Lee and O'Tuathaigh 1982: 12). While de Valera was to become the acknowledged outstanding political figure in modern Irish history, his most prominent cabinet minister and obvious heir apparent, Sean Lemass, came in time to be credited with being 'the main architect of industrialisation' in the country's economic development (Lee 1979a: 16).

The de Valera administration came to power with a very definite vision of the kind of Ireland that it wanted to create. He wanted to make the country as economically self-sufficient as possible and to recover as much of the country's cultural distinctiveness as was salvageable after many centuries of English hegemony. Economic prosperity was of secondary importance. The society that he wanted to create was to be essentially rural, gaelic, Catholic in ethos, and secure from unwanted outside influences.

De Valera was obsessed with sovereignty. After he came to power in 1932 he succeeded with amazing speed and considerable political skill in removing piece by piece the remaining constraints on the political sovereignty of the Irish state that had been the most contentious elements of the 1921 Treaty. He managed to do this with relatively little overall political fall-out in Anglo-Irish relations other than a period of mutual economic sanctions, known in Ireland as the Economic War. He first of all abolished the controversial Oath of Allegiance. Then he systematically watered down the powers and status of the British Governor General in Ireland. He eventually abolished the role completely, taking advantage of the abdication crisis of 1936 to remove all remaining references to the Crown and to the Crown's representative in the Free State Constitution. Finally, in 1937, he drew up a new constitution for the Irish state which, 'while stopping short of actually proclaiming a full republic, gave concrete form to the concept of popular sovereignty in Ireland' (Lee and O'Tuathaigh 1982: 72).

While de Valera was pre-occupied with the issue of political sovereignty Lemass set about the task of trying to develop an industrial base in the country. Under its general economic policy of self-sufficiency the de Valera administration planned to develop new native industries through an initial emphasis on import substitution. These industries were to be encouraged and protected in the formative phase by the selective use of import tariffs. In spite of the clear commitment to a protectionist economic policy private investment for industrial projects remained low and sluggish. In these circumstances Lemass showed little hesitation in using public capital to accelerate the development of a native industrial base. During the 1932–1948 period the number of state-owned enterprises, or semi-state bodies as they became known in Ireland, quadrupled from 6 to 24 and state enterprise became a firmly established part of the wider economic structure. Among the semi-states set up during the 1932–50 period were Aer Lingus, the national airline, and Aer Rianta, the airport management authority; the Irish Life Assurance Company; Irish Shipping; CIE, the national transport authority; Bord Na Mona, the peat processor; and CSET, the sugar company.

Economic pragmatism, rather than socialist ideology, underlay the foundation of these companies. As Sean Lemass (1959: 278) was later to explain,

in contrast to many countries where similar State-sponsored organisations have been created as part of a deliberate policy of State socialism, they developed in this country in a haphazard way to meet particular needs and opportunities as they arose, when no other course appeared to be practicable.

They were never intended to compete with, or displace, private enterprise. These organisations played a formative role in the development of native managerial and technical skills. As C. S. (Todd) Andrews (1959: 299), the first chief executive of Bord Na Mona publicly declared, these companies gave to Irish managers and technologists 'opportunities for advancement which would never have been available to them in an economy where the family-owned firm was dominant and the crown prince blocked promotion to the top posts'. They also 'introduced into Ireland modernity in mechanisation and in management methods, in industrial environment and in the training of staff'. Men like Andrews were handpicked by Lemass for the task of leading these semi-state organisations at this formative stage in the industrialisation of the national economy because of his conviction that 'in a small society with no inherent momentum of its own' the 'initiative or lack of it of a handful of individuals could make or mar important institutions for a generation (cited in Lee 1979a: 24).

Lemass and his colleagues had to thread carefully in their use of state enterprise at this time because the Catholic Church was extremely wary of any extension of the state apparatus into the social and economic affairs of the country. The Church had become alarmed at the rise of socialism and fascism throughout Europe in the 1930s and at the spread of atheistic materialism that seemed to be an inherent part of any statist or socialist philosophy. In 1931 Pope Pius XI produced the papal encyclical, *Quadragesimo Anno*, to update and reaffirm Catholic social thinking on the proper organisation of society. Central to this philosophy was a rejection of the inevitability of the class struggle and the advocation of vocationalism or corporatism as an approach to social organisation that could, instead, foster class harmony. The solution that it proposed, as summarised by Whyte (1980: 67), was 'that members of each industry or profession be organised in "vocational groups" or "corporations" in which employers and workers would collaborate to further their common interests'. This would 'restore the State' to 'its rightful place' to 'direct, watch, urge, and restrain subsidiary organisations' in accordance with the 'basic principle' in social philosophy of 'subsidiary function'. Catholic social thinking was at its most influential in Ireland during the 1940s and 1950s.

Fianna Fail left office in 1948 after sixteen years in government. This first lengthy tenure was a tribute to de Valera's leadership and to his personal capacity, in tough times, to mobilise the 'national will'. Ireland's ability to pursue a policy of neutrality during the Second World War, and to maintain it in the face of enormous pressure from Britain and the United States, was confirmation of her status as a politically independent entity, both to her own people and to the outside world. The period from 1948 to 1957 saw three further changes of government, involving two short-lived inter-party coalition administrations under J. A. Costello, interspersed with a brief return to power by Fianna Fail. The 1957 General Election brought Fianna Fail back into office once more for another sixteen-year tenure. When the first Costello administration broke the final formal linkage with the British Commonwealth in 1949 and declared Ireland a republic there was little reaction in either Britain or Ireland to a move that was merely institutionalising the *de facto* position.

In spite of the best efforts of Lemass and his colleagues, general economic development remained sluggish until 1957. Up to the early 1950s the new state could be said to have never experienced 'normal' socio-economic conditions. The political turmoil of the 1921–31 period, the Economic War and war-time Emergency of the 1932–48 period meant that there were always extraneous factors to point to when any critical assessment of prosperity or economic performance since independence arose. In the more normal conditions of the 1950s, however, the short-comings of the economic self-sufficiency policy and the structural weaknesses of the Irish economy began to be thrown into sharper relief. The new enterprises that were fostered under the protectionist policy of self-sufficiency were not providing enough industrial employment to compensate for the migration from the land that came with the advancing mechanisation of agricultural production. Emigration in the mid-1950s reached alarming levels. The material aspirations of many Irish people were clearly not to be satisfied by the de Valera rural idyll of frugal comfort and traditional values. The prevailing mood in the country, when Fianna Fail came back into office in 1957, was one of despondency. Their previous attempt to close the country off from outside influences, and to keep as many people on the land as possible, had led to general economic and cultural stagnation. The people had lost confidence in the ability of their leaders to control the economic destiny of the country and to provide for its inhabitants.

ECONOMIC REVIVAL AND NEW DIRECTIONS 1958–79

The national despondency and self-doubt of the late 1950s was to change dramatically within a relatively short time. There is general agreement among modern Irish historians that the decade of the 1960s 'marked some kind of watershed in Irish history'. It was 'one of those pivotal periods when a society swings on its axis to face in a new direction', with the years from 1945 to 1960 appearing 'as an epilogue to a traditional Ireland' (Lee 1979b: 166). The momentum generated during this axial shift was to bring Ireland into the European Economic Community and to continue through most of the first decade of its 'Europeanisation'.

Economic expansion 1958–79

The first major change came in the economic sphere. After returning his party to power in 1957 de Valera retired in mid-term and passed the mantle of leadership to Sean Lemass. Lemass led the country through the front end of its axial shift. He provided the political leadership for a bold economic revival strategy formulated by the young Secretary of the Department of Finance, T. K. Whitaker, and published in his now historic study *Economic Development* (Whitaker 1958).

Whitaker concluded that whatever the merits of economic self-sufficiency as a national policy for former times it was no longer suited to the Ireland of the late 1950s. Sooner or later 'protection would have to go and the challenge of free trade be accepted'. He was convinced that real growth in national income could come only from 'capital and labour being devoted to industrial and agricultural production for export, rather than for the provision of welfare services for home consumption'. He recognised, however, that increased capital investment alone would not be enough. More fundamental changes in the general levels of education, health and skill, along with the willingness to embrace change and encourage initiative and the adoption of new techniques and new ideas based on scientific advances, would be necessary. As he saw it nothing less than a general 'dynamic' had to be found and released that could help revitalise the whole economy (Whitaker 1958: paragraphs 4,5,7 and 18).

To release this 'dynamic' what Whitaker proposed was the 'setting up of targets of national endeavour which appear to be mutually attainable and reasonably consistent'. This is precisely what the Lemass administration did when it produced its First Programme for Economic Expansion 1958–63. The approach was based on the model of national indicative planning that had worked so well in post-war France. Whitaker was very perceptive in recognising that there was a 'sound "psychological" reason' for having such 'an integrated development programme' and it was aimed at no less than encouraging 'a general resurgence of will' across the nation to 'buttress confidence in the country's future' (Whitaker 1958: paragraph 12). Overall it was a bold and imaginative strategy for economic development and it needed a political leader that was bold and imaginative to put it into effect. Lemass was 'pragmatic' and 'intelligent' with an almost 'instinctive' understanding of economic problems. He was prepared to embark on 'a momentous mission' to 'create a viable Irish society, self-confident without being unduly self-righteous'. In the stagnant society that was the Ireland of the time this amounted to nothing less than an attempt to 'transform a people's self-image and even their very character' which only 'a conquistador of the spirit' could have undertaken with any degree of confidence and conviction (Lee 1979a: 22). For Lemass, himself, it was 'the historic task' of that particular generation of Irishmen 'to secure the economic foundation of independence' (Dail Debates 3/6/59).

The new economic strategy opened out the economy, and with it Irish social and economic life in general, to new investment, new ideas and new markets. In a dramatic reversal of the protectionist self-sufficiency policy the new emphasis was on freer trade and export-led growth. In line with this new approach it was decided to seek entry into the European Common Market at the earliest possible opportunity. The fundamental change in national economic strategy allowed the country to take full advantage of the general improvement in economic conditions then prevailing in international trade, and the Irish economy expanded at an unprecedented rate throughout the decade. Fiscal policy shifted from protectionism, which had tended to encourage complacency and inefficiency, to tax incentives for exporting activity, which were designed to encourage initiative, expansion and efficiency. This policy was extended to the active encouragement of direct foreign investment in order to help accelerate the industrialisation and modernisation of the Irish economy. The foreign-owned projects were targeted at areas that tended to complement indigenous capital rather than displace it and so they helped to create a more diversified export-oriented economy.

The country's transition during the 1960s went far beyond the economic sphere. It extended into all aspects of the social and cultural fabric. Irish society became everywhere more empirical and less traditional throughout the decade with 'new emphasis on information' (Lee 1979a: 171). Lemass's own pragmatic and empirical approach to the nation's economic development was reflected in an unprecedented quest for knowledge through scientific research and analysis. The economic development strategy channelled public investment into industrial, agricultural and economic research in order to help provide an empirically sounder basis for developing industry and agriculture and for the management of the national economy. This was accompanied by unprecedented levels of public investment in general education, based on the first scientific in depth study of the Irish educational system since independence. New emphasis was given to science and technology in recognition of their importance in the development of a modern economy (Coolahan 1984). In the most radical reform of the education system since the foundation of the State both the second and third level sectors were greatly expanded to make it possible for all young people of whatever means to progress to their highest level of capability (Sheehan 1979). Under the development strategy public investment was also increased in the areas of industrial training and management development.

The transition from traditionalism to modernity during the 1960s was also influenced by the advent of television and by the radical changes in the Catholic Church brought about by the Second Vatican Council. Television brought mass access to new ideas and new influences and was increasingly used to subject traditional authority figures and their religious, political and economic dogmas to mass scrutiny. Vatican II played its part in encouraging more openness and modernity in Irish social life by encouraging a more empirical, more questioning and more involved approach to Church doctrine and practice among all Catholics and a more open and ecumenical approach to other religious persuasions and beliefs. This itself was culturally very significant in a predominantly Catholic country.

Indeed the transition extended to the very leadership of Irish society itself as the revolutionary generation gradually gave way to the post-revolutionary generation in political and commercial life. The average age in Cosgrave's 1921 administration was 33; in de Valera's 1932 government it was 41. In de Valera's later 1951 cabinet the average age had risen to 57. The young revolutionary generation of newly independent Ireland had grown old in power without any significant renewal up to the 1950s (Cohan 1972). Lemass accelerated the process of renewal within Fianna Fail and put a premium on demonstrated talent, which he used his junior ministries to grow and prune. Similar renewal occurred in the other political parties at this time. The post-revolutionary generation of politicians was more pragmatic and careerist in orientation. This new breed came to power not because they were men of destiny but because they had chosen politics as their preferred career and they were men of ambition (Tobin 1984). More generally the era of Lemass heralded a new national hero to replace the revolutionary patriot. This new hero was the professional manager or politician, committed to economic development and efficiency, willing to be judged on the merit of his performance, and modern in his attitude to management ideas and the use of empirical data in decision processes.

Living standards in the country rose by over 50 per cent during the 1960s and Ireland became 'a net gainer from migration for the first time in recorded history' (Walsh 1979: 35). However, the unprecedented growth introduced new pressures into the country's economic and social life and existing institutions were found to be inadequate to deal with them. Progressive urbanisation and industrialisation brought with them new tensions between town and country, between farmers and industrial wage-earners. The economy became more diversified as it grew and old certainties and old relativities were challenged by the emergence of new classes and categories of workers and salaried professionals. The decade was characterised by a series of major industrial disputes that were notable for their protractedness and bitterness. Few sectors were left untouched. These disputes were diverse and involved at various times throughout the decade the busmen, the building workers, the power workers, the teachers, the bankers and the maintenance workers. It was believed in some quarters of Irish society that there was some kind of concerted movement linking these disputes, but McCarthy (1973), after detailed empirical examination of them, rejected this view and concluded that they were essentially empirical adjustments to the general economic and social upheaval that the country as a whole experienced during the transitionary 1960s.

Industrial relations in Ireland had been based, since the start, on voluntarism and collective bargaining (Hillery 1980). They had largely followed the British pattern in terms of traditions and organisation (Fogarty 1980). New initiatives were taken in the general industrial relations machinery in the late 1960s in order to cope with the tensions which had been released through the process of economic growth and which threatened seriously to undermine this process and slow it down. The responsibilities of the Labour Court, set up in 1946, were redefined in 1969 to bring them more up to date. Furthermore, the Employer-Labour Conference was reconstituted in 1970 and came to play a major role in the centralised development of a series of sophisticated national wage agreements that allowed the country to deal with the inflationary pressures that came to be an enduring feature of the 1970s.

The Northern troubles, Europe and oil crises – Ireland in the 1970s

The processes of transition in Irish life, that were set in motion during the 1960s, continued to transform the structure and texture of Irish economic and social life on through to the 1980s. What was new and exciting in the 1960s, however, became more 'normal' in the 1970s and the process of transition became the backdrop against which new issues were to come to prominence. Chief among these new issues were the Northern troubles, Ireland's accession to the European Economic Community and the inflationary pressures unleashed on all oil-dependent economies by the oil crises of 1973 and 1979.

The Northern troubles and the national aspiration

The troubles that broke out in Northern Ireland in the late 1960s took most people in the South completely by surprise. With the exception of those Southerners who lived in border areas, most people in the Republic felt quite remote from their nationalist brethren in the North and were generally ignorant of the conditions under which they lived (O'Malley 1983: 75). There was still a strong aspiration for national unity in the Republic but in the forty or more years since the Anglo-Irish Treaty of 1921 there had been no political movement, and little hope of movement, towards this ideal on the ground. There had been sporadic campaigns by the then marginalised IRA but the 1956–62 campaign had been a demoralising non-event for the extremists due mainly to the lack of nationalist support for the effort within Northern Ireland itself.

In the early 1960s Lemass, himself a veteran of the 1916 Rebellion and of the War of Independence, refocused the energies of committed Southern nationalists onto the process of economic revival and expansion and linked the 'historic task' of that decade's generation of Irishmen to the national aspiration for unity. According to Brown (1985: 280), Lemass 'gave Irishmen and Irishwomen to understand that work for economic renewal was the best way to serve the national aim and the most practical form of nationalism' in the belief that 'it would make the southern state attractive to the northern unionist that had in the past ample reason to reject incorporation into a state which could not even maintain its own population'. In 1965 Lemass broke new ground when he exchanged visits with his counterpart Northern Prime Minister Captain Terence O'Neill to open up a pragmatic *rapprochement* on economic cooperation. This was the first inter-governmental contact at that level since the 1921 settlement. Most people in the South welcomed the move as heralding a new era in North–South relations. It was hoped by both men that a new spirit of cooperation between North and South might also help to heal the long standing divisions within the North itself.

The process was soon to be completely over-shadowed, however, by the turn that events were to take within Northern Ireland itself. The problems that gave rise to the outbreak of civil strife in the North were endemic to the divided society in that part of the island and were deeply embedded in the social and political structure of the region. Protestant-unionist ascendancy was established at the beginning, but given the particular nature of the political divide Northern Ireland remained a one-party state. Later evidence would clearly show that there was widespread systematic discrimination against the nationalist community in relation to political representation, state housing and state-sector employment (Buckland 1981).

In the late 1960s a new generation of Northern nationalists, more articulate and better educated than their parents, and inspired by contemporary events in the United States, took to the streets in mass protest to demand their civil rights. The political challenge posed by the Civil Rights Movement and the heavy-handed response that it drew from hard-line unionists in the Northern Ireland administration eventually led to seriously political instability. Civil rights marchers were inadequately protected from violent attacks by extreme unionist mobs. In some notorious instances the police baton-charged the marchers and followed them into nationalist areas causing indiscriminate damage to persons and property. The deteriorating situation led to the emergence of the Provisional IRA. When 5 Catholics were killed and 150 Catholic homes burned to the ground on one night in August 1969 the nationalist community throughout the whole island became alarmed and the protection of nationalists in West Belfast became an urgent priority. With little help forthcoming or expected from the mainly sectarian security forces within Northern Ireland they looked to their own resources and to the South for support.

Lemass had retired from politics in 1966. He was succeeded by Jack Lynch. Lynch was a compromise choice in an attempt to avoid a potentially divisive leadership contest between two able and ambitious rivals for the position, Charles Haughey and George Colley. Lynch surprised many people by turning out to be an electoral asset in his own right. In August 1969 he and his government came under enormous pressure to intervene in some way on behalf of the nationalists in the North. His cabinet was deeply divided on what action should be taken. From this division a crisis developed, which as Lyons (1973: 587) has described, with due care, 'led to the resignation of two ministers, Mr. O'Morain and Mr. K. Boland, and the dismissal of two others, Mr. Charles Haughey and Mr. Neil Blaney'. The two dismissed ministers' names 'had been persistently mentioned in connection with an alleged plot' to 'smuggle arms into Northern Ireland, with the obvious intention that these should find their way into nationalist hands' and 'one of them, Mr. Haughey, was brought to trial on charges arising out of the allegations' and was 'subsequently acquitted'. Despite his exoneration by the courts this episode helped consign Haughey to the political wilderness for most of the 1970s. It also continued to haunt him on his return to prominence in the 1980s. This episode demonstrates a recurring feature of the Irish context, that when the 'national question' moves to centre stage it often tends to dominate and to divert energy away from the processes of social and economic development.

The outbreak of violence in Northern Ireland in the late 1960s, and the continuation of these troubles ever since, posed some awkward questions about the contemporary nature of Irish nationalism, particularly in the

South. The years since 1970 have been marked by the emergence of a strong revisionist strand among modern Irish historians and by a notable change in general attitudes towards the 'national aspiration' among the community at large. For example, Shaw (1972: 117–118), in a very influential article, challenged what he called the cannon of Irish history since the 1916 Rising that 'honours one group of Irishmen by denying honour to others that merit it no less' and that 'teaches that only the Fenians and the separatists had the good of the country at heart, that all others were either deluded or in one degree or another sold out to the enemy'. The most obvious example was the way in which the heroism and sacrifice of the many thousands of Irishmen, North and South, that had fought at the Somme in 1916 had been shamefully ignored while official adulation was solely reserved for the heroism of the 1,500 rebels that had taken active part in the 1916 rebellion. O'Brien (1972) went further and publicly challenged the central tenet of Irish nationalism, the concept of an Irish nation whole and indivisible, and argued that Ireland was really two nations, a reality with which nationalists North and South would eventually have to come to terms.

Ever since the outbreak of the Northern troubles nationalism as a cultural bonding force in the South has been on the decline. Survey after survey have in recent times revealed a growing 'chasm between the level of aspiration to unity and the depth of commitment to it' when 'unification is demystified, robbed of its heroic pretensions, and examined harshly in the context of real alternatives' (O'Malley 1983: 79). The 75th anniversary of the Easter Rising in 1991 was a deliberately low-key affair. It was marked by open debates about the wisdom of the Rising and its real legacy to modern Irish life, particularly in the context of the continuing violence in the North. This was in stark contrast to the triumphalism that marked the 50th anniversary in 1966, when such debates would have been considered heretical and when even Shaw's article, quoted earlier, was considered to be too controversial to publish and its eventual appearance delayed for six years.

The economy – EC entry and oil crises

Ireland's decision to join the European Economic Community, affirmed by an overwhelming 83 per cent to 17 per cent vote in favour in a national referendum on the issue, had already been anticipated in the programmes for economic expansion initiated by Lemass in 1958. When accession finally came in 1972 (along with the United Kingdom and Denmark) it was relatively undramatic though it was potentially the most far-reaching choice that the country had made since independence. From an economic point of view Ireland had already tried the isolationist self-sufficiency approach and had abandoned it as a dismal failure. EEC entry had then become the logical extension of the new, more outward-looking, economic policy that had been in operation since the beginning of the 1960s. When Ireland's initial application for entry to the Common Market was turned down, in tandem with Britain's in 1963, the country was already committed to a more liberal and less protectionist trading policy as part of the overall economic strategy of pursuing export-led growth. Undeterred by this temporary set-back, Lemass continued to prepare the national economy for eventual EEC Common Market conditions by concluding the Anglo-Irish Free Trade Agreement with the country's biggest trading partner in 1965.

Ireland expected EEC entry to help sustain and accelerate the process of the country's economic development and modernisation. Membership of the Community also offered the Irish economy the opportunity to overcome its dependence on the British market which in 1972 accounted for a larger share of Irish exports than all of the other EEC states taken together, including Denmark, by a ratio of over four to one (Coombes 1983). On the political front EEC entry was seen by most Irish people as a positive expression of their sovereignty rather than a diminution. It represented a positive affirmation of the country's independence and nationhood and one completely consonant with the outward-looking Ireland of the post-1958 era. The Republic of Ireland, by virtue of its independent status, was to be directly represented in the institutions and policy making bodies of the European Community in its own right, something that would not have happened had it remained an integral part of the United Kingdom. In this way it gave her historical struggle for independence new legitimacy. Moreover, by bringing the two parts of the island into closer economic and political union, EEC entry appeared to many Irish people, North and South, to offer a more positive context within which the age-old problem of Northern Ireland might eventually be resolved.

EEC entry did help to sustain the process of economic development until 1979. However, the positive effects of Community membership were quickly dampened by the sudden recessionary and inflationary effects of the first major oil crisis in 1973. Over the 1957–72 period the average annual growth in GNP was 4 per cent and the average growth in output per head was 3.9 per cent. Over the 1973–80 period, the average annual growth rate in GNP was 3.2 per cent but because of net population increase the average annual growth in net output per head was only 2.1 per cent. Furthermore, while the expansion rate in the economy had slowed down somewhat, it had also become more volatile, ranging from 1.2 per cent in 1976 to 6.1 per cent in 1977 (Blackwell 1982). The most immediate economic impact of EEC membership was felt, where it was expected to be felt, in the agriculture sector. Gross agricultural product grew, under the price-support incentives of the Common Agricultural Policy, by over 35 per cent in the 1970–78 period. The major expansion was in dairy production and processing, which in 1978 was almost 60 per cent higher than in 1970. The crisis in the world beef industry in 1974, unfortunately, considerably undermined the positive effects of Community membership to this important sector. Overall, however, farm incomes which had generally remained at 85 per cent of the average industrial wage throughout the 1960s rose to exceed parity by the late 1970s.

In manufacturing industry the most notable consequence of EEC entry during the 1970s was the rapid growth in the foreign sector. In 1969 the remit of the Industrial Development Authority (IDA) was extended to cover the negotiation and allocation of state incentives to foreign-sourced industrial projects. Under the dynamic leadership of Michael Killeen the IDA began to market the country as an attractive EEC industrial base with great skill and the agency became a model of its kind. By 1980 foreign-owned firms in Ireland employed about 80,000 people or close to 34 per cent of the total manufacturing workforce. Nearly 10,000 of these jobs were provided by over 70 multi-national companies in the electrical and electronic sectors. Over the 1973–80 period there was a net increase of 22,000 jobs in the foreign sector. In contrast, EEC entry did not stimulate the indigenous sector to anything like the same extent and there was a net increase of only 2,000 jobs in this sector over the same period

The growth in manufacturing employment and the growth in GDP that occurred throughout the 1970s would not have been possible without the contribution of the foreign sector. However, by the early 1980s the need to refocus the thrust of future industrial policy more towards the revitalisation of the indigenous sector became increasingly apparent. This was the primary message delivered to national policy makers by the international consultants, Telesis, in their commissioned review of Irish industrial policy in which they pointed out that no country 'had successfully achieved high incomes without a strong base of indigenously owned resource-based or manufacturing companies in traded businesses' (Telesis 1982: 26). The industrial programme of the 1970s had not gone 'far enough in developing native skills in technology and marketing' and the 'foundations of the industrial superstructure' still 'lacked depth' (Kennedy 1986: 48–49).

On the political front there were two general elections in the 1970s and both resulted in changes of government. In 1973 Fianna Fail went into opposition for the first time in sixteen years. The new incoming National Coalition Government, led by Liam Cosgrave, son of the country's first Taoiseach, was a partnership between Fine Gael (the modern name for Cumann na Gael) and the Labour Party. This coalition of the right and left in Irish politics held together remarkably well until 1977 in very difficult economic circumstances. It was only months in office when the Western world was hit by the sudden quadrupling in oil prices by OPEC. The Cosgrave Government took strict remedial measures to try to contain the inflationary pressures unleashed by the 1973 oil crisis which together with the temporary depression in world demand put a brake on the rate of Irish economic growth.

The country, however, grew tired of the 'economic hairshirt'. There was a lot of pent-up demand in the economy and a widespread impatience for a return to economic growth. When the Cosgrave administration called an election in 1977 the Fianna Fail Party presented the electorate with a reflationary economic package, involving a dramatic increase in government borrowing, which was designed to revitalise the economy. It was an election-winning formula which brought the party back to power with a majority of over twenty seats, its best ever electoral performance. However, whereas the economic strategy of Lemass in the early 1960s had heralded the end of a form of economic nationalism based on inward-looking self-sufficiency, its very success had, over the years since Lemass's departure from the scene, become associated with a 'different but equally dangerous form', the 'tendency to exaggerate our ability to control our own destiny'. Fianna Fail's latest programme for economic revival was, in the circumstances of the time, a 'brave strategy but a risky one' which 'gambled on continued economic growth in the rest of the world' and on 'Irish workers being willing to accept lower wage increases than our competitor countries' (Neary 1984: 71–73). In the wake of the 1979 Oil Crisis both bets lost and Ireland entered the recessionary 1980s with an unsustainable level of foreign borrowing and little flexibility to deal the new and very difficult economic challenges of the period.

RETRENCHMENT AND REALIGNMENT – THE 1980s

World trade went into recession, deepening into depression, in the wake of the oil crisis of 1979. The situation was particularly difficult in the Irish case because the country entered the low growth 1980s with a high level of public borrowing. As the decade progressed the state of the public finances deteriorated, reaching critical proportions in 1986. For much of the decade the country's economy was in the grips of a vicious cycle that successive governments seemed incapable of arresting and turning around. The debt to GNP ratio grew from 29 per cent in 1976 to 70 per cent by 1985, much of it denominated in strong foreign currencies. By 1986 the already high, and still rising, level of public debt had become the single greatest obstacle to any return to economic growth, keeping interest rates and the level of personal taxation at inordinately high levels and acting as a general brake on economic recovery. Tackling the major problems of the high level of public debt, the low level of economic activity and the high level of unemployment proved to be difficult for a number of reasons. Prominent among these reasons were the changes that had taken place in the structure of the economy since the 1960s, the resistance and inertia of sectional interests, the weakening of traditional cultural bonds and, up to 1987, the failure of the political system to produce a government with sufficient strength and imagination to be able to turn the situation around successfully.

By the 1980s the structure of the Irish economy had changed considerably since the policy of economic self-sufficiency was officially abandoned in 1958. The Lemass strategy of the late 1950s opened out the economy and in doing so led it inexorably to a much greater degree of integration with the international trading environment. Irish exports as a percentage of GNP had risen from 25 per cent in 1960 to over 60 per cent by 1985. International linkages became more extensive as the United Kingdom market became less dominant in the export pattern, its share of Irish exports falling from 75 per cent in 1960 to less than 35 per cent by 1984. As McAleese (1986: 19) remarked 'the fact of integration is indisputable' and 'not confined to the exchange of goods' with 'foreign manufacturing subsidiaries' accounting for 'four out of every ten jobs in Irish industry', the Irish government borrowing 'extensively abroad' and Irish capital and labour 'internationally mobile'. The overall effect of this increasing integration was that the decision making framework for Irish firms in general and for the national economy as a whole was becoming more complex, more dependent on external factors and less responsive to unilateral action at the level of national economic and fiscal policy. Nowhere was this more evident than in the strategically important agri-sector where the policy making focus had shifted from Dublin to Brussels. Community over-production and the reform of the Common Agricultural Policy, which included the progressive reduction in price-supports and the eventual introduction of quotas and cutbacks, became the major strategic issues for this sector as a whole and for the producers and processors in particular.

As well as having become more integrated into the international trading environment the underlying structure of the Irish economy had undergone significant change over the 1960s and 1970s. In particular the economy had become more developed and diversified with significant consequences for the underlying social and political structure of the country. Agriculture's share of GDP dropped from 22 per cent to 15 per cent over the 1960–79 period; industry's share rose from 28 per cent to 38 per cent over the same period. Over the 1961–78 period employment in agriculture fell from 397,500 to 229,000, employment in industry rose from 257,000 to 319,000 and employment in services grew from 416,000 to 500,000. Over the same period the proportion of those at work classified as employees rose overall from 56 per cent to 69 per cent. The proportion of those classified as professionals or managers rose from 7.6 per cent to 13.3 per cent and the class profile of all of those in the employee category had changed from 36 per cent middle class, 20 per cent skilled manual workers and 44 per cent unskilled manual workers to 50 per cent, 29 per cent and 22 per cent respectively. As Rottman and O'Connell (1982: 63) concluded from these data 'by 1979, Ireland had clearly ceased to be characterised as petit bourgeois: the predominant categories were of large scale employers and of well-qualified employees'.

The public service had also become enlarged and more diversified in line with the general expansion in the rest of the economy during the 1960s and 1970s. Public authority spending had increased from 24 per cent of GNP to 42 per cent over the 1958–78 period while over the same two decades the numbers employed in the public sector had risen from 182,000 to 295,000. Furthermore, around forty new state-sponsored bodies and agencies had been created over the same period with responsibilities ranging from the marketing of Irish dairy products abroad to the improvement of public health. State spending on health, education and social welfare had also expanded in line with the general expansion of the economy over the 1960s and 1970s. Furthermore, the country entered the low growth 1980s with a level of dependency that was increasing in relative terms due to a net population growth of 20 per cent over the 1960–80 period, an increase in the under-25 age group from 45 per cent of the population to 47.9 per cent and a decline in the working cohort from 43.8 per cent to 41.4 per cent. This legacy of the halcyon decades of growth became an increasingly unbearable burden on a contracting private sector as the economy moved deeper and deeper into recession.

Economic recovery was hampered by the strong sectional interests (Lee 1980; Farrell 1986) that had evolved through the processes of economic growth and modernisation and emerged in the development of a more differentiated and diversified socio-economic structure. Many of these sectional interests were vocational, like the hospital consultants and veterinary surgeons, who were anxious to preserve the privileges that they had derived from an enlarged public sector. Others were representative organisations, like the professional, technical and general trade unions and the farming bodies, that were capable of mobilising substantial sectional political power in defence of their claims on the public purse. Still others were state agencies that had over their histories developed and consolidated for themselves positions of considerable autonomy and power in both public policy formulation and in the acquisition and allocation of public funds.

Side by side with the emergence of these sectional interests the years of economic growth saw the progressive weakening of the two strongest cultural bonds, nationalism and Catholicism, which held traditional Ireland together and enabled its leaders to mobilise the 'national will' in the interests of the community as a whole. As noted earlier, ever since the outbreak of the troubles in Northern Ireland nationalism as a cultural bonding force had been on the decline. The influence of religion had also declined with the growth of materialism and secularism that accompanied the processes of economic development and modernisation. This left the country in a position where there was 'no large group of people in the society' who had 'the trust of the population' and could 'get its cooperation for medium- or long-term goals' (Garvin 1982: 32). What Lee (1982: 13) noted as the 'peculiarly weak sense of identity by European standards' that characterised the Ireland of the 1980s had been further diluted by the unrelenting shift that was taking place in educational emphasis away from the arts and humanities towards business, technology and the professions. This shift tended to elevate the material, the empirical and the contingent at the expense of the spiritual, the cultural and the universal.

Tough decisions were needed to restore order to the public finances in the early 1980s. However, the political system failed to provide a government with enough political strength or will to tackle this problem head-on in the face of these strong sectional interests and weakened cultural bonds. Lynch retired in 1979. The succession contest between Charles Haughey and George Colley was bitter and divisive. Haughey had been restored to Lynch's cabinet in 1977 but remained an outsider. He narrowly won the succession race with strong back-bench support but mistrust and antipathy for Haughey remained rife among his former cabinet colleagues. This continued to weaken his political authority up to 1987. Indeed, between 1979 and 1982 there were three concerted efforts to remove him. Some of the dissidents left after the failure of these attempts to help form a new party, the Progressive Democrats. This weakened Fianna Fail's overall electoral position.

Over the 1979–87 period Irish governments alternated between internally strained Haughey-led Fianna Fail administrations and Fine Gael-Labour coalitions led by Garret FitzGerald that were weakened by inter-party differences over economic and fiscal policy. There were three changes of power between June 1981 and November 1982 as all the major political parties found themselves having to desperately court popularity, and form unstable minority governments, at a time when unpopular but necessary measures were called for in the national interest. The general election of November 1982 returned a FitzGerald-led coalition of Fine Gael and Labour that remained in office for over four years.

The FitzGerald coalition of 1982–87 had only limited success in dealing with the growing crisis in the public finances because of ideological tensions between the coalition partners. Consequently FitzGerald was forced to confine himself to piecemeal containment action. Increases in indirect taxation on tobacco and alcohol soon reached the level of diminishing returns. Across the board cutbacks in non-salary public expenditure shared the pain but were not deep enough to achieve the level of rationalisation necessary. The major political achievement of this government was the securing of the Anglo-Irish Agreement of 1985. This went some way towards trying to improve British–Irish relations over the Northern problem and reducing the alienation and isolation of the Northern nationalists, though Unionists saw it as a weakening of their position and were bitterly opposed to it. On the economic front, however, the FitzGerald coalition was largely seen as ineffective.

It took a change of government in 1987 and a growing sense of national crisis to produce the conditions that eventually made tough action possible. The 1987 election brought a Haughey-led minority administration into power. Haughey was finally leading a party that was fairly united behind his leadership. His political position was strengthened by the public commitment of Fine Gael in opposition to support any fiscal programme through at least two budgetary periods which promised to deal decisively with the country's financial crisis. His government pursued fiscal rectitude with all the zeal of the convert. Over the 1987–89 period it brought in two very tough budgets which significantly reduced the level of public expenditure. It also brought about a radical restructuring of the public sector, closing down some of the smaller agencies and merging many of the larger ones.

The Haughey administration was able to persuade the employers, the unions and the main farming organisations to join with it, as social partners, in an agreed Programme for National Recovery. This move made tough rationalisation measures possible without major conflict. The need to stabilise the national debt and strengthen the overall competitiveness of the Irish economy took on new urgency with the ratification of the Single European Act in 1987 and the determination within the European Community to complete the internal market by the end of 1992. The Programme for National Recovery soon began to show substantial results. Within two years the Government had exceeded its own ambitious target for debt reduction and looked set to stabilise the debt as a percentage of GNP well ahead of schedule. In late 1988 inflation was running at under 2 per cent, its lowest level for 25 years and well below the EC average of 2.8 per cent. Against the background of an economy that was improving in nearly all respects Haughey decided to go to the country in 1989. He failed to win the elusive overall majority and found himself ironically having to form a coalition with the Progressive Democrats who were even more market-oriented in their economic ideology than the Fianna Fail of fiscal rectitude.

The process of economic recovery continued under this coalition through the end of the 1980s. Radical reform of the public sector was moved beyond rationalisation to the privatisation of a number of state enterprises. For the country as a whole the one major weakness in the recovery process was its sluggishness in creating new employment opportunities. Rising unemployment and the far-reaching fundamental changes heralded by the 'brave new world' of greater European integration looked set to be among the major challenges facing the country as the 1990s began.

CONCLUSION

In this chapter we examined the main phases in the evolution of the common context of the organisations in our study in its own terms at the national level of analysis. This separate analysis of the national context is an integral element of our multi-level approach to the analysis of the leadership-context-strategy inter-relationship. In the next four chapters we go on to examine the strategic histories of the organisations themselves as viewed at industry and firm levels.

4   A state agency – An Foras Taluntais

INTRODUCTION

In this and in the following three chapters we see strategy and leadership in interaction in four organisations over their histories. These organisations, taken together, are representative of the four main organisational forms to be found in Ireland's small, open and mixed national economy. The four are An Foras Taluntais (AFT), the state sector agricultural research institute; Irish Distillers Group (IDG) Ltd, a large public limited company; Comhlucht Siuicre Eireann Teoranta (CSET), the state-owned sugar company; and Golden Vale Coop Creameries Ltd, one of the country's largest dairy processors and a cooperative organisation. We start with the case of An Foras Taluntais.

AN FORAS TALUNTAIS IN BRIEF

An Foras Taluntais (AFT), also known as The Agricultural Institute, was a public service agency set up by the Government through an Act of Dail Eireann in 1958. Its general functions, as described in the Act, were to 'review, facilitate, encourage, assist, coordinate, promote and undertake agricultural research'. AFT ceased to exist as an independent organisation in 1988 when it merged with the advisory services into a new entity called Teagasc.

AFT was essentially an infrastructural research organisation for Irish agriculture funded by the State. Its main resource was professional staff and its main activities were research projects. As one senior manager succinctly described it 'we have one product, information; and we only have one source, ideas'. In 1986, when the field work for this study began, AFT had around 1,200 personnel. Of these 236 were researchers. The remainder were technical, administrative and general support staff. There were around 700 discrete projects in the overall research programme of the Institute.

The following narrative describes the main phases in AFT's thirty year history as an independent entity.

ORIGIN AND FORMATION 1945–58

Though the State had been directly involved in Irish agriculture since 1899 the idea of establishing a national agricultural institute first took root in the immediate post-World War Two period. Soil fertility had suffered over the years of shortage and economic depression that had characterised the 1930–45 period. In 1948 a visiting grassland expert from New Zealand, a man called Holmes, reported that 'the country's grasslands were producing the minimum possible under an Irish sky' (Bolger 1977: 244). At the same time the Marshall Aid Program for European recovery and reconstruction was underway. Special delegates had been assigned by the US Government to each country in Europe to administer the programme. In 1948, the Irish delegate, a man named Carrigan, was invited to speak at a meeting of the Agricultural Science Society, an undergraduate society, in University College Dublin. He used this platform to argue that Ireland was too small a country to have multiple agencies conducting research in agriculture without coordination. At the time the Department of Agriculture, the universities and some public and private enterprises were independently engaged in agricultural research without any overall coherent strategy. Carrigan's proposal was that the US Government would be favourably disposed to lending financial and other support, through the Marshall Aid Program, for the establishment of a national agricultural institute that would be responsible for 'teaching at University level in agriculture, veterinary science, horticulture and forestry; research in these subjects; the dissemination of research results' and would also 'take over the advisory services' (O'Sullivan 1973: 158).

This proposal gave rise to much conflict and controversy and it was to be nearly ten years before the new national Institute finally opened its doors. The proposal threatened a number of powerful interests that were already engaged in the activities earmarked for the new Institute under the American model. Among these interests were the universities, the Catholic Hierarchy, the Department of Agriculture and some farming bodies. Conflict arose mainly over the proposed domain of the new Institute and over the form of control. By 1954 the governments of the US and Ireland had concluded their formal arrangements and in 1955 the Minister for Agriculture, Mr James Dillon, publicly announced his plan for the reorganisation of higher agricultural education in Ireland. Essentially what the Minister wanted was to centralise all third-level teaching and research in agriculture into a single institution modelled on the Dutch agricultural university at Wageningen.

University and farming interests were the main opponents of the Minister's plan but they managed to harness powerful support from the Catholic Hierarchy. They appealed to Catholic social teaching on the organisation of society, as then most recently ennunciated in the papal encyclical of Pope Pius XI, *Quadragesimo Anno*, published in 1931. During the 1946 to 1958 period the influence of this social philosophy was at its zenith in Ireland and there was great wariness by Church leaders of any extension of the state apparatus into the organisation of society. By harnessing this concern the university and farming interests were able to mobilise a number of influential Irish bishops in their opposition to the Minister's plan. In voicing these worries at a public meeting the Bishop of Cork was convinced that the people of Ireland 'would vote down a government that openly committed itself to a policy of Socialisation' but that 'socialisation can be a gradual, hidden and undeclared process'. That was why, in his view, it was 'so necessary to examine the proposed Institute and see if it be part of the larger trend' towards 'out-and-out Statism' (quoted in Whyte 1980: 310).

In the face of opposition on such a scale, the Minister had to modify his proposal. The teaching function was dropped and left with the universities. The advisory services were left with the Department of Agriculture. In the end the supporters of the new Institute had to fight even to retain an active research brief. There were many who wanted it to be reduced to a mere coordinating body, with no direct research activity. There were also many who questioned the need for the new Institute to be an autonomous body. Some senior AFT staff recalled that 'there was tremendous political activity by the Department of Agriculture in particular, and possibly by the Department of Finance, to deny the autonomy that the American Government was particularly anxious to assign to the new institute'. In the end the government of the day set up AFT as an independent institution but excluded from its remit responsibility for university teaching, veterinary research and the advisory services.

THE WALSH ERA 1958–79

Establishment and early growth 1958–68

Dr Tom Walsh was seconded from the research staff at the Department of Agriculture to be the new Institute's first director. The initial funding for AFT came from the Marshall Aid fund in the form of a capital grant of £840,000 and an endowment fund of £1m. The interest from the endowment fund was meant to contribute towards the operating expenses of AFT. However, it was always accepted that an annual grant-in-aid would be needed from the State to supplement it.

The early development of AFT was critically watched by many of those interests that were earlier embroiled in the controversy surrounding its establishment. In Walsh's own words AFT expanded quickly and 'this fact raised the ire of some people in the Department and in the Universities'. Right from the word go 'the Doc', as Dr Walsh came to be known by all his staff, had to fight for his operational freedom. As he saw it the Institute was set up to develop the agriculture of the country and 'this did not mean just farming'. There were objections to him setting up a rural economy division because 'it was said that the Institute's focus was production' but the Doc 'never saw it that way'. His efforts to get the Department to transfer its cereal breeding research activities to AFT failed, in spite of the strong representations made by him and his council to government.

Undaunted by these difficulties the Doc quickly set about defining the major elements in the research programme. He created a structure with five main operating divisions to reflect these elements. They were Soils, Animal Production, Plant Sciences and Crop Husbandry, Horticulture and Forestry, and Rural Economy. In his initial structure he also established two special liaison activities. The first of these, Scientific Liaison, was set up to maintain ready access to relevant scientific developments at home and abroad in order to make the acquisition and production of knowledge as efficient as possible. Agricultural Liaison, the other one, was intended to help the organisation to keep in close touch with the primary users of its services in order to ensure the efficient dissemination and application of the knowledge acquired or generated. He was clear on what he wanted. The role of AFT, as he saw it, 'did not just mean farming' but 'brought in the socio-economic structure and the behavioural sciences as well'. His 'model' was the State college of agriculture as operated in the United States.

The Doc assembled the physical and human resources to fulfil his vision for AFT with the minimum of bureaucratic procedure. He negotiated personally for the transfer of existing facilities and staff from the Department and from the universities. Decisions were often made at a single informal meeting between himself and the other principals involved. With the Marshall Aid money, he and his senior staff went out and bought land and buildings in the same informal way, haggling personally over the terms and conditions as if they were dealing for themselves. In this way the initial resources for AFT were quickly acquired and assembled. He hired a mix of experienced graduates, some of them non-nationals, and a crop of fresh young Irish graduates. He sent scores of these young graduates off on

Kellogg Foundation scholarships to take higher degrees at reputable US universities in order to bring his scientific base as quickly as possible up to the highest of international standards.

By 1961 AFT had already grown to 705 personnel and by 1967 this had expanded further to 1,076. According to one senior manager 'officially the Department of Agriculture were very alarmed at the rate of AFT's early expansion' and clearly had never intended nor expected that it would grow so large, so fast.

AFT's rapid growth during the 1958–68 period was due to a number of factors. Firstly, the early work of AFT had 'an immediate impact' on raising the productivity of Irish farming because the whole research effort was 'starting out from such a low base'. Secondly, AFT had 'emerged at a time of revolutionary thinking in national policy' (O'Sullivan 1973: 158). The Institute was finally established in the same year that the Lemass/Whitaker strategy for economic development was drawn up and the First Programme for Economic Expansion launched. The export-earning potential of agriculture was a cornerstone of the overall strategy. Foreign exchange was needed to help expand the manufacturing base because it was recognised that such expansion was going to necessitate the importation of capital equipment and raw materials. AFT's Annual Report of 1963–64 recorded that the Institute's early development was 'in line with the objectives of the (First) Programme'. When the Second Programme for Economic Expansion came to be formulated the Institute was required to advise on the research needs for agriculture up to 1970. AFT's proposed programme for research, on approval by the Government, was directly incorporated as an integral element in the Second Programme's plans and objectives for the agricultural sector. During the period covered by the Second Programme the Institute got a three-year financial commitment from the Government to support its planned development over the 1963–66 period, the only time in its history that such a multi-year commitment was ever made.

AFT was also fortunate during this general expansionary period in 'having an advocate in court' to counterbalance the less than satisfactory relationship between the Institute and the Department of Agriculture. As the Doc put it 'the Department were not friendly' and 'there wasn't the right level of goodwill between the Institute and the Department'. However he 'knew Ken Whitaker and the Minister Jim Ryan in the Department of Finance'. This 'in' with the Department of Finance was a help in securing the multi-year funding over the 1963–66 period. In general there seemed to be sufficient funding to support any worthwhile project and the financial scope to keep the young and talented researchers well-motivated and rewarded. As one senior researcher recalled 'there was great growth and buoyancy associated with the Programme for Economic Expansion'. The 'rising tide was raising all boats' and 'it raised our boat'.

A third factor of significance was the Marshall Aid funding and the Institute's control over its disposition. According to AFT's Finance Officer the capital fund 'was entirely under AFT control and this bought the farms and built the buildings'. It gave the Institute 'the freedom to expand as it did without having to refer back to the State'. When this funding ran out it had 'a noticeable effect on AFT's rate of expansion'. The operating freedom that the Marshall Aid fund and inter-governmental-agreement gave AFT in its early years was particularly important given the attitude and concern that appeared to exist within the Department of Agriculture to the new Institute and its first director. The Doc recalled that 'there was a certain resentment within the Department to the Institute'. The Department wanted him to 'go cap-in-hand to them' while he was 'operating the autonomy of the Institute'. It was 'a continual struggle day in, day out'.

Last, but not least, within AFT itself there is little doubt that the personal characteristics, beliefs and operating style of the Institute's first director, Dr Tom Walsh, had a decisive influence on AFT's early expansion and ultimate size. As one senior manager, in AFT since its foundation, recalled nearly three decades later 'the Doc was the driving force'. 'If it had not been for the Doc' AFT would 'never have been as big as it is' or 'what it is today'. To another Walsh was 'the outstanding character'. This second manager went on to remark that when he and others looked back in later years over the rapid rate of AFT's early expansion and development they had often asked themselves 'who else could have done it?'. The Doc was growth-oriented and 'anything that anybody was doing in agriculture, food or environment Doc Walsh threw his beady eye on it', always 'arguing against fragmentation'. He 'just grew and grew in not a very planned manner' and 'was an opportunist'. He 'had no concept of, and did not want discussed, when the end of the expansion of AFT was to be'. His strategy around recruiting was to 'get the best people, motivate them, turn them loose and they will define the programme'. He was aided in this by having control of the salary structure of AFT during the early years and not being unduly constrained by general public service rates. He was a cavalier and a builder who attracted like-minded people into AFT and encouraged them to be innovative and to build up their departments and programmes. With the ferment that he generated it was almost inevitable that difficulties would arise. Some people in key positions were moved, others resigned. Some were not cavalier enough, others were too much so. 'The main thing was to get the job done.' Walsh fired his young staff up with a belief in themselves and in the importance of their mission to the nation. He was driven by his own deep nationalist convictions. In characterising his own leadership role the Doc saw his 'main job' as 'building morale', as getting 'to know each person and their capacity', as helping them to see that 'they had a national job to do' and that while 'they might have thought that they were small cogs' nevertherless 'the work that they were doing was important'.

He had, as senior staff recalled in interview, 'a charisma of leadership where young scientists identified for themselves individually and collectively a mission in the revival of Irish agriculture'. He infused in them a spirit and a belief that 'as scientists, even though from a small country', they were 'equal to the best and better than most'. He saw himself and his young staff as 'bringing science to the people'. He believed passionately in the potential of the application of science to help develop Irish agriculture in the national interest. He 'had the idea that there was no problem that could not be solved by AFT'. His attitude was that 'science and technology could be harnessed to do anything and to hell with the politicians and people who got in the way'. He saw 'no limit to the growth of agriculture in Ireland and he saw agriculture as the primary engine of the economy'.

The Doc continually pointed to native renewable resources as a primary source of the nation's wealth. One of his favourite metaphors for Irish agriculture was 'the mine on the top of the land'. The Doc always saw AFT as part of a larger national effort. Many of the young pioneering scientists that he had attracted to AFT in the early days later left to take up key positions in the meat and dairy processing industries which, as Institute scientists, they had been helping to develop and modernise. This was a matter of pride for the Doc who looked on this process as a natural extension and valuable by-product of the developmental role of AFT. To him it was part of the 'whole thing about the intellectual investment', about 'the resource pool', and he saw that the development of staff within AFT 'provided a pool of scientifically trained manpower to this country in a real sense' even if some of it migrated beyond the organisation itself.

Review and reorganisation 1968–73

AFT began to face some new issues in the late 1960s. The organisation had grown to over 1,000 personnel and the research programme had elaborated and diversified into hundreds of discrete projects and activities. By this time also the easy gains from applying science to the problems of agriculture had been made and it had become harder to demonstrate to the economy the value of AFT's research programme. Furthermore, the Marshall Aid capital fund was effectively spent and the endowment fund was providing a declining proportion of the Institute's annual expenditure. A new council was appointed for AFT in 1968. It included two officials from the Department of Agriculture, 'the two men that the Department put in to control me' as the Doc saw it.

The Doc met the new situation by setting up a major review of AFT's programme for relevance and scientific quality. He involved major external interest groups and highly reputable external scientific expertise in these reviews. From this major review a five year plan for AFT, 'Research for Agriculture 1970–75', was produced and published. The plan called for moderate expansion at a rate of 5 per cent per annum over the period covered. This major review and the five-year plan that emerged from it were seen within AFT as 'Walsh's reposte to the new situation that the Government had imposed'. The Doc 'knew he was going to have a new chairman and a new council that were going to be difficult; the question was how to contend with this' and 'how to keep them at arm's length'. His answer 'was to draw up a charter'. As the Doc himself recalled the 1970–75 plan was 'addressed at the government of the day to get more money'. Its impact fell far short of his own aspirations in this regard.

As part of this major review process the Doc and his council decided to look at the question of the organisation's structure. There were general concerns throughout the Institute that 'the system had begun to creak' under the strains of growth. The Doc was worried that 'the organisation had settled down too much' and that it 'was getting too structured in terms of mobility and action'. He was particularly concerned that 'the divisional structure had created a sense of division' and wanted to ensure a better 'flow of knowledge across divisions'. He persuaded the Council to engage the help of Dr J. A. Anderson from the University of Manitoba in this appraisal.

The main structural change that emerged from the review was an overall reorganisation from six divisions to seven research centres. Whereas before the divisions had been focused on scientific disciplines, five of the new research centres were focused on commodities. These were the beef, dairying, horticulture, soils/grasslands and tillage crop centres. A sixth centre was devoted to rural economics and welfare. The seventh centre was focused on the needs of the western region of the country and represented a major departure from the rationale for the rest of the structural change. It is clear from his own later writings (Walsh 1981) that the Doc had deep personal convictions about the need to focus national research attention on the needs of the west. In raising it to full centre status in the new structure he felt that AFT was 'raising the development of the land in the west to a national priority'.

The reorganisation went beyond this structural change to introduce some new decision making structures. A central directorate was set up consisting of the Director, a Deputy Director, a number of Associate Directors at AFT headquarters and the heads of the new research centres. The concept of this central directorate was one 'where the head of centre was part of the corporate management team'. The Doc had become concerned that the division directors under the old structure 'were beginning to run these divisions as independent entities', in effect, 'running several institutes instead of one'. He felt that he 'wanted more cohesion and sharing in the administration of the Institute'. A 'consultative management committee' which was 'representative of all categories of staff' at each centre was also to be set up under the new structure in order to ensure 'staff participation in programme development, evaluation and review'. The post of Deputy Director was another novel feature of the reorganisation. A further development was the setting up of the Planning and Information Analysis Department to help to ensure that 'the right decisions are made on research priorities, having regard for the resources available'. An early contribution from this new staff department was the introduction of the ARMIS system, the computerised Agricultural Research Management Information System, which was intended to 'provide a comprehensive database on programme activities for all staff in the organisation' (Higgins 1973: 182).

The 1970–71 reorganisation was not an unqualified success for a number of reasons. There was serious controversy over the appointment of one of the new Centre directors which led to the resignation of one of the Doc's most talented cavaliers. The Doc and one of his senior staff clashed openly over the latter's appointment to the newly established Western Centre. This able executive had wanted, and had been generally expected to get, the directorship of the Dairy Centre at Moorepark. This was one of the two most prominent centres and the one in which he had personally played a key role in developing to full centre status. He refused to accept the outcome of the Doc's reorganisation. After months of controversy, which extended beyond the Institute into the media and the political system, this senior figure eventually resigned. When the irresistable force met the immovable object in this reorganisation episode AFT lost a talent that in the Doc's own view 'had the attributes' and had 'a good chance of being a future Director' of AFT. The Doc's credibility with his own staff was damaged by this episode.

There were further difficulties which tended to undermine the effectiveness of the reorganisation. The Doc, by personality, was not suited to the participative structures that emerged from the Anderson recommendations. His dominating style meant that none of the new administrative supports, the Deputy Directorship, the Central Directorate nor the consultative committees, were used to anywhere near full effect under his leadership. The Doc came in time to regret the reorganisation of 1970–71 in that it went too far too fast. It was not primarily new structures that he wanted out of the reorganisation process; these were somewhat forced upon him by the Anderson study. What he really wanted was to 'keep the pot stirring in some ways' because of his conviction that 'in any research organisation there has to be agitation or nothing will get done'. He later came to feel that 'there was a mistake made in terms of reorganising all at one time' instead of reviewing and reorganising one department or centre each year just to keep things on the boil. Furthermore, the ARMIS system never really came to full fruition during the Doc's regime. He wanted AFT to be seen to have a comprehensive formal planning system but he also wanted to retain the flexibility to manage intuitively and opportunistically as he had always done. According to one former senior executive, the Doc 'never believed that he needed all the planning paraphernalia' but was convinced that 'research was managed best through the personal touch'.

EEC and contract funding 1973–79

Three developments dominated the remainder of the Doc's tenure at the top. These were Ireland's entry into the European Economic Community (EEC) and its implications for the development of Irish agriculture; the growing contribution of AFT to its own running costs through a distinct shift in emphasis towards user-funded research; and the abortive attempt by government to establish the National Agricultural Authority (NAA).

Ireland's entry into the EEC provided AFT with new opportunities to expand the range and scope of its activities and the Doc was quick to avail himself of them. Access to the large Community market, at stable and favourable prices under the regime of the Common Agricultural Policy, gave Irish agriculture considerable scope and incentive for further expansion in production and processing activities. It also gave the Institute a renewed sense of national mission in helping to contribute to this growth. With such bright prospects for agriculture the government of the day, under acute fiscal pressure following the inflationary 1973 Oil Crisis, let it be widely known that there would be no further expansion in AFT's research activities without the sector itself providing a substantial share of the additional funding required. The Doc quickly took the initiative and went out in search of user funding in order to continue to develop the Institute and its programme. With some users, like the sugar company, the mechanism employed was direct user-defined contract research. With others, like the dairy industry, it took the form of a commodity levy with industry participation in the determination of research priorities. EEC entry also provided AFT with an expanded market for agri-policy research and the Institute began to seek, and be sought for, Community-funded projects.

AFT continued to grow over the 1970s, though at a more modest rate than in the previous decade. Most of this growth was funded by these new revenue-generating activities. 'If a man from Mars was to look at the Institute from the beginning', according to a senior finance officer, 'the growth in the Institute's contribution to its own finances' would have been 'the most significant change' to strike him.

The final drama in the Doc's tenure at the top was the episode of the National Agricultural Authority. The Minister for Agriculture in the National Coalition Government of 1973–77 put on public record early on his belief 'that there should be close working arrangements between the research, development, advisory and educational agencies' involved in supporting Irish agriculture and that he looked forward to 'the early integration and streamlining of the various services available to the farmer'. He later drew up proposed legislation for the formation of the National Agricultural Authority (NAA) to give effect to this policy. The proposed NAA was to involve a merger between AFT and the advisory services which were then under the joint administration of the Department of Agriculture and the local County Councils.

The Doc strongly supported the proposal and saw it as a way to enlarge his organisation's influence within the sector. His researchers as a body opposed the move. They felt that the proposed merger threatened the status of the research activity. They also believed that research could lose out in the competition for resources and be 'starved' in times of stringency in favour of the more politically visible and sensitive advisory services. They believed that the Doc did not understand their concerns because 'he was after power' and 'wanted to expand his power base'. The issue was fought out in public, in the media and in the Dail chamber. The Fianna Fail opposition spokesman supported the position of the staff. In the end the proposed merger was aborted, but only because the Fianna Fail Party was returned to power before the enabling legislation had been enacted. This incoming administration set up the advisory services as a separate state agency, ACOT, and the Doc left AFT in 1979 to become the new agency's first director.

THE RYAN ERA 1979–88

New challenges and programme transformation 1980–85

The Doc was succeeded at AFT by Dr Pierce Ryan, the man who had been the Deputy Director since the reorganisation of 1970/71. Ryan was one of the young Irish scientists that the Doc had attracted to AFT in the 1960s. He had headed up the Soils Division prior to 1971. The two most immediate effects of the succession were a change in the style of leadership and a change in the distribution of power within AFT.

In contrast to the direct, driving, expansionist, authoritative style of Walsh, the Ryan style was characterised by AFT executives as 'quieter but equally committed to the advances that science and technology (could) make'. Ryan was seen as a leader who had 'a vision' and 'a more balanced view of where the Institute should be going', a man whose inclination was towards a 'more collegial approach', a 'logician, systems-man, and diplomat'.

Ryan appointed three new deputy directors at AFT headquarters and shared power with them. Each was given a strategic focus, one on resource allocation and control of the organisation as an effective director of operations; another, as the architect of the research programme, on keeping the programme as a whole and the scientific base of the organisation relevant and up-to-date; and the third on external relations with a particular brief to develop the links with the EEC. The role of deputy director under Walsh's leadership was perceived to have had relatively little impact on strategic issues like 'programme composition' because of the Doc's tendency to keep power at the centre. The Doc had been a 'dominant Director who had a deputy director in name only'. He had tended to delegate only 'the things that he did not want to handle himself' like 'personnel' issues. Under Ryan's leadership the role of deputy director had real content, clout and responsibility. These changes in structure on Pierce Ryan's accession to the leadership were, in the view of one senior executive, even 'more significant' in their impact on the real redistribution of power within AFT than the more extensive reorganisation of 1970/71.

The new leader and his new directorate came to the helm of AFT at a time of dramatic change in their organisation's environment. They were faced with some very difficult challenges and threatening developments. The most important were the dramatic changes in EEC policy towards agricultural production and the related changes in national agri-product strategy, the gathering crisis in the state of the country's public finances, and the ageing of the professional research base within the organisation itself.

The Common Agricultural Policy (CAP) of the EEC came under increasing pressure from the early 1980s onwards and this had major implications for AFT's research programme. By 1980 the EEC had moved beyond self-sufficiency in most commodities, after years of expansion in agricultural production throughout the Community under the price support system of the CAP. This expansion was mirrored right across the world's major food producing blocks so that the international situation in the 1980s became broadly one of increasing supply and falling demand. Commodity surpluses began to build up to unsustainable levels and became an unacceptable drain on the Community's budget. Throughout the 1980s the Commission adopted a series of measures, each one more drastic than the last, which were designed to curtail production and to control the surpluses. The Commission first reduced the price supports and followed this by introducing quotas, and later still, cutbacks. These developments had major implications for AFT. The restrictions and cutbacks on agricultural production meant that the traditional emphasis on production research in AFT's programme, aimed at helping to increase the output of Irish agriculture, had to undergo major reorientation. The development of more efficient production systems designed to improve producer margins rather than to increase output became the new priority in production research. In addition, the new imperative on the processing and marketing side became the need to reduce the industry's dependence on commodities and to develop more consumer-oriented products with higher levels of value-added. This was 'an absolutely new ballgame', a 'whole revolution' with 'enormous implications for (agricultural) research'.

In facing the need to bring about a transformation in its overall research programme there were some significant difficulties to be confronted. The first of these was finance. The Institute saw its grant-in-aid from the government decline in real terms during the 1980s as the state of the public finances deteriorated into crisis. This forced AFT to keep increasing its revenue-raising activities in order to preserve its resource base from cutbacks. At the same time public sector agencies in general came under increasing pressure to justify their existence and AFT found itself included in the *Sunday Independent*'s (27/4/83) own list of state agencies that 'test the taxpayer's tolerance'. Such developments affected staff morale. Long-serving professionals began to question why AFT's grant was being reduced and concluded that 'either there are no votes in it or they do not see us as contributing'. With the grant-in-aid on the decline there was no longer any financial slack within which to try to transform the programme without major reallocation of the existing resource base.

The second difficulty was the serious imbalance that had developed in the Institute's internal demographics by the early 1980s. The cohort of young scientists that the Doc had brought into AFT during the 1960s had aged with the organisation. The average AFT researcher was by 1980 in his late forties or early fifties. The scientific base of the Institute was made up largely of specialists with 15 to 20 years of cumulative knowledge, experience and reputation in areas that were the priorities when the expansion of agricultural output had been the national goal. The need to reassign such people to the new research priorities, involving newer scientific disciplines, presented major problems.

There were, in addition, internal ideological and political difficulties to be overcome. The increasing pressure on AFT to become more self-financing meant that over time the emphasis in the overall programme had shifted significantly away from basic research towards short-term, problem-solving, user-funded projects. AFT's mission was being changed by this process without any conscious change of policy. Many of the researchers found this ideologically hard to accept. To them the distinctive character of the Institute, its overall sense of national purpose and the quality of its scientific base were all threatened by this development. There was, moreover, the political difficulty posed by the need to change the primary emphasis of the programme as this threatened the traditional pre-eminence of the production researchers and their units within the Institute.

To try to overcome these difficulties Pierce Ryan and the directorate carried out a major review of AFT's activities. The approach was very different to that of the Doc in the late 1960s. The Ryan process was designed to involve all of the professional staff in a comprehensive effort to systematically evaluate the programme and develop a fair degree of consensus around future priorities. Under his patient and persistent leadership the Institute began to make steady, if slow, progress in the task of transforming the programme. In fact the ARMIS system, which had 'done just about enough to keep it alive over the years' since its introduction, was revitalised by Ryan and his team as one of the procedures used in this overall transformation effort. One major challenge was to get the need for change widely recognised throughout AFT in order to generate the momentum needed to bring it about. As one dramatic change followed another in EEC agricultural policy, and as the resourcing environment became more stringent, the sense of urgency became more widespread and the need for change more widely accepted. This was vital in helping to get the process underway.

By 1985 Ryan and his team had already achieved a fair measure of rationalisation and realignment involving the closure of 6 research stations, a reduction in staff of over 140 and the redeployment of a further 55. Within the programme itself 69 per cent of the discrete projects were new. The ratio of production to process research had already been reduced to 60/40 and a sustained effort was underway to realign it still further towards a 50/50 balance. Though the redeployment of resources across departments and centres still remained relatively small in scale, considerable progress had been made in transforming the programme at the discrete project level.

From the Cashman Report to the merger with ACOT 1985–88

The pace of events quickened for AFT as the country's fiscal problems became more acute. In April 1985 the FitzGerald Government set up a commission, under the chairmanship of farm leader Donal Cashman, to examine the operations of AFT and of ACOT, the advisory service. Cashman's brief was to recommend how the existing levels of state investment in the two bodies might be better deployed and coordinated. This was the first major review of the Institute's activities to be commissioned by a government in the lifetime of the organisation and was itself a manifestation of the new realities facing AFT. Successive governments had kept the operation of the Institute at arm's length for most of its history. However, as public funds became more scarce, and control of expenditure in the public sector more stringent, commissioned reviews of the affairs and operations of state agencies became more prevalent. In relation to AFT the Cashman study addressed itself primarily to the issue of how the research activities of the Institute might be expanded and extended into new areas without the need for any increase in overall resource input from the State.

The Cashman Report highlighted publicly some of the structural difficulties that were besetting the organisation and impairing its performance, including the age imbalance of AFT researchers and the low ratio of research to non-research staff. He lay the responsibility for the reform of these problems primarily with AFT management. In the wake of this study the organisation came under public pressure to speed up the process of transformation, whatever the internal difficulties.

In December 1986 the Director and the Council decided to accelerate the process. AFT's morale had been badly dented at a meeting of agricultural interests convened by the FitzGerald Government in late 1986 at which the influential chief executive of one of the country's largest dairy cooperatives publicly dismissed the Institute's effort in food research as largely ineffective. Though AFT could fairly question the objective merits of this sweeping criticism, it was a damaging blow to the Institute's public image. Ryan and the Council reacted quickly to restore credibility. They introduced substantial changes in the primary thrust of the Institute's research programme to deal with the major changes in EEC policy. New priorities were identified in areas such as the development of alternative uses for land, the improvement of efficiency in the food processing industry, the identification of new non-food applications for agricultural products and the support of the sector's efforts to expand exports particularly in Europe.

One of the most significant changes to emerge from this exercise was the decision to set up the new National Centre for Food Research. Prior to this food research had been carried on right across the Institute in a number of the commodity-focused centres. The Institute had been stressing the need to give this activity more attention in its overall programme for over two decades. It had, however, always stopped short of setting up a separate centre for food research because of the internal political problems involved in redeployment and relocation. Such an initiative also posed the risk of a public dispute with the Institute for Industrial Research and Standards, which had long since been advancing its own claims on this domain. However, in the context of late 1986, Ryan and the Council considered the situation critical enough to confront these difficulties head on.

The Haughey-led Fianna Fail administration which came to power in the 1987 General Election brought even more dramatic change for AFT. This new government was determined to turn the economy around and had sufficient political strength to take tough decisions that were necessary to restore order to the public finances. It conditioned the whole public sector for radical rationalisation by closing down completely one of the smaller public agencies. Within months of taking office this government announced its intention to merge AFT with ACOT and to rationalise and streamline the whole area of public sector agricultural research and advisory services in the process. Just a decade earlier essentially the same proposed merger was successfully resisted because of the joint opposition of AFT professional staff and of Fianna Fail. Ten years later the same party in government succeeded in pushing through the merger with little opposition from within AFT or throughout the wider political system. There was, perhaps, no more graphic example of how much the organisation and its environment had changed over the interim period. The new entity, Teagasc, was targeted for a cutback of 500 staff and an annual budgetary reduction of 33 per cent over the pre-merger situation. The difficult challenge of implementing the merger, with the attendant need for rationalisation and for forging two disparate cultures into a new corporate entity with a unified sense of national mission, was entrusted to Pierce Ryan.

5   A public limited company – Irish
Distillers Group

The second case in this study of strategy and leadership in interaction concerns Irish Distillers Group Plc and the Irish distilling industry. The narrative concentrates mainly on the period from 1966 to 1988.

IRISH DISTILLERS IN BRIEF

In 1966 the three dominant producers of Irish whiskey in the Republic of Ireland merged to form the forerunner of what later came to be known as Irish Distillers Group (IDG). IDG's dominance of Irish whiskey production on the island of Ireland became complete in 1974 with the acquisition of a controlling interest in Northern Ireland's sole producer, the long-established Bushmills company. In November 1988 IDG became a wholly-owned part of the Pernod Ricard Group, the white knight in a takeover battle also involving Grand Metropolitan of the United Kingdom. Since the takeover Irish Distillers has continued to operate in a largely autonomous way. The company has two distilleries, one of the world's most modern plants at Midleton in County Cork, and the world's oldest distillery at Bushmills in County Antrim. In addition to providing stocks for its own brands, IDG also supplies a whiskey-based ingredient for the production of a range of Irish liqueurs, including the well-known Bailey's Irish Cream. Irish whiskey is a unique generic type in its own right and the company's flagship brands include Power, Paddy, Jameson, Bushmills and Tullamore Dew. The full IDG product line also includes other spirits, such as vodka and gin, a range of liqueurs and some lighter wine-based products.

IDG dominates its domestic market, accounting for two-thirds of spirit sales. After considerable growth throughout the previous two decades the domestic market for spirits was largely stagnant throughout the 1980s. From the 1966 merger to the 1988 takeover the company concentrated on the United States as its main export market. Throughout the 1980s, however, the company had been strongly developing the European market and shipments to Europe were rising to US levels by the end of the decade.

We now turn to examine the strategic history of IDG under the leadership of Kevin McCourt and Richard Burrows over the 1966 to 1988 period. Before we do that, however, we will first briefly review the history of the Irish distilling industry up to the merger in 1966, drawing heavily on the excellent histories of the industry by McGuire (1973) and Magee (1980).

IRISH DISTILLING UP TO 1966

The history of whiskey distilling in Ireland stretches back into the mists of time. It is believed that the art of distilling was brought to the country by Irish missionaries on their return from the Mediterranean region during the first millennium and that the early use of the spirits that they produced was for curative purposes. It is also believed by some that the word 'whiskey' was coined by the soldiers of King Henry II during the first Norman conquest of Ireland as their best attempt at pronouncing the full Gaelic name of *uisce beatha* ('water of life').

The main developments in the modern history of Irish distilling date back to the end of the eighteenth century when, by then, the distillation and drinking of whiskey was widespread. The first excise duty on whiskey was imposed in 1661 and since then the stake of the State in the development of the industry has remained one of its notable characteristics. Excise collection was a major influence in transforming the industry from a cottage-based to a factory-based structure in the late 1700s. In 1757 the Government introduced legislation prescribing a legal minimum capacity for a commercial still. This measure was taken in order to control the proliferation of small illegal operations and to facilitate the collection of excise duty. Growth in the size of individual distilleries was also encouraged by the expansion in the overall domestic market for home-produced spirits from less than 200,000 to over 1 million gallons over the 1730 to 1777 period (McGuire 1973). The larger units tended to develop close to the large ports and Dublin soon emerged as the main distilling centre. The city provided a large concentrated local market. Furthermore, the large ports provided more economic access to imported coal and grain than inland centres. In 1779 the Government accelerated the process of industry consolidation by introducing a minimum still charge on commercial producers regardless of throughput. This effectively made small legal operations economically unviable.

By 1823 the system of minimum still charges was discredited, having given rise to a number of questionable practices which threatened to undermine the whole industry. However, it had helped to force consolidation. During its 40 years of operation the total number of legal distillers had fallen from over 1,200 to just 40. It was at this time that the now famous family firms of Power and Jameson first came to prominence. Throughout the nineteenth century the domestic market for whiskey grew as the quality of the product improved. Whiskey became the preferred drink, outstripping beer, wine and rum along the way. Developments in engineering, and in transportation and communication, also encouraged the evolution of larger scale units. In 1823 a total of 40 distilleries produced 3 million proof gallons. By 1900 the number of distilleries had reduced to 30 but total output had increased by nearly five-fold. The most significant of the mergers that took place during this period of consolidation was the formation of Cork Distillers Company Limited (CDC) in 1868, involving the family firm of Murphy (founded in 1825) and four other companies.

The one major technological development in the history of the distilling industry happened around 1830 when an Irish excise officer, Aeneas Coffey, invented a fundamentally new type of distillation process. The Coffey still became known in the industry as the continuous column-still to distinguish it from the traditional pot-still. The column-still proved to be a more efficient process for the distillation of alcohol and was capable of producing very pure spirit even from low grade agricultural inputs. This was also its major drawback because it distilled out the flavouring elements that gave a whiskey its unique character. It seems likely that Coffey invented the column-still for the production of industrial alcohol only. However, within twenty years Andrew Usher, an Edinburgh merchant, began to experiment in the blending of neutral column-stilled and flavouring pot-stilled spirits. The blending industry of the Scottish lowlands was born. The initial reaction of the traditional pot-stillers in Ireland and the Scottish Highlands was to reject the new blended whiskey as an inferior product. They fought a thirty-year campaign to have the blended product legally excluded from the right to be called whiskey. By the time the campaign had finally failed, in 1909, several reputable brands had begun to find favour with an expanding base of consumers. In 1877 six leading firms in the blended Scotch industry consolidated to form the Distillers Company. During the 1920s the industry was further strengthened when the Distillers Company was expanded to incorporate the Dewar, Haig, Walker and Buchanan brands.

In the early 1900s, at the height of the great whiskey controversy, Irish was still the 'sovereign whiskey' at home and abroad and more Irish whiskey was exported than any other type (Magee 1980). By the 1950s Irish whiskey exports had all but totally collapsed and paled into insignificance compared with those of blended Scotch. The inter-war years had been extremely difficult for all whiskey producers. The prohibition of the 1920s in the United States was followed by the general depression of the 1930s. Irish economic policy during the 1930s and 1940s prioritised self-sufficiency and import-substitution, and the protectionist 'Economic War' with Britain was a further blow to whiskey exports. During the 1939–45 period the Government curtailed the production of whiskey in order to conserve cerials for food stocks. It also curtailed the export of the limited output in order to maintain excise revenue. This was in sharp contrast to the policy of the British Government which prioritised the dollar exports of Scotch at the risk of domestic shortage. By the early 1950s the consolidated and market-oriented blended Scotch industry was well-positioned for dramatic export-led growth particularly in the US. By contrast Irish distilling remained fragmented, production-oriented and inward-looking. By 1952 exports of Scotch whiskey had already exceeded £32.5m while those of Irish whiskey languished at only £0.5m, having fallen ten-fold in gallonage terms since 1925. This poor export performance, and the slim prospects for improvement under the existing industry structure, prompted the three leading Irish distillers towards merger in 1966.

THE McCOURT ERA 1967–77

By the early 1960s the distilling industry in Ireland was concentrated in the hands of four main players, Power and Sons, Jameson and Sons and Cork Distilleries Company in Southern Ireland and the firm of Bushmills in the North. Yet all of these players were small in scale in relation to the international market and their independent efforts to develop Irish whiskey exports remained paltry and largely ineffective. In 1966 the three Southern firms finally came together after many years of discussions to form a new public limited company, the United Distillers of Ireland (UDI). Behind the merger lay the conviction that the future growth of the Irish whiskey industry rested firmly on exporting. The formidable challenge of revitalising, and fully exploiting, the export potential of Irish whiskey would require the combined efforts and resources of all of the players.

The wave of fresh thinking in the industry that finally brought about this merger was influenced by a number of contemporary developments. The spectacular post-war success of the Scotch industry had provided a clear demonstration of the export potential. In the late 1950s the dramatic change in national outlook brought about by the Lemass programmes for economic expansion pinned the future economic development of the country as a whole on export-led growth. Each sector of the economy with real export potential, including distilling, was publicly challenged to play its full part.

There were also defensive considerations. As national policy changed to embrace free trade and direct foreign investment a number of leading British brewing concerns entered the wholesale and distribution end of the Irish drinks sector. Bass Charrington acquired Bushmills in 1964. By then Allied Brewers had acquired a number of wine and spirits merchants and the Irish distilling companies had become increasingly vulnerable to such a concentration of buying power in the industry. Finally there were fears that the publicly quoted firm of Jameson had become financially weak and vulnerable to takeover (Brophy 1985).

Merging legally and making the merger work operationally proved, however, to be two different matters. As one executive recalled 'for some time after the merger, no merger took place except on paper'. Each company 'went its own separate way'. There was 'little attempt at rationalisation'. The problems of trying to forge a unitary organisation from three disparate cultures went right up to board level. For a start there were different expectations among the three parties about how far the operationalisation of the merger should extend. The main difficulty was with the Cork Distilleries Company (CDC). Prior to the merger CDC was a family firm headed up by Norbert Murphy. Murphy was a strong independent-minded force in the industry. He was a far-sighted and progressive distiller who had diversified CDC into white spirits using column-still technology, and he had developed the brand leader in gin on the home market. By the mid-1960s he had come to accept the need for the three Irish distilling companies to pool their efforts, in order to secure and develop their industry. However, in the aftermath of the merger he remained reluctant to surrender any of his former operational control over CDC to the new corporate entity. As one senior executive recalled, 'Cork looked on UDI as a trade protection association' and 'as a joint venture on exports'.

Frank O'Reilly, as one of the architects of the merger, was an uncontentious choice for the chairmanship of the new company. However, for some months after the merger there was a 'struggle for supremacy' among the parties involved. It soon became clear to O'Reilly that little progress would be made on realising the potential benefits of the merger until a professional manager, 'with no axe to grind' and no traditional loyalties to any of the pre-merger entities, was brought in to manage the new entity. In 1968 Kevin McCourt was hired in as Managing Director on a ten-year contract. He was an experienced chief executive whose early career was spent in sales and marketing with a large Irish tobacco company. His most recent appointment had been Director General of the national television service. The partnership of O'Reilly and McCourt proved to be important in getting the merger to work. While O'Reilly, as Chairman, skilfully managed to 'smooth oil on troubled waters' in the boardroom, McCourt is remembered as 'the man for the time' who 'brought through some very difficult decisions' and 'forced the families to agree'. 'I don't think that the need for an external managing director was seen before the merger', recalled one senior executive. He also did not think 'that Norbert Murphy bargained for Kevin McCourt' nor did Murphy 'forsee a unitary hierarchy developing as quickly as it did'.

The first strategic move made by McCourt was to bypass the wholesale blending and bottling network and sell a distillery-bottled product direct to the publican. This move gave the company more direct control over product quality and brand promotion at the point-of-sale. It also enabled the company to reduce its dependence on the traditional wholesale channels that were gradually becoming more concentrated in the hands of large British-based brewing companies. There were risks. Apart from invoking a 'vitriolic' response in the wholesale trade the strategy also involved a large investment in working capital and wider exposure to bad debt.

Kevin McCourt brought a new level of professionalism to the organisation and management of UDI. With O'Reilly's backing he quickly put in place a senior executive structure. He designed it around the three primary functions of marketing, finance and production and set about forging UDI into an integrated corporate entity in earnest. The traditional strength of the Irish distillers was production and he inherited inside expertise to head up this function. For marketing and finance, however, he hired in two experienced professionals with proven track records. These two functions were to be integrated and the problems were formidable. The three salesforces had been competing with each other for years, 'indoctrinated in the belief that their company brands were superior' to each other. In the finance area 'you just would not believe that three systems could be so different', recalled the new controller, and integration took nearly three years. However, some of the most formidable obstacles to forging a new unitary organisation and culture were at board level where Power was the most 'committed to complete integration and rationalisation' but Cork 'wanted it to go away'. 'After you got together', as one senior manager acutely observed, 'no matter how much you may have felt you misunderstood each other, you now had a responsibility to the shareholders' of the new company to forge ahead with full implementation.

The main thrust of the McCourt/O'Reilly overall strategy was two-fold. Irish as a generic whiskey accounted for less than 1 per cent of the US market and an even more minute percentage of worldwide whiskey sales. The export potential was enormous. The domestic market, in contrast, offered limited potential. The strategy was to secure and strengthen the company's dominant position in the domestic market and use the cash flow from this market to fuel a strategy of export-led growth. As outlined by the Chairman in the 1972 Annual Report the 'two fundamental aims' were to develop the capability to produce products 'at costs which will be competitive in both home and export markets' and to 'make our industry capable of greatly enlarging our export trade', which he recognised was 'of great importance to the Irish economy'.

During the early 1970s the McCourt/O'Reilly partnership began to strengthen the market orientation of the company. In 1971 the corporate name was changed to Irish Distillers Ltd to present a corporate image that was more readily identifiable at home and abroad. In the same year the first new corporate brands appeared as the product line was extended to include gin, rum and vodka. The new emphasis on marketing was carried onto the export front. The company introduced new lighter blends of Jameson and Tullamore Dew to cater for the preferences of the North American market. This was a significant departure from the long production-dominated tradition of marked reluctance to 'interfere' with the flagship brands. The Chairman underlined the changing emphasis in the 1971 Annual Report when he told the shareholders that 'we must all be salesmen for our products' because 'we operate in an increasingly competitive world'. On the home front competition was set to intensify when the protective duties on imported Scotch were due to be eliminated under the terms of the 1965 Anglo-Irish Free Trade Agreement. At the same time the company gained more open access to the large United Kingdom spirits market, an opportunity that could be fully exploited only through a more market-led approach.

Midleton – the rationalisation and modernisation of distilling

The strategic move to rationalise production and concentrate all of the company's distilling operations in a new custom-built complex in Midleton, County Cork, 'dominated' the 1970 to 1975 period under McCourt's leadership. The alternative was to develop and modernise some or all of the company's four existing distilleries. The proposed complex offered advantages in both operating costs and production flexibility. The 'main' problem with the existing distilleries was that they 'did not have the flexibility to tailor or to fine-tune the whiskey production to meet the demands of marketing for a smoother product'. The possibility of such a major rationalisation of operations was not foreseen by all of the parties to the merger, 'particularly Cork' though 'it was a lot more difficult for Jameson and Power to accept' because they 'had to see their 150-year old distilleries close'. International consultants A. D. Little were brought in to advise on distilling operations strategy. However, their role was perceived as largely 'to confirm the Board's innate feeling that they needed to do something' and to help 'take the personal politics out of the situation'. As a senior executive elaborated 'if you bring someone as expensive as A. D. Little in and pay them large fees you cannot walk away from the decision after that'. Midleton was not the only site considered but the company already had land there, and a distilling tradition. These factors swung the decision in its favour.

The shareholders were informed of the decision in 1969. However, work did not commence until 1973 and the new operation was not fully commissioned until 1976. The issues were complex, quite apart from the political difficulties at board level. It involved accepting the write-off of the traditional distilleries with little salvage value relative to the cost of the new facility. Moreover the initial cost estimate at £2m was way too low. This had to be revised upwards to £6m during the detailed planning phase and the final cost turned out at £9m because of rampant inflation during most of the building period. There were also serious concerns that the nature of the product itself, and the customers' perception of it, might be compromised because the 'transfer of the process to new shiny facilities' made it seem to some more 'like chemical processing' than traditional distilling. A related concern was that consumers might 'perceive that Power, Jameson and Paddy were now the same product, coming from the same distilling process'. The Chairman, in the 1972 Annual Report, took care to reassure the shareholders and the public that Midleton would be 'effectively a number of distilleries in one' so that the company might continue to produce 'the whiskeys of unique character and flavour' for which it 'was famous'.

There were further difficulties and concerns. The new facility was designed to be more energy intensive, and less labour intensive, than the old distilleries. The project was already underway when the 1973 Oil Crisis developed. This undermined some of the economic rationale for the new facility as well as greatly inflating its capital cost. The Midleton decision also meant the end of a centuries-old link between the distilling industry and certain inner city communities in Dublin, where the 'last members of the St. Patrick's Guild of Coopers' belonged to 'a trade founded in 1501' (*Irish Times* 30/7/76). Midleton later proved to provide a much tougher industrial relations climate than had been anticipated. Nevertheless once the decision was made there was no attempt to turn back. A senior finance executive characterised the process as 'like a Japanese decision' which 'took a long time to reach decision point' but 'once there everyone was committed to it'. 'Confidence in Cotter [the project leader], Ryan [the production director] and McCourt was a major element in the whole thing'.

The association with Seagrams and the acquisition of Bushmills

The other main development during the early 1970s was the formation of an association with Distillers-Seagrams, the world's largest distiller. Seagrams was initially interested in the full acquisition of Irish Distillers but the board was determined to retain the ownership and control of the company in Irish hands. Seagrams settled for a 15 per cent stake with an agreement to limit its extension to 20 per cent. Irish Distillers, for its part, acquired through the deal a 25 per cent interest in Old Bushmills which had been a recent addition to the Distillers-Seagrams portfolio. The association was also expected to make 'additional resources, outlets and promotional support' available to Irish Distillers in 'major export markets' which would have taken the company 'incalculable time to attain' through its own efforts and financial resources (Annual Report 1972).

In 1974 Irish Distillers raised its equity in Old Bushmills to a controlling interest of 80 per cent. The year was heralded as one of the 'four major dates in the history of the Irish whiskey industry' (Annual Report 1974) alongside the foundation of the Power and Jameson companies in the late 1700s, the formation of Cork Distillers Company in 1968 and the merger of 1966. The main strategic significance of this acquisition was the consolidation of the total production of Irish whiskey in one corporate entity, which facilitated the concerted marketing of the product as a distinct generic type. The acquisition had other benefits. The Bushmills brands were already well established in the US and UK markets. In addition the Bushmills distillery was the oldest in the world. This had a certain market value in an industry in which tradition plays an important part in the overall image of the product. Moreover, the traditional distillery was well located in a rural setting with a pure and plentiful water supply. It was also efficient by industry standards as a result of the modernisation programme which Seagrams had implemented. Finally, it provided Irish Distillers with a second production location which helped to mitigate the industrial relations risk associated with the centralisation of the rest of its distilling operations in the modern Midleton complex. The stake in Bushmills was eventually raised to 100 per cent ownership in 1977.

The relationship with Seagrams was expected to help accelerate the growth of Irish whiskey in the American market. However, as the 1970s progressed a large body of the shareholders began publicly to question the benefits of the arrangement to Irish Distillers. Over successive annual general meetings they demanded that their board provide them with exact figures for exports to North America. The Chairman persisted in withholding this information on the grounds that 'they would be very advantageous to our competitors' (quoted in *The Irish Times* 1/3/75). The shareholders' concerns were shared by the press. As one senior executive recalled 'the press' had 'given us a hard time on the US involvement over the years' because it had 'not developed as fast as hoped, thus challenging the wisdom of the strategy'. Unrealised expectations from the Seagrams association were not the only reason. The strategic assault on the North American market began at a time when the underlying trend in that market was shifting away from brown to white spirits, and from spirits in general to lower alcohol drinks. There were also some internal organisational problems hindering the company's efforts to develop this key market.

Kevin McCourt was in his late fifties when his ten-year contract expired. He retired from the management of the company in 1977. Much had been achieved under his leadership. The company had carried through a major rationalisation of the domestic sales and distribution activity. It had also rationalised and modernised its distilling capacity, with sufficient capacity established to handle the expected growth in exports for some years ahead. It had acquired Bushmills and consolidated the production of Irish whiskey under one corporate entity. Corporate turnover had grown in real terms by nearly 90 per cent, PBIT by over 220 per cent, productivity by nearly 300 per cent and output by over 260 per cent. One surprising element over the period had been the unexpected buoyancy in domestic sales, which had grown by over 160 per cent largely on the strength of the rise in farm incomes that followed from Ireland's entry into the EEC. Much progress had been made on expanding export sales, and though the company had not yet reached lift-off in the important US market, nevertheless it was looking forward to the future with confidence as he handed over the reins.

THE BURROWS ERA 1977 –

Kevin McCourt was succeeded as Managing Director by Richard Burrows. Burrows was brought into IDG headquarters as McCourt's 'right hand man' for twelve months of grooming for succession. He was a chartered accountant by profession and had family connections with the industry. When Seagrams acquired Bushmills it had hired in Richard Burrows as Managing Director and he was credited with bringing 'the twentieth century' into Ireland's oldest distilling company. He became leader of IDG at just 31 years of age. Though there were to be changes in style, structure and tactics to follow, his appointment signalled continuity rather than change in broad strategic thrust. O'Reilly was still Chairman of the board and remained so until 1981. McCourt remained a board member until 1982.

The year 1979 was a watershed in the fortunes of the company. Sales on the domestic market had reached a record level and exports to all markets outside the Republic of Ireland had passed the level of 1m cases. The company had embarked on a £30m development programme and the two distilleries were on full seven-day operation. Management were looking to the future with confidence. Within a year the environment changed dramatically. Richard Burrows and his team found themselves confronted with tough new challenges which undermined their company's future prospects and threatened the whole basis of the post-merger strategy. The company experienced new pressures on both the domestic and the export fronts.

Contraction and stagnation in the domestic market

In the wake of the 1979 Oil Crisis the international trading economy went into prolonged recession with low growth and high inflation. In Ireland these problems were compounded by the high level of public sector debt. Domestic demand for the company's products was largely determined by population trends, the level of consumer expenditure and the price of spirits relative to other consumer goods. The recession brought with it a sharp decline in real incomes. Rapidly rising government debt led to rapidly rising levels of personal taxation and to steep increases in excise duties. In addition, there was a dramatic slowdown in the rate of population growth to one third of the level prevailing throughout the 1970s. As a result domestic demand for spirits was stagnant or in decline throughout most of the 1980s.

The company was in little doubt that the sharp rise in excise duty was the most serious of these problems. 'Throughout the history of distilling', as one senior executive remarked, 'the single constant factor which has brought change to the industry has been excise'. The government's take in excise duty rose from £39.9m to £66.8m over the 1979 to 1981 period. By 1983 the onward rise in excise duty had passed the point of diminishing returns as the overall contribution fell to £55m. In 1984 the Government was persuaded to reduce excise duty by 20 per cent and the company's domestic sales recovered by 15 per cent. Further recovery was delayed by a seven week strike. In 1986 the increasingly hard-pressed Government again raised the excise rate and once again depressed demand. By the end of 1987 the company's sales of branded goods to the domestic market were 20 per cent lower than in 1981. This erosion of the domestic market undermined the profit platform on which the company's whole export-led development strategy was based.

The acquisition of BWG

Over the 1968–84 period the structure of the industry, downstream of the company, had been undergoing substantial change. There was a distinct shift away from the public house as the dominant retail outlet towards the off-licence and the supermarket. While the large multiples tended to deal directly with the company, much of the smaller supermarket and off-licence trade came through independent cash and carry wholesalers. This mode of distribution continued to develop throughout the 1980s. In 1984 Burrows and his company acquired BWG for its nationwide wholesale cash and carry business at a net cost of £10m. The acquisition strengthened the company's control over domestic marketing and distribution. Richard Burrows explained that the acquisition had been made to 'consolidate' the 'home base' in the face of falling domestic demand (quoted in the *Sunday Tribune* 8/4/84).

The acquisition was perceived as defensive by the Stock Market. It met with a 'torrent of criticism from the press' and was 'attacked' as 'dull and unimaginative' because of the substantial investment that it represented in a stagnant home market (*Sunday Tribune* 8/4/84). The Stock Market wanted to see more focus on exports and the BWG move marked a turning point in its attitude to the company. Up to 1984 the Market had been relatively uncritical of the company and had kept faith with its basic strategic thrust. Progress on exports had continued to be promising. After a sharp fall in EPS over the 1979–81 period the company's profit performance recovered by 1983 in very difficult trading conditions. The Market responded very favourably to this recovery. The quadrupling of IDG's stock price over the 1982–84 period reflected the Market's confidence in the company's future export potential. After the BWG acquisition investors began to lose faith in the will or capability of the management team to realise IDG's export potential and the company's stock began to trail the general market index.

Decline in the US market and revision of marketing strategy

Stagnant demand in the domestic market was not the only problem that the company faced during the 1980s. Demand for whiskey in the company's main export market was also in decline. Over the 1970–79 period the US market for alcoholic beverages had enjoyed general growth as a result of increasing population and rising disposable incomes. Within this general pattern there was a marked sluggishness in the growth of spirits sales compared with those of beer and wine. This reflected a growing concern with fitness and health, a trend which continued apace during the 1980s and spread throughout the international market. World recession after 1979 led to further problems and the general market for spirits declined by 13 per cent over the 1979–87 period. The position for whiskey was even more difficult as its share of the spirits segment, which had been as high as 76 per cent in 1960, fell to 40 per cent by 1986.

In spite of these unfavourable trends, however, the potential for the generically distinct Irish product still appeared vast in what remained the world's largest whiskey market. Even in decline the US market still accounted for over 40 per cent of the global total at 68m cases per annum. IDG had still less than a half a percentage of this market in the early 1980s, where every 1 per cent gain would have been an increase of one third in IDG's total turnover. By the 1980s the company had already reached an annual volume of 0.35m cases in the US, up from 0.04m at the time of the 1966 merger. Over the 1976–82 period Irish whiskey was the fastest growing mature spirit in this market, albeit starting from a very low base. It is not surprising that the company and the Stock Market continued to view the future potential for Irish whiskey on this market as huge, even in the early 1980s.

The company's marketing efforts at this time were hampered by organisational problems. In 1982 Richard Burrows hired a new marketing director to add organisational strength to this vital area. However, the new man did not fit in with the culture of IDG and left quietly within a year. Meanwhile the company had difficulties with its US organisation. The company had chosen a strategy of relying on different importers to handle US sales and distribution for each of its flagship brands: Seagrams for Jameson, Brown-Forman for Bushmills and Heublein for Tullamore Dew. In 1981 it set up a direct marketing presence to give it closer involvement in the promotional and marketing efforts of the importers. This operation had three different coordinators over the 1981–86 period. Then it was scaled down and relocated. The company struggled to find the most effective way to sustain the momentum and keep the importers motivated when many of their allies' own brands were faltering under difficult market conditions.

The company's exports to the US continued to expand until 1984. After that they stagnated at around 0.3m cases and then declined, in the wake of a 19 per cent rise in federal tax, to 0.27m in 1987. This stagnation added to the doubts of the business community, following the BWG acquisition, that the company really had the will or ability to make a real breakthrough on exports. The performance of Irish whiskey continued to look lacklustre when compared with the phenomenal success of Baileys Irish Cream. The cream liqueur concept had been developed in the early 1970s by Gilbeys, a Dublin merchant which shortly afterwards became part of the Grand Metropolitan Group. By 1987 over 2.5m cases of Baileys were being exported annually, which exceeded the total exports of the Irish Distillers brands by a wide margin.

In 1985 Richard Burrows and his board carried out a full review of the company's marketing strategy. The premium brands had withstood the market decline in the US much better than the lower-priced products. Moreover, the experimental two-brand strategy in the United Kingdom market was proving very successful. Following this review Burrows and his team decided to put more emphasis on their growing European markets and to adopt a more focused approach in all major overseas markets, including the United States. They targeted the German, French and Dutch markets for special attention on mainland Europe and over the 1984–87 period case sales to these countries increased in total by around 45 per cent from a combined base of 0.062m. In the US the promotional effort was concentrated behind the Jameson and Bushmills premium brands as the 'rifle' approach replaced the 'shotgun'. The US effort was further concentrated on the five states that the company's analysts felt offered the best opportunity for real market breakthrough: California, Colorado, Florida, Illinois and Massachusetts.

Rationalisation and takeover

Over the 1980–87 period Burrows and his team implemented a series of rationalisation measures designed to improve the competitiveness of the company and to reduce overheads. In 1985 they invested almost £1.5m in streamlining the transport operation. In 1987 they invested a further £10m in a cost reduction programme which reduced the workforce in the main trading operation by almost one-third. This was designed to yield a 25 per cent improvement in pre-tax earnings.

By 1987 Irish Distillers had, under Richard Burrows, become a leaner operation with a more focused export marketing strategy and it had done this against the background of an international market for spirits which was in decline. Meanwhile, most of the large players, with much greater exposure to this decline, were looking to acquisitions to help maintain their earnings growth. As a result the spirits industry became more consolidated with the top six players accounting for over 35 per cent of the market by 1987. The effect was even more pronounced in the whiskey segment where the top five, Distillers (Guinness), Seagrams, Suntory, Allied Lyons-Hiram Walker, and IDV, had by then gained control of over 60 per cent of the global market. Speculation began to grow that Irish Distillers, with its monopoly of a generic but under-exploited product, was ripe for takeover. It heightened in November 1987 when FII-Fyffes, the large fruit importer, acquired a 20 per cent interest in the company.

Richard Burrows, his Chairman Joe McCabe and the board moved swiftly to mitigate any takeover threat and met with the company's major institutional investors. These investors had reportedly been 'disenchanted for several months with IDG, which they saw as going nowhere' (the *Sunday Independent*, 8/11/87). The presentation of the company's rationalisation programme and new marketing strategy went far towards restoring investor confidence in the short term. No public takeover moves were made by FII-Fyffes. Its Chief Executive, Neil McCann, refused to be drawn on his precise intentions for the IDG holding other than that it was a strategic investment. IDG's half yearly performance figures, published on May 26 1988, began to show the positive effects of the rationalisation and marketing changes with a half yearly improvement of 37 per cent in EPS over the same period in 1987.

Then at 7am on Monday May 30th 1988 a new joint venture company, GC&C Brands, announced that it was making a takeover bid for IDG at 315p per share. IDG described the bid as 'ill-conceived, unsolicited and unwelcome'. GC&C had already secured the pledge of FII-Fyffes' full stake at the bid price. The two principals of GC&C were Irish subsidiaries of British-based conglomerates, Gilbeys of Grand Metropolitan and Cantrell and Cochrane of Allied Lyons (51 per cent) and Guinness (49 per cent). The bidder's public rationale was that IDG 'had a very small hand to play' in trying to exploit the potential of Irish whiskey when what was required was 'an investment beyond' its capacity (*Sunday Tribune* 5/6/88). IDG retorted that the bid was highly opportunistic and sought to acquire future control over Irish whiskey on the cheap. The drinks sector analyst of the London *Evening Standard* was among those who echoed the company's view that this bid was coming 'just as the fruits' of what the management were doing were 'coming through' and the prospects for IDG were 'better than for a decade' (31/5/88).

There was a great deal of public, as well as commercial, interest in the takeover bid. The *Irish Times* (editorial 31/5/88) predicted that the drama would be 'followed with avid interest' by a public which feels that it has a 'personal interest' in the fortunes of a company whose products were 'quintessentially Irish' and which 'is – or should be – one of the jewels in the crown' of Irish manufacturing industry. For some commentators it was a portent of things to come, with major implications for future industrial policy. 'Will nothing be sacred in the brave new world of the single European market?' asked economics columnist, Maev-Ann Wren, in the *Irish Times* (4/6/88). 'If Irish Distillers can pass into foreign ownership what will be left?', she went on to ask, and 'why bother struggling to build up strong Irish firms, if they will immediately fall to foreign predators?'. In the wake of the country's ratification of the Single European Act in 1987, the scope for the company to play the 'green card' in defence of its independence was more limited than ever before.

The takeover bid threatened the whole future of IDG as an entity because the partners in GC&C made it publicly known that they intended to divide the company's flagship brands between them. Initially Burrows and the board tried to fend off the bid by their own efforts. The market valuation of IDG just before the bid was around £176m. The initial bid valued the company at £198m. IDG successfully persuaded its shareholders to reject it. The company also referred the bid to the European Commission. The Commission ruled that the bid was concerted and forced the break up of the GC&C consortium. A second GC&C bid was allowed when it was clear that the venture now involved just one principal, Gilbeys of the Grand Metropolitan Group. The new offer was made on 19/8/88 and valued the company at £235m or 400p per share. At this price the takeover battle entered a new phase. The only viable defence became a counter offer. IDG's days as an independent company were numbered. The company persuaded Pernod Ricard, the French drinks giant, to be its white knight.

Pernod Ricard entered the contest on condition that its offer of 450p per share would be assured of success. It was not prepared to become involved in an auction with GC&C. Over the first weekend of September the financial advisers to IDG and Pernod Ricard obtained irrevocable undertakings from various IDG investors, including the FII-Fyffes shareholding, that guaranteed the French company over 50 per cent control. GC&C responded with a bid of 525p. The contest entered its final phase which involved the Irish Courts and the London Stock Exchange Takeover Panel in a complex dispute about the status of the Fyffes' undertakings to Pernod Ricard. The Courts and the Takeover Panel ruled that these undertakings, though verbal, were in order and legally binding. Pernod Ricard became the new owner of Irish Distillers.

Throughout the takeover process Richard Burrows, his Chairman and his board had shown considerable ingenuity and deftness in their fight to preserve the integrity of IDG as a business entity. In the process they surprised many of their supporters, and confounded most of their critics, as they succeeded against all the odds in fighting off a powerful and determined predator. The IDG board and management expected that Pernod Ricard would operate IDG as an autonomous and integral subsidiary of the new parent company, preserving the unity of the company and the existing structure of the Irish distilling industry, and this has been the case to date. The GC&C takeover, had it succeeded, would have involved the disintegration of the company and a fundamental change in the structure of the Irish distilling industry. Though the full strategic impact of the Pernod Ricard takeover will take some time to emerge, the takeover battle of 1988 was clearly an important watershed in the history of IDG. It marked the beginning of a new phase in the future development of the company and the industry.

6 A state-owned enterprise – Comhlucht Siuicre Eireann Teoranta (CSET)

For most of its almost sixty-year history to date the third organisation featured in our study, CSET, was a state-owned enterprise (SOE). The company was privatised in 1990 and is now known as Greencore. The narrative to follow covers the history of CSET from foundation to privatisation. CSET was the sole producer of sugar in the country and sugar was the company's main product line. For most of its history CSET dominated the domestic market for sugar but in more recent times began to come under increasing competitive pressure due to rising imports from other EEC countries.

CSET IN BRIEF

In the late 1980s, prior to privatisation, CSET had five main divisions. Sugar, as the core business, was the largest. The others were Food, Engineering, Agrichemicals and Quarries. The food division began as a major diversification in the 1960s. However, its subsequent development fell far short of the high aspirations set for it in that period. By the late 1980s it was a profitable business which accounted for around 11 per cent of company revenues. The other three activities were closely related to the core business. The company was founded to develop an indigenous sugar-beet processing industry which gave it a unique relationship with beet growing communities. The company's operations were organised regionally around sugar processing plants in Carlow, Thurles, Mallow and Tuam. Carlow, Thurles and Mallow are in the Southern region of the country and Tuam is in the west. In 1980 the company started to report losses in profit before tax after forty-five years of almost uninterrupted profitability. In turning this situation around it consolidated its operations around the Carlow and Mallow plants. The closures of the Tuam and Thurles operations, in the face of considerable political pressure, were significant milestones on the way to privatisation.

The Stock Market launch of Greencore, Ireland's first major privatisation, was highly successful. However, questionable practices by some senior executives in the lead up to privatisation subsequently came to light and led to serious public disquiet, the forced resignation of the managing director and a public inquiry into the whole episode.

THE FIRST DECADE 1934–45

As early as 1660 sugar from cane was refined in Ireland. By 1766 there were forty sugar refineries operating in the country. In 1842 the first acres of sugar beet were grown in County Antrim, and in 1851 the first sugar beet factory was built at Mountmellick by the Royal Irish Beet-Root Sugar Company. This early production of home-grown sugar failed in 1862. In 1911 momentum began to build up for another attempt at establishing an indigenous sugar industry. This led to the establishment of the Irish Sugar Manufacturing Company, a private enterprise, in 1925. The following year this company opened a production facility in Carlow and began a beet growing campaign in the locality. By 1932 it was producing 13,400 tons of sugar, over 7 per cent of the national requirement. The new enterprise then ran into commercial difficulties, but not before it had clearly established that quality sugar could be produced in Ireland from beet grown locally.

When the first Fianna Fail Government came to office in 1932 it was committed to a policy of economic self-sufficiency. Sean Lemass, the new Minister for Industry and Commerce, was determined to accelerate the development of indigenous industry, using public capital if necessary. He decided to rescue the failing sugar enterprise and was determined not only to save the Carlow operation but to develop it. He recognised that to make the country self-sufficient in this basic commodity was going to involve a much larger scale of concern. In doing this he was fully aware that 'in no country in the world' was beet sugar an economic proposition when viewed 'from a purely accountancy point of view'. A measure of protection would be needed to make it viable. However, he justified this on the basis that it would 'provide employment', be a 'cash crop for farmers' and 'indirectly create new business for quite a number of industries', and all this 'at a cost to the community of an additional halfpenny a pound on sugar' (quoted in Foy 1976: 141). A new state-owned enterprise, Comhlucht Siuicre Eireann Teoranta (The Irish Sugar Company), was established. It acquired the Carlow factory and opened three new factories at Thurles, Mallow and Tuam. In a country which until then had little regional industry outside of farming these new factories were economically and socially very significant. At the sod-cutting ceremony for the Thurles Plant in May 1933 the Taoiseach, Mr Eamonn de Valera, declared that 'in establishing factories such as these we are making the way for a self-sufficient, self-supporting state' (quoted in Foy 1976: 40).

The early direction of CSET was placed in the hands of a civil servant. Both he and his successor were described by one senior executive as 'administrators and custodians'. The early operation depended heavily on imported skills right down to the level of the factory foreman. Meanwhile a number of young Irish graduates were sent abroad to learn about sugar technology. All of these men were to play significant roles in the future development of a native sugar industry. When war broke out in 1939 the Belgian, Austrian, German and other central European technologists returned to their homelands. Full responsibility for the operation passed into Irish hands much sooner than had been expected. While Ireland remained neutral during the war it was affected by general wartime stringencies and scarcities. However, the young company managed to supply the country's basic sugar requirements during this period in the face of severe scarcities of spare parts, grease, oil, formalin, beet knives and imported beet seed. In being able to do so it seemed to demonstrate the wisdom of the national policy of economic self-sufficiency

At the end of the war CSET was ready for further development. The company and the industry had emerged from this period 'in a state of near exhaustion' after many years of 'stop gap measures'. The fields had been over-tilled and the factories were in need of modernisation. The saving of the beet crop remained very labour intensive and the crop itself was threatened by all kinds of pests and diseases. Company and industry were in need of revitalisation.

THE COSTELLO ERA 1945–66

In 1945 the Government appointed Lieutenant-General Michael J. Costello as General Manager of CSET. At the time, according to Lynch (1986: 12), Lemass and his associated ministers 'were looking around for a man who had proved himself not alone as possessing the ability and strength of character to shoulder a major industrial appointment, but who had proven his patriotism to the hilt'.

The General, as he was widely known, came to CSET with impressive credentials. In the year following the Treaty Costello was promoted to Colonel Commandant of the new Free State Army. He was not yet 20 years old. It was a time when young men of exceptional ability were being called upon to play major roles in the development of the fledgling state. He was to rise to General Officer Commanding of the First Division South before he retired from the army in 1945 at the age of 41. During his army career he had been selected for a special two-year training programme at the US military academy for senior officers at Fort Leavenworth, Kansas. What Lemass wanted in selecting Costello, according to one senior executive, was someone to 'loosen the grip of the Civil Service' on the company.

Securing the supply side 1945–59

The late Michael Foy (1986: 18–23), CSET's own historian, presented the following graphic picture of the General's initial impact at the company:

> The General on joining, took a general's view. A 'campaign' was needed. The fields must be made fertile if the industry was to have a future. The programme he set had research as the key. That soon brought to light a bewildering range of problems: disease in the beet was rife and threatening the industry's very existence. So were the pests. Appalling shortages of essential limes on the beet fields showed. No suitable fertiliser system existed – indeed no system existed. Beet seed purity was at a low level. An unsustainable high labour input per acre was involved (660 manhours in 1945 as against 22 manhours in 1986); soil testing (was) non-existent.
>
> The General set up field stations at each factory. They became the country's first soil-testing units. The tests showed just how lacking in lime Ireland was – and while there were private quarries in existence, the General saw the need was greater than their collective capacity. He opened quarries on a scale not known here but then found the farmers had not the equipment or the resources to avail of them as the need demanded. The General had recruited for the company a group of army officers who had served under him. One of them was his director of transport, Capt. John O'Brien. Soon the sugar company had purchased 300 British army trucks (which had seen service in the North African campaign against Rommel and had become surplus). These were fitted with spreading equipment and they not alone took the lime to the farms but spread it as well. The war on want of lime was on, weather conditions were ignored. Work on Irish farms now spanned the four seasons. A new excitement gripped farming Ireland.

The General also brought mechanisation to Irish beet harvesting. This was necessary because a growing shortage of farm labour threatened to hold back the expansion of the industry. When the harvesting machinery in use abroad proved unsuitable for Irish soil conditions the General engaged the help of Austin Armer, an eminent American technologist. Under the latter's expert guidance a beet harvester, the Armer MK1, was developed in CSET's Carlow facility. 'It wasn't the invention of the harvester which caused us the most trouble', the General was later to recall, but 'convincing the farmer to let us in to test it on his crop' (quoted in Foy 1976: 74). The company was to further develop its line of beet processing equipment not only for Irish use but also for export. The General came in time to be one of the best known figures in the European sugar-beet industry and to serve as President of the International Institute for Beet Research. His was a fully integrated and cooperative approach to the production and processing of sugar.

The General was a benevolent autocrat who took full charge of the company's direction while at the helm. He believed in consultation and communication, and he was willing to be influenced by good ideas from whatever quarter. He 'attracted the best into the industry and extracted the best from those attracted'. He knew his employees and suppliers well and kept close links with them. 'He was not a man to pass a dirty beet field without stopping to find the owner'. He 'organised so many competitions' and 'presented so many prizes in the course of helping his growers towards excellence' that he 'knew their fields almost as well as themselves' (Foy 1986: 23). He established Works Committees at the plants to give each employee a say in the running of their sections. He established the magazine *Biatas – The Tillage Farmer* to keep the farmers informed. The cornerstone of his managerial philosophy was that 'the cooperative theories of Horace Plunkett' were 'superior to communism or capitalism' (CSET 1986: 32).

Up to 1959 the General had concentrated on trying to meet the national needs of industry and the consumer for sugar. The marketing of the commodity remained in the hands of companies that had been major importers and distributors before the establishment of CSET. By the end of the 1950s the country was self-sufficient in this product. There was little prospect of exporting sugar because the international market was dominated by Britain and the United States, and each had plentiful supplies of a relatively cheap product.

Diversification into food 1960–66

In the late 1950s the General and his company were already seriously searching for opportunities to diversify when national economic policy dramatically changed. They responded to the Lemass initiative of the period in a brave and imaginative way, considering it their 'duty in the national interest' to utilise their 'special knowledge and very considerable technological resources to exploit the vast opportunities for economic expansion offered by the convenience food business' (Annual Report 1964). Through diversification into food processing the General and his board 'hoped to build up this new business' to a scale that would 'be larger than any industrial activity' then carried on in Ireland (Annual Report 1962). This project turned out to be more difficult than expected and never made the hoped-for impact. As one senior executive reflected 'from the early 60s until 1972 food almost dominated the strategic thinking' and in that period 'could be said to have both developed and declined'.

The General led CSET into food processing with great energy and conviction. Food processing plants were established in the company's main sugar processing centres. A new R&D facility was established in Carlow in 1961 and expanded in 1964. The world's first commercial plant using accelerated freeze-drying technology, a revolutionary dehydration process, was opened in Mallow. The Taoiseach, Sean Lemass, performed the opening ceremony. The first commercial product, instant potato flakes, appeared in 1962 and the new product line was quickly extended. The government increased its equity to provide funds for facilities but the other major development costs, including R&D and marketing, were met by cash flow from the sugar business. Initial national and international reaction to the project was highly favourable. Lemass publicly praised the company's 'very positive' response to the national challenge in the Dail, and the press in Britain, the primary target market, was generally high in its acclaim for the new initiative.

The food activity grew initially within the existing organisational structure, with an area general manager responsible for the sugar and food operations in each of CSET's four main processing centres. In 1964 the Government set up Erin Foods Limited, a new subsidiary with its own board, to be the marketing organisation for the food operation. Henry Roth, a high-level marketing manager from the Grace Corporation, was seconded as its first managing director to bring some international expertise to the initial marketing effort. The General and the CSET board retained control of the overall strategy of the food business.

The task of reaching a self-sustaining breakthrough on the British food market proved more difficult than anticipated. The market was huge at £1b per annum, and the winning of even a small percentage of it would have been a significant boost to company growth and national exports. However, it was a market already dominated by large international food companies and was highly competitive. The costs involved in developing and maintaining a well-motivated salesforce, generating brand awareness and consumer support, and securing wide, efficient distribution gave the initial marketing strategy a high break-even point, requiring a large volume of sales to succeed. The task was made more difficult by the restriction placed on the company in the Irish market. It could not offer more than 10 per cent of its total turnover for sale at home because the State 'was anxious that state enterprise would not discommode private enterprise', as one senior executive explained. This put the project 'on an uneven keel from the word go', with no domestic profit base of its own to help fuel the growth of exports beyond the break-even level. By 1965 sales were growing rapidly but operating losses were accumulating. The General and his board still considered these 'development costs' but the civil servants began to get seriously concerned about the future viability of the project. The development costs/losses were, by then, absorbing nearly all of CSET's total cash flow from operations.

The General resigned in October of 1966. It was widely believed within CSET and beyond that his departure was manoeuvred. Some of the more able and ambitious of the young career-politicians in Lemass's cabinet already saw the General as 'yesterday's man', as one senior CSET executive recalled. When the General tendered his resignation over what he saw as a withdrawal of support for his food strategy, a tactic which he had successfully used in the past to get his own way, word of his letter was deliberately leaked to the media which promptly carried the news to the nation at large. The General had little option but to stand over it or face public ridicule.

THE O'REILLY ERA 1966–69

The autumn of 1966 was a period of high drama for CSET. Immediately following the General's resignation B. T. (Bart) Daly was appointed by the board as General Manager. Daly was one of the pioneers of the industry and 'very much a traditional sugar man rather than food man'. A senior executive recalled what happened next as follows:

> Within two months four stories appeared simultaneously in the four daily newspapers saying that Tony O'Reilly was to become chief of the Sugar Company. This caused consternation within Irish Sugar. Daly spoke to me about it and said he was appalled and that the chairman was on his way to refute it. Before 12 noon the chairman discovered that O'Reilly was offered the managing directorship of both Sugar and Food. B. T. Daly was left with his title and O'Reilly came in. The workers and management were so stunned by the events of those six weeks that they never really recovered from them.

O'Reilly came to CSET from An Bord Bainne, the Irish Dairy Board. He was closely associated with the successful launch of the generic 'kerrygold' brand for Irish dairy exports to the UK market. He was seen by the Government as having the kind of marketing flair that was needed to turn the Erin Foods project around and bring it to profitability. O'Reilly remained with CSET for only three years before moving on to a career in the Heinz Corporation that was to take him all the way to chairman and chief executive. He was the first person outside of the Heinz family to be appointed chairman in its 117-year history. He also found the time and energy along the way to complete a PhD thesis in marketing based on the kerrygold experience.

We now know of Tony O'Reilly's extraordinary abilities in hindsight. When he arrived at CSET he was still only at the beginning of his career. As with many marketing geniuses, with one success behind them, there were those who wondered whether there was really much substance behind the image. He was playing international rugby and was on social terms with senior politicians. Some insiders viewed his arrival with a sense of excitement. Others viewed it with some cynicism and suspicion. He was a professional businessman rather than a nation builder. His national pride expressed itself in the competitive arena, in business and on the field of play. As with any professional, each specific job was taken on primarily for the personal challenge that it offered and the contribution that it could make to his development and advancement. As a professional manager he was mobile and open to better offers.

In 1965, while the General was still at the helm, the board had engaged the firm of A. D. Little (ADL) to advise on strategy for the food project. ADL suggested three options. The first involved staying with the existing strategy of building up a consumer franchise for Erin Foods through the company's own efforts. The consultants estimated that the company would have to invest a further £15m and sustain losses of £5m over six years before an operating profit could be expected. The second option was to reduce the level of general activity, particularly in branded sales. The final option was to seek a joint venture which might secure the company's growth objectives with much less risk, if also less profit potential. O'Reilly led the company into an alliance with the Heinz Corporation. Under the arrangement Erin Foods continued to produce the products and develop the product line, the Heinz organisation in the UK began to distribute and sell the products and a new jointly financed company, Heinz Erin, took on the responsibility for promotion and advertising. The Minister for Finance, Charles Haughey, introduced the arrangement to the Dail in April 1967. He emphasised that it was 'a commercial arrangement between two commercial companies' and that 'perhaps the best service' the Dail could render the country was 'to recognise the commercial nature of the undertaking' and give it a 'reasonable opportunity' to achieve the hoped-for results.

Tony O'Reilly focused his energies on the food business. During his tenure at the top he expanded sales from £2.5m to over £7m. The average level of employment in the food business rose from 989 to 1,384, and the acreage sown from 4,300 to 9,200. He extended the product line through the acquisition of Mattersons, a meat processing and canning company. The operating losses on the project were reduced from £1.9m to £0.3m, which was very close to break-even on a cash flow basis. CSET was showing an after-tax profit for the first time in four years and the food project was no longer a drain on company reserves. The leadership of O'Reilly, and the joint-venture arrangement with Heinz, appeared to be having the hoped-for effect.

Then in 1969, in 'a major surprise to the politicians who put him in' and to company and country in general, Tony O'Reilly resigned to take up a senior position with the Heinz Corporation in the United Kingdom. He remained on as a board member of CSET until 1972. In that year the affairs of Erin Foods, along with its assets and liabilities, were reintegrated with the other CSET business activities under a single board. Food revenues had reached £8.9m, with trading losses at £0.76m. Food had passed its peak of 28 per cent of company revenues in 1970, and was already declining as a percentage of the total business. The great dream that Erin Foods would be the primary agency in the development of a national food industry was over. CSET continued to be involved in food but by 1987 it was to account for only 11 per cent of total revenues. Would it have been different if the General had not resigned in 1966, or Tony O'Reilly in 1969? Was the strategy flawed and beyond the ability of even these exceptionally able men to make it succeed? These questions are still debated by company executives and business analysts alike to this day.

The 1960–72 period was very significant in the life of CSET. The company's high profile diversification kept it in the national limelight throughout. The food project brought new people with new skills and outlooks to CSET. The young scientists and marketing professionals involved 'were speaking a language not known' in the sugar industry. They 'looked differently, dressed differently and had different interests and pressures'. This 'created its own boundaries'. The food project introduced a new commercial emphasis into CSET which challenged the developmental ideology that had been dominant up to then. For almost two decades, up to privatisation, this ideological tension continued to energise the debate about the company's long-term mission.

When Tony O'Reilly arrived on the scene the differences between the cultures of the sugar and food activities became, if anything, even more pronounced. 'There was a buzz in the place and a market-oriented approach to the development of the food business' which made food 'the fast track' and sugar look 'archaic by comparison'. O'Reilly was seen as an 'interloper' by many in the sugar division. These sugar executives 'were forceful and tough men who had fought the battles and built the industry'.

O'Reilly 'left them alone' while he 'went with the areas where he was strong'. When he moved to Heinz a number of his senior team on the Erin Foods project left CSET soon afterwards. By 1972 the sugar men had regained control over the company and one of the most dramatic episodes in its history was over. It left a deep imprint on the company's culture that went on to influence its strategy well into the future.

THE DALY ERA 1969–74

Following Tony O'Reilly's dramatic departure after only three years as Managing Director the politicians had got 'such a land' that their 'golden boy' had gone off to Heinz that they appeared to back away from the company. His departure was an embarrassment to them and the food project became seen as a political liability. In the late 1960s the Industrial Development Authority, under the brilliant leadership of Michael Killeen, was successfully marketing the country as an attractive location for direct inward investment in high-technology 'sunrise' industries. Political interest in the 'old concept of the state company' like CSET 'as an engine for growth' began to wane in comparison.

The company was left to its own devices to appoint a successor and Bart Daly once more became head of CSET. He was close to retirement when he took up the helm for the second time and his period of leadership is remembered as one when the company 'ticked over'. Daly largely 'maintained the status quo' and 'did not initiate' any major new departures.

It was a period of reassessment after the drama of the O'Reilly years. The consultants A. D. Little were once again brought in to review the food business. They advised CSET to concentrate on 'added-value formulated goods, combined with selling bulk products of high quality to specific major customers' (Annual Report 1973). Rationalisation plans were developed for the reintegration of the food and sugar activities but were to be implemented gradually with due regard to 'the national position regarding unemployment' and in 'the context of alternative opportunities becoming available for growers and employees' (Annual Report 1972). In 1972 the Heinz–Erin joint-venture began to trade profitably for the first time.

Ireland's accession to the European Economic Community in 1972 had major implications for the core sugar business. The sugar industry entered a 'new era' and faced the full force of 'the cold winds of competition' for the first time (Annual Report 1973). Production was constrained by a national quota set under the Common Agricultural Policy at 150,000 tons per annum and enforced through heavy levies on excess output. The company was already operating at this level in the early 1970s and the failure to get a higher quota made it hesitant about further development and investment. Even the existing acreage came under threat as farmers began to shift land use to respond to the better opportunities offered at the time by beef and dairy production.

During the 1960s there was little reinvestment in the sugar business as all available funds were being channelled into food. By 1971 the food business, with 28 per cent of the total turnover, had 49 per cent of the company's net assets in plant and equipment. Between 1967 and 1973 the net assets of the sugar and related activities had fallen from 32 per cent to 18 per cent of total turnover. Plant and equipment had become old and run down. A four-year modernisation programme for the sugar business was set in train. However, the approach was conservative and the capital programme was 'restricted to modernising [the] factories' out of retained earnings (Annual Report 1973). Bart Daly retired from CSET in 1974.

THE SHEEHY ERA 1974–84

Maurice Sheehy became the new Chief Executive of CSET after a very divisive succession process. When Daly was due to retire the Government remained at arm's length, and the board decided to advertise the post. This, recalled one executive, was 'the worst investment' that his industry ever made because of 'all the confusion and the trauma of the previous few years since the General had left'. The board initially offered the position to an outsider but the compensation package was not attractive enough to secure him. Two 'big camps' emerged around the most prominent of the inside candidates, Maurice Sheehy and Chris Comerford.

The process by which the board eventually came to its decision was loosely structured and highly political. Both sides actively lobbied behind the scenes. The board became as deeply divided as the management in its support for the two candidates and eventually selected Sheehy by a very narrow margin, in somewhat controversial circumstances. The divisiveness engendered by the whole process continued to affect the management of the company far into the future.

In 1976 Denis Coakley became Chairman of the board. Coakley was 'a man of exceptional energy and of concern for the advancement of his country and its people' (Foy 1987: 405). Coakley and Sheehy together faced up to the full implications of EEC entry and made bold moves to secure the company's future in this more competitive environment. In 1976 they went abroad with the Minister for Agriculture to study 'at first hand the changing face of the European sugar beet industry'. They found the levels of investment being poured into the streamlining and modernistaion of facilities in Europe to be 'simply staggering' (Annual Report 1976). Coakley and Sheehy duly made the international competitiveness of the sugar business the dominant theme of their regime. They fully recognised the limited potential for growth offered by the core business and saw the 'need to diversify' into some 'complementary area'. However, they were convinced that they would be 'tempting fate' and 'risking the future' of the sugar industry if they were not prepared to reinvest heavily in it (Annual Report 1977).

Under Coakley and Sheehy the company spent over £40m on modernising the factories and by the end of Coakley's term as Chairman there were plans in place to spend a further £50m. Over the years the State had provided little extra capital. In 1979 its equity was only £6.5m and funds flowing from retained earnings fell far short of the £90m needed for the modernisation programme. Coakley went to the Government in search of further equity but had to be content with letters of comfort that offered state-guarantees for further debt-financing. Both men recognised the dangers involved in having to fund the modernisation programme out of increased borrowing but did not baulk at what they felt had to be done. The modernisation programme quickly made an impact on factory costs and efficiency, and involved the major refurbishment of 50 year-old facilities. However, with the massive additions to company debt, CSET became severely under-capitalised by normal commercial criteria. When Coakley retired as Chairman in 1980 the modernisation of the sugar business was already well advanced. However, CSET entered the difficult trading conditions of the early 1980s with an enormous interest burden and suffered its first overall loss since the late 1960s.

New equity and rationalisation 1980–84

In the early 1980s the resourcing environment for all public enterprises and agencies became more stringent as the problems in the nation's finances became acute. This environment 'generated – in political and official circles and in the public media – increased questioning' as to whether Irish society was 'getting value for money from its state-sponsored sector' (Bristow 1982: 173). CSET's first trading loss in over a decade brought it under public scrutiny and led to fundamental questions about its future role and mission. Denis Coakley, in his final report as Chairman, warned of the damage that 'popular' and 'sometimes shallow' criticism from those with 'little respect for, or understanding of national enterprise' might do. There was, he argued, an urgent need for 'aims' to be 'restated', 'guidelines agreed' and 'ambiguity removed' so that companies like CSET might be more clearly focused and fairly judged (Annual Report 1980).

This debate about the primary role of public enterprise in the changed circumstances of the 1980s had been active within CSET itself for some time past. The food project had brought the seeds of a commercial ideology into the company and allowed them to take root. Later, as the winds of competition began to affect the core sugar business, this ideology began to spread throughout the organisation. From the late 1970s, as one senior manager recalled, the company went through a 'major mind-set change from thinking of itself as a development organisation towards thinking of itself as a commercial' business. The arrival of James Fitzpatrick as the new Chairman, in succession to Coakley, brought about 'a major change in the company's way of looking at itself' where 'there was less emphasis on the performance of an activity as an end in itself and the future viability of the business was the focus'. The more commercially-minded managers inside the enterprise just 'did not like publishing losses' when they knew that their business was viable if free to run on purely commercial grounds. Outside influences also facilitated this transition. Civil servants had 'started to speak the [commercial] truth' to their ministers, and to support change, rather than try to manage state enterprises 'in such a way as to minimise political hassle'. Finally governments of the 1980s had become 'more amenable' to the commercial ideology. 'If they had wanted to focus on, and emphasise, employment' the company could not have transformed itself in the way that it did throughout most of the 1980s.

In fact a number of state-sponsored bodies all started to record losses around the same time at the end of the 1970s. This refocused the attention of the Government and the civil service on the whole semi-state sector after a decade of arm's length management. The civil service began to look for corporate plans from these bodies in addition to the usual annual estimates. A joint committee of the Oireachtais (representative of the two houses of parliament, the Dail and the Senate) was set up to review a number of state companies. It reported on CSET in December 1980. The company, in its submission, presented its financial statements in a way that clearly highlighted two major contributors to its overall losses. One was the 'Tuam Cost Penalty' of £2m per annum to keep the uneconomic Tuam plant in operation. The other was 'The Shareholder Deficiency Account' which showed the negative impact that a debt/equity ratio of more than twice the commercial norm was having on the company's profit performance.

The company argued that a more balanced capital structure and the freedom to rationalise uneconomic operations would make it commercially viable. The Report of the Joint Committee (1980: 72–76) was broadly supportive. It called on the State to make 'an immediate injection of £25m' and to provide for further equity investment over the following three years to 'support the prudent financing of the additional £40m investment programme'. It further recommended 'that the company should in future concentrate its sugar operations on its most viable plants'. It also argued that the company should not be held directly responsible for the provision of alternative employment for those affected by the rationalisation of uneconomic operations. While CSET had, in earlier times, 'pioneered rural industrialisation' it was 'more difficult to justify this pioneering role now given the diffusion of industrial employment opportunities throughout rural areas over the last decade'. This was a matter for industrial strategy or policy at overall state or regional level. However, the Committee did recognise that from the State's point of view any plant closures should be delayed 'until alternative employment opportunities have come on stream'.

The Tuam controversy

Securing fresh equity from the State and closing unviable operations became the twin aims of the company's overall strategy in the early 1980s. Armed with the broad support of the Joint Committee CSET set about closing the Tuam plant. The process took five years and was of national, as well as company, significance. In September 1981 the CSET board announced its decision to cease sugar processing at the plant at the end of the 1981/82 season. Tuam was losing money because there was no longer sufficient acreage under beet in its hinterland. The board's announcement was followed by 'thirteen days of controversy' (Foy 1981: 161) which ended in the Government deciding that the factory would remain in operation for a further season. The issue was hotly debated in the national newspapers and on the airwaves. There were delegations to politicians and Ministers, as community and Church leaders got involved on behalf of Tuam and the employees. As a *Sunday Independent* editorial (20/9/81) sharply defined it:

> The dilemma is this. Are semi-State companies to be run commercially or as development agencies? Incredibly, as in the Sugar Company, nobody has formally told them what role they are to play. If they behave commercially and sack workers, all hell breaks loose. If they pursue social objectives and lose money they get hammered. That's a catch 22 with vengeance. Somebody had better clear up this contradiction.

The Chairman, James Fitzpatrick, appealed to 'all interests' to recognise that CSET was a 'commercial company' and to understand 'the commercial pressures' that CSET was under. He warned that 'in the Ireland of the 1980s' these pressures were such that any attempt to maintain commercially unviable activities would eventually 'bring down the whole industry' (Annual Report 1981). Tuam was closed eventually. The process took four more years and cost the company a further £8m in losses in addition to rationalisation expenses. Its attempt to implement the closure was not helped by the political instability of the period which saw three changes of government, and much prevarication at national level, over the 1981–82 period. The company had notably less difficulty with other rationalisation measures. It closed Mattersons, a Limerick-based meat processing operation, with little of the fallout experienced over the Tuam decision. Mattersons had been a commercial acquisition, made by the company when the food project was at its height. Its closure was a relatively straightforward commercial process. Tuam was one of CSET's four original processing centres. Its closure had much deeper national and regional significance. When it finally happened it was a historic milestone in the company's modern transition from a development agency to a commercial enterprise.

In the 1980–86 period the company managed to secure more equity from the State, though it fell short of stated requirements. The modernisation programme continued but at a slower pace than the company would have wished. Major rationalisation was carried out in many of CSET's activities in addition to the Tuam closure, as the average number employed by the company declined from 3,615 to 2,205 over the 1979 to 1986 period. A reduction of this scale and in this timeframe would have been unthinkable prior to the 1980s. The political context had indeed changed dramatically. In 1985 the FitzGerald Government enshrined this change in its programme 'Building on Reality 1985–87' (FitzGerald Government 1985: 67) in which it was committed to 'an entirely new approach to the role and function of state enterprise' where the 'primary emphasis' would be 'placed on developing modern industry with emphasis on commercial viability and profits'.

THE COMERFORD ERA 1985–91

Maurice Sheehy retired as Managing Director of CSET in early 1985 and was succeeded by his old rival Chris Comerford. In one capacity or another Comerford had a major bearing on the strategic direction of CSET from the mid-1970s to the early 1990s. He was particularly influential in spearheading the transition within CSET from a developmental to a commercial ideology, which culminated in the successful privatisation of the company in 1991.

Shortly after Maurice Sheehy won the divisive succession contest in 1974 the board had appointed Comerford to the position of Deputy Chief Executive in an attempt to restore harmony. When James Fitzpatrick became Chairman of CSET in 1980 he quickly sensed the difficulty faced by both men in this arrangement. He persuaded Comerford to move out of Sheehy's direct line and take responsibility for group strategic planning and corporate development. This inspired move turned out to be of considerable benefit to both Comerford and the company. The new planning group played a crucial role in the successful presentation of the company's case to the Joint Committee of the Oireachtais, and through it to the Government and the public at large. 'In the excellence of what they did', and 'through the forcefulness of Comerford', the planning group 'won the right to bring their plans to the main Board directly and to defend them at that level', one senior executive recalled, and 'it was on the strength of the planning department's plans that we eventually got the equity that we were looking for'.

Comerford was more committed to the commercial ideology for state enterprise than his predecessor. His operating style was also more direct. Sheehy 'always tested the water everywhere before going ahead' and was more 'responsive to political persuasion' than his successor. Comerford and his new Chairman, Bernard Cahill, were more prepared to take decisive commercial action and deal with the political fallout on a *post-hoc* basis. Comerford 'went through the company like a tornado', as a *Sunday Independent* feature article (8/9/91) described his tenure at the top, and 'any lingering notion that the Sugar Company was a public service' was 'set aside with a succession of major rationalisations and plant closures'. Comerford's 'drive and ambition' raised the company's net profit performance from around 1 per cent of total turnover in 1985 to nearly 10 per cent by 1990. Comerford and Cahill moved quickly to close the uneconomic Tuam plant in 1986. They followed this by a determined bid to consolidate the sugar operations around a two-plant configuration in order to make the business competitive in European terms. They succeeded in closing the Thurles plant in 1989, despite a pre-election promise by the incoming Minister for Agriculture, a local representative, to keep it open.

Having dramatically improved the size and quality of the core business's profit flow, Comerford and Cahill turned their attention to the future growth and development of the company. Expansion in the sugar business remained restricted under the EEC regime. For the first time in nearly two decades the company in the late 1980s was once again in a position to pursue a major diversification strategy. In 1989 the company acquired a 50 per cent stake in the Odlums flour milling group for £17.6m with a clear intention to increase its ownership to 100 per cent as quickly as possible. This was followed by the acquisition of Grassland Fertilizers for £11m. Comerford was one of the first chief executives in the state sector to publicly enter the privatisation debate and advocate the privatisation of his company. Under his aggressive, commercial style of leadership, the company was successfully privatised in April 1990 under the new name of Greencore. The Stock Market flotation was Ireland's first major privatisation of a state enterprise. By then the company's dependence on the core business had already been reduced through the acquisition strategy to under 50 per cent of turnover. This left it well poised for future growth in its two other main business activities of food processing and agricultural trading.

Chris Comerford had spent his working life at the company and looked certain to lead it to greater commercial success well into the 1990s. However, he was forced to resign in very dramatic fashion in September 1991. The dubious circumstances surrounding the sale in 1990 of a 49 per cent stake in Sugar Distributors Limited (SDL) to CSET, the 51 per cent stockholder, came to light only six months after privatisation. The 49 per cent stake of SDL had been acquired in a management buy-out in 1989 for £3.2m and sold to CSET just over a year later for £9.5m (figures quoted in the *Sunday Independent*, 8/3/92). Comerford's involvement began when he was being head-hunted with a lucrative offer by the Goodman-owned conglomerate Food Industries to become its Chief Executive at around the time of the SDL buy-out moves. Comerford himself has described what happened next to the *Sunday Independent*, 8/3/92:

> I was going to Goodman, Tuam was closed, Thurles wasn't. They [SDL executives] came to me and told me they realised I was badly paid. They said we will give you a top-up salary and a share of the management buy-out. I was assured that everything was alright.

The questionable practices involved in the dealings between Comerford and the parties to the management buy-out led to serious public controversy and a sudden slump in market confidence. Comerford's personal position with the company had become untenable and his leadership of the new plc, to which he had contributed so much over his career, was brought to a premature end.

7 A producer cooperative – Golden Vale Cooperative Creameries Ltd

GOLDEN VALE IN BRIEF

Golden Vale Cooperative Creameries Ltd, our fourth and final case, has been one of Ireland's leading dairy processors since the early 1970s. In 1990, its first year as a public limited company, Golden Vale plc had a turnover of £209m and a net profit of £12m. In that same year it had 4,153 suppliers and processed 95m gallons of milk, around 10 per cent of the national total. Its main traditional catchment area has been the south west of the country serving counties Clare, Limerick and Cork. Its corporate headquarters and main processing complex are located in Charleville in north County Cork.

In 1990 food processing, mainly dairy products, accounted for 87 per cent of turnover. Agricultural trading and milling accounted for most of the remaining 13 per cent. Export sales were 53 per cent of the company's total. Competition between the processors in the Irish dairy industry has largely been confined to the sale of end products on the home market. The long-standing norm in the industry has been to discourage competition for supply, though this has been breached on a number of occasions, giving rise to so-called 'milk wars'. Most of the industry's export sales have been channelled through An Bord Bainne (the Irish Dairy Board) and marketed under the generic 'kerrygold' brand or sold into intervention as commodities under the Common Agricultural Policy (CAP) of the European Community.

Golden Vale Cooperative Creameries Ltd was formed in 1947, as a federation of small independent creameries to manufacture and market processed cheese. By that time the industry as a whole was dominated by the cooperative movement but remained fairly fragmented. We now trace the evolution of the industry, leading up to the foundation of the company.

THE IRISH DAIRY INDUSTRY UP TO 1947

Dairying has been a key sector of Irish agriculture for many centuries. The first major change in the organisation of the dairy industry came in the late 1800s when Sir Horace Plunkett recognised that the advent of the mechanical cream separator was about to transform it from a farm-based to a creamery-based structure. He was concerned to ensure that the producers retained control over the value of their produce in this transition and he promoted the widespread adoption of the cooperative form of organisation in the industry. For Plunkett the preservation and enhancement of producer spending power was vital, not only to the welfare of the farmers and the communities that depended on it but also to the whole process of national economic development.

With the changes in organisation and technology the industry grew rapidly over the 1890 to 1920 period. In 1894 Plunkett and his associates set up the Irish Agricultural Organisation Society (IAOS) to coordinate the further development of the cooperative movement at national level. By 1910 the number of cooperative societies had already grown to over 1,000 and over the 1914–19 period their combined turnover quadrupled. The influence of the cooperative movement in the dairy industry came to exceed by far that in any other sector. Plunkett and a group of fellow parliamentarians also succeeded in persuading the Westminster Government of the day to set up the Department of Agriculture and Technical Instruction (DATI) for Ireland in 1889. The national cooperative movement and the new state department together did much to improve the overall image and quality of Irish dairy produce and to develop the skill base of the industry.

The foundation of the new Irish Free State in 1922 coincided with the beginning of a serious and prolonged slump in demand for dairy products in Britain, the industry's main export market. The economic policy of the first Free State administration was broadly *laissez-faire*. As the 1920s progressed the situation in the dairy industry grew to crisis proportions. The slump in export demand left the industry with severe over-capacity and unbridled competition for milk supply threatened its future. The cooperative creameries, even though in the majority, were the most vulnerable to shake-out. In 1927 the Government was persuaded by Dr Henry Kennedy, the then Secretary of the IAOS, to intervene and bring about an ordered rationalisation to stabilise the situation.

The Government set up the state-owned Dairy Disposal Company (DCC) to act as a vehicle for buying out the remaining proprietary interests in the dairy sector and arranging for their eventual transfer to cooperative ownership. The DCC also rationalised many of the cooperative creameries most severely weakened by the slump. In addition Kennedy persuaded the

Government to set up the state-owned Agricultural Credit Corporation in order to provide the much needed capital for the further development of Irish agriculture. The one 'really disgraceful episode' of the period was the failure of the cooperative societies to adequately support a new federation set up by Kennedy and the IAOS to coordinate the generic export marketing of Irish dairy produce (Bolger 1977: 220).

During the 1930s and 1940s the industry continued to stagnate. In 1932 the incoming Fianna Fail administration was committed to a policy of economic self-sufficiency based on protectionism. This new policy prioritised import substitution at the expense of export development. The intention was to create a national economy less exposed to the volatility of export markets, especially the British food market. The difficulties posed by this new policy for the export-dependent dairy industry were further exacerbated by the Economic War with Britain over the 1932–38 period. The outbreak of World War Two further reinforced the isolationist, self-sufficiency, approach and seemed to confirm the wisdom of the policy on strategic as well as economic grounds. The Government diverted resources away from dairying during the war years through a policy of compulsory tillage.

National milk production grew by just 30 per cent over the period from 1922 to 1945. In spite of this general stagnation, however, there were some major developments within the dairy sector during these two decades. Industry rationalisation continued and by the late 1940s the total number of processors had been reduced to 200, down from 580 at the height of the crisis in the 1920s. A number of large commercially efficient processors had emerged to play a leading role in the industry's future. Many of these were developed by men like Eamonn Roche of Mitchelstown who had proven their leadership qualities during the War of Independence. By 1951 the five largest processors, Mitchelstown, Ballyclough, Dungarvan, Killeshandra and Drinagh, already accounted for over 20 per cent of the industry's total output. However, the industry remained under-developed on the production side and was producing what a visiting New Zealand expert characterised as 'the minimum possible under an Irish sky'. This was the situation into which Golden Vale came into existence.

GOLDEN VALE – FORMATION AND EARLY GROWTH 1947–56

Golden Vale Cooperative Creameries Ltd was formed through the initiative of Captain David John Barry, a former revolutionary. In 1947 Barry, who was then the Secretary of the Cheese Manufacturers Association, persuaded a number of small processors around the Charleville area to set up a federation to manufacture and market processed cheese. The twelve processors involved had been concerned about the potential loss of milk supplies to the larger, more diversified operators within their catchment area, particularly to Mitchelstown and Ballyclough. At the time Mitchelstown had the only licence in the country to manufacture processed cheese using technology imported from continental Europe.

Golden Vale's new processed cheese facility was opened in 1948. The members of the federation still retained much of their autonomy. They continued to operate independently of each other in the manufacture of butter and Cheddar cheese, and in the disposition of their excess milk. However, their new federation gave them more control over this disposition at more favourable prices than before. This gave them better profits and the scope to pay more competitive prices to their farmer-producers to secure their milk supply.

The first two leaders of Golden Vale were essentially technical men who had relatively short tenures at the top. In 1956 the board was unhappy with the overall rate of development and and brought in Dave O'Loughlin as Chief Executive. O'Loughlin led the company until his untimely death in 1971 and is the legendary figure in Golden Vale's history. He is credited with the main developments that set the company on the road from being a small joint-venture with a turnover of less than £0.5m to becoming number two in the industry, and a £70m business, by the mid-1970s. His father was the manager of one of the federated creameries so Dave had a background in the industry. He was well qualified academically, with an MSc in Dairy Science, and had worked as a senior representative with a dairy engineering firm before taking over the helm at Golden Vale.

THE O'LOUGHLIN ERA 1956–71

Golden Vale's rise to prominence

O'Loughlin's first venture was to develop an engineering division. There had been a small engineering activity at Golden Vale before he arrived but he 'developed this at a fierce rate, a rate of knots'. He was able to exploit the opportunities created by general expansion in the industry and by the introduction of new regulations on pasteurisation which required the greater use of stainless steel in pumps, tanks and piping throughout the processing sector. As a result Engineering 'grew like topsy' for a number of years to become a £3m business by the early 1970s.

The period from 1950 to 1980 saw major and sustained expansion in the dairy industry as national milk supply for manufactured products grew from 130m to over 900m gallons. The expansion came in three waves. The initial surge, over the 1948–58 period, was unleashed by the arrival of the mechanical and chemical revolutions to Irish dairy farming. The increasing availability of a plentiful supply of relatively inexpensive fertiliser; the growing adoption of the milking machine; the development of infrastructure, especially road improvements and the extension of rural electrification; developments in farm mechanisation generally and the spread of motorised transport with cheap fuel; developments in the education of farmers; and the establishment of a dedicated national research back-up, all played their parts. The programmes for economic expansion in the early 1960s created the second surge, which maintained the momentum, and EEC entry in 1972 created the third.

The expansion at farm level put pressure on the members of the federation to find new applications for the growing milk supply. At the same time new requirements for the grading of natural cheese, introduced by the Government to improve the quality and consistency of Irish dairy produce, proved difficult for small-scale processors to meet. O'Loughlin responded by expanding Golden Vale's processing capabilities in order to relieve the pressure on his member creameries and to provide them with a better service. He established a central facility for the processing of natural cheese in 1960. In 1962 he began diversifying into the production of skim-milk powder. This latest move helped to increase the profile of the company and project it into the 'big league' with Ballyclough, Dungarvan and Mitchelstown, as they worked together to coordinate the marketing of Irish milk powder in the British market in association with the giant Unigate company.

The early 1960s was a time of great movement and development in Irish dairying, with 'a big drive to add value' and 'to upgrade the industry' as an integral element of the First Programme for Economic Expansion. The setting up of An Bord Bainne in 1961 to market Irish dairy products abroad gave further impetus to the industry as the Lemass 'rising tide' started to lift all the boats. The new state agency recorded a major breakthrough with the successful launching of the generic 'kerrygold' brand on the British market. Overall there 'was a surge of forward thinking' as industry statesmen like Captain D. J. Barry encouraged young creamery managers to go on management courses and on overseas trips to study at first hand best practice abroad. This 'was a real eye-opener' which 'accelerated and encouraged their thinking'.

Throughout the 1960s Golden Vale, under O'Loughlin, expanded in all of its major product lines. Turnover increased by 473 per cent to £2.6m over the 1960–66 period. In 1966 the company won the accolade for the best European Cheddar Cheese at the World contest in Wisconsin. The engineering activity continued to expand and won major contracts from the distilling and soft drinks industries which was evidence of 'the high quality' of the company's products, 'allied to the unique technical and marketing skill of the personnel' (Annual Report 1966). O'Loughlin continued to expand the company's milk drying capacity and to lead it in a policy of 'active diversification'. He expanded the federation itself by attracting nine new members, which enlarged the milk pool and encouraged even further development. He then diversified into fat-filled milk powder, a new process involving the substitution of a lower-cost fat like sunflower oil for cream in the production of milk powder. He was the first to develop this process into a large-scale commercial activity in Irish dairying. The new 'Golden Maverick' line of milk-replacers for calves, based on this initiative, became the company's flagship brand.

Amalgamation and physical development

The 1958–74 period was a time of major structural change in the Irish dairy industry. The process was initiated by the Lemass administration when it decided, as part of its economic development strategy, to seek entry into the European Economic Community at the earliest possible opportunity. The export-earning potential of the dairy industry was pivotal to the national strategy and Lemass was concerned about the sector's readiness to meet the challenges of free trade. He commissioned an extensive study of the industry and the Dairy Products Survey Team submitted their report in early 1963.

The Survey Team's study (Byrne *et al.* 1963) was extensive. It surveyed 210 processors in the industry and examined the dairy industries of the six EEC countries and those of the UK, Denmark and Norway. France, West Germany, Holland and Denmark were investigated 'on-the-spot'. The Team's report stressed the need for the industry to be restructured and consolidated around larger, more resourceful and flexible units in line with the developments taking place elsewhere. The structure it envisaged was a national milk pool of 300m gallons being organised around 30 or so large units controlling 10m to 15m gallons each. The Team raised serious doubts about whether the corporate body of the cooperative movement, the IAOS, had sufficient influence over the industry and its members to provide the leadership necessary to bring about this structural consolidation in a timely fashion.

The Lemass administration was anxious to get the reorganisation of the industry underway but preferred to do it under the aegis of the cooperative movement. It immediately commissioned a general appraisement of the movement to see how it might be strengthened and its influence increased. Dr Joseph Knapp, the US expert chosen on the recommendation of the IAOS, reported in early 1964. He confirmed the need for structural consolidation but urged that it be implemented from the bottom up rather than from the top down. He further recommended that the IAOS should be given full responsibility for working out general reorganisation plans for the industry. He also offered advice on how the IAOS might be reorganised to strengthen its central role in the future development of the cooperative movement (Knapp 1964).

Following the publication of both reports the IAOS came under increasing pressure to develop a set of proposals for restructuring the industry. In the Second Programme for Economic Expansion Lemass publicly chartered the organisation with the responsibility for encouraging the cooperative creamery societies to achieve the desired voluntary consolidations. At the same time the IAOS was getting 'quiet but firm warnings' that it could not 'sit on [its] hands forever' and that state enterprise would be used if needed. It published its first 'Proposals for Re-Organisation of the Dairying Industry' (IAOS 1966) in February 1966 and met with 'big opposition' from the management committees of many of the cooperatives and from the Irish Creamery Milk Suppliers Association (ICMSA). The debate centred on not only whether there should be consolidations but also whether the mechanism should be through federation or amalgamation. The final study commissioned by the Government in 1968, the Cook and Sprague Report (1968), confirmed the wisdom of consolidation by amalgamation.

When the IAOS's amalgamation blueprint first came out Dave O'Loughlin 'on the surface vehemently opposed it because his owners vehemently opposed it', as a senior IAOS executive recalled. However he 'very quickly' came to see 'the advantages in amalgamation' through what would be, in effect, the 'reverse take-over of his owners'. Under the existing structure of Golden Vale the federated creameries were free to supply milk elsewhere. O'Loughlin had major plans for development in a country that was becoming increasingly short of milk processing capacity. The federal type of organisation did not give him the type of control over milk supply on which to base a major development programme.

O'Loughlin approached the IAOS for professional help in bringing amalgamation about and secured the services of Gerry Curley, one of its senior executives. Gerry graphically described, in interview, how they did it:

> We started early in January 1968. In 5 days we had meetings with members of about 20 member committees. We got a reasonable reception from them but there were a lot that were totally opposed to it. It was a general softening up situation. What O'Loughlin did was that he got the idea and started to do lots of homework . . . sort of what would

happen if we got all the milk supply . . . what sort of facilities would be needed here . . . what would it cost and what were the benefits.

O'Loughlin took the bull by the horns and more or less decided that he was going to provide the facilities anyway. Again, at the same time, he was developing the 'Maverick' fat-filled products. He was in more and more need of milk. The people outside [the small creamery managers] were beginning to let their plants run down with all the talk of amalgamation, consciously or unconsciously. O'Loughlin then set up the Structural Subcommittee chartered to progress the amalgamation. It consisted of the managers and chairmen who had agreed to look at the possibility of amalgamation. While ostensibly the purpose was to progress amalgamation, it was really to indoctrinate the chairmen and societies who were leaning towards, waivering towards, amalgamation on the benefits of amalgamation. . . . At the same time O'Loughlin, Hyland and Curley were going to the AGMs of the member societies to get the 'principle' accepted, never forcing a vote if we thought it would go against us.

While the end result was economic in its nature the means by which we did it was political. All the time we were trying to get the thought leaders committed all along the line, a sort of preaching the gospel effort. . . . It was attrition the whole time. Often you had a guy 5/8ths of the way and he would fall back to 4/8ths. You just kept at it and at it. Between O'Loughlin, Hyland and myself we must have attended 500 meetings. . . . That went on for three years before we got any real breaks. . . . At the same time this complex was being developed and he [O'Loughlin] was pushing forward with that and sailing very close to the financial wind. He had an extraordinary capacity to take risks . . . pushing the debt/equity ratio at an enormous rate. . . . The critical thing was O'Loughlin's initial decision to develop the place with large scale capital expenditure and an uncommitted milk supply.

The change that was taking place in the industry at that time had significant sociological, as well as economic, implications, and it is little wonder that it proved to be so difficult to bring about. The farmers were split on the issue. The younger, more specialised, ones could see the economic advantages of bigger units. The older ones were concerned about the break up of the parish-based creamery structure which to them had become a way of life. The National Farmers Association (NFA) supported the rationalisation, the Irish Creamery Milk Suppliers Association opposed it. The younger generation of creamery managers perceived more interesting and enhanced career prospects from the larger units. Many of the older managers were deeply wedded to the traditional parish-based structure in which they were as central and valued as the local teacher or the parish priest.

In 1972 the IAOS issued its second, and final, blueprint for amalgamation (IAOS 1972) to bring the plan up to date with the general developments which had taken place in the industry since 1966. This plan essentially confirmed the pre-eminence of those processors that had already taken the initiative on the ground. Six major players emerged from the process: Ballyclough, Golden Vale, Avonmore, Mitchelstown, Waterford and Kerry. The big six continued to lead the industry over the following two decades. The process was far from smooth and there were problems and disappointments along the way. The final shape of the industry in 1974 accorded fairly closely with the IAOS plan. However, there were many cases where the economic logic of geography broke down. Quite a number of small creameries decided to amalgamate with processors other than those to which they were assigned or to remain independent.

Golden Vale's emergence as a major growth centre was a significant achievement for an organisation that came on the scene late on in the industry's evolution and started as a federation of small players. The amalgamation was not a total success for the company. A number of the thirty-six societies assigned to it under the IAOS plan did not amalgamate. Dave O'Loughlin, the architect of the process, did not survive to see his plans realised. He died suddenly in the summer of 1971 just as the final stage of the amalgamation process was about to get underway. It was left to his successor to complete the process and see the O'Loughlin vision for the company through to reality.

THE LENIHAN ERA 1972–80

After O'Loughlin's untimely death there was a six-month 'interregnum period' while the search for a successor went on. 'The twelve apostles [the original members of the federation] held control' so one 'can imagine the schemozzle and the canvassing that went on for the job', recalled a senior executive. Early in 1972 the company selected Mick Lenihan for the position.

Mick Lenihan was the Manager of the Shandrum Coop, one of the larger creameries in the original federation. He was not as highly qualified as his predecessor academically, nor was he seen as a builder or a strategist in the O'Loughlin mould. He was a conservative choice who 'looked at his whole function as carrying out O'Loughlin's plan'. Insiders recalled the contrast between the two men in various ways. 'The general perception was that Dave O'Loughlin was standing way above the whole lot' and was 'very much the boss'. He was 'forceful' and 'driven', a 'risk taker' whose 'basic strategic decisions were very right'. Lenihan, on the other hand, was regarded as somewhat of 'an outsider' by the management team that he inherited. He was less dominant and directive than O'Loughlin and 'not as technically strong'. He is remembered more as a good operator who was well versed in the politics of the farmer–processor relationship, a crucial attribute in this 'sound man' business. He was 'probably more astute' than O'Loughlin and 'a political man'.

Lenihan is mainly credited within Golden Vale for his role in implementing the amalgamation process. His standing with the managers of the targeted creameries was a major factor in moving the process towards its conclusion. These creamery managers had regarded O'Loughlin highly but were somewhat intimidated by his forceful and driving style and he 'was not one of the creamery manager types'. Lenihan, on the other hand, was 'one of their own'. He did the final deals with them on the specific terms for amalgamation 'on his own personal touch, over pints' because he 'knew what made them tick and how to allay their fears'.

Financial crisis, turnaround and expansion

In spite of the painstaking efforts of O'Loughlin and Lenihan only 25 of the 36 societies targeted for Golden Vale had amalgamated with it by early 1973. The total milk pool owned by the company was 47m gallons, 30m short of the capacity being planned for in the company's development programme. However, Golden Vale gained access, under contract, to the milk supply of 6 further societies that had chosen to remain independent. By year-end the company had processed a total of 66m gallons which was stretching its existing capacity (after completion of the first two phases of its development programme) to the limit. Since milk yields were expected to increase considerably throughout the remainder of the decade, under the incentives of the Common Agricultural Policy, Lenihan and his board decided to go ahead with the final development phase designed to bring capacity up to 94.5m gallons.

Milk yields, however, fell sharply in 1974 as confidence in the industry slumped due to a crisis in the cattle trade and the steep rise in input costs that came in the wake of the 1973 Oil Crisis. The effects of this set-back in national milk supply were compounded when five of Golden Vale's independent suppliers decided to amalgamate with other processors. In a somewhat desperate move to maintain overall volume the company acquired Clare Creameries to secure an extra 18m gallons for its milk pool. This was at the cost of extending its operations over a wider geographical area with unfavourable cost implications for its overall operational configuration. Even with this addition the company processed only 61m gallons in 1974 which was 18 per cent lower than planned.

In early 1975 the company was in financial crisis. Trading profit for the previous year had fallen below the level of the interest on the company's rising debt. Its capital structure was seriously out of balance with £15m in borrowings, £10.5m of which was in the form of bank overdraft, and only £6.5m in shareholders' funds. While the crisis was precipitated by the unexpected fall in milk volume its onset revealed some fundamental weaknesses in the company's overall operations. In addition to its unsound capital structure the company had achieved very little in the way of downstream rationalisation economies since the amalgamation process was concluded. Furthermore it had failed to develop the kind of systems and structures appropriate to its large size and diversified activities.

The crisis was the catalyst for an outburst of frenetic activity. 'The bankers came in first', as one senior executive recalled, and 'they were toing and froing with rapid speed for about six months'. There was 'a need for systems' and 'the place was over-run with consultants recommending this, that, and the other about organisation, accounts, procedures, financial structure, board structure' and the rest. It was a critical time in the company's history and there was a great risk that it could lose the backing of the banking community and the confidence of its supplier-shareholders. To many of those involved the Chairman, Martin Flanagan, was the steady hand at the tiller during this difficult period. 'It was the bank's confidence in Flanagan', recalled one senior insider, 'that persuaded them to continue its support of Golden Vale'. Flanagan, a farmer from West Limerick, is remembered as the 'outstanding chairman' in the company's history.

Lenihan's leadership came under pressure from the farmer-shareholders. Flanagan backed his chief executive and management team at a critical board meeting in August 1975. He exhorted his board to 'run this business on a business-like footing' and 'to stand over their decisions', which 'must be business-decisions' based on 'a global understanding of the problems' facing the company and 'not a parochial one' (Board meeting minutes August 1975). He embarked the company on a major rationalisation programme to turn the situation around. It involved the centralisation of processing activities, the elimination of uneconomic product lines and the streamlining of milk assembly operations. In all 400 jobs were eliminated at a cost of £1.3m. A new 10 per cent convertable loan stock scheme was developed to strengthen the capital structure through the addition of £4.9m of equity over a five year period. This innovation was necessary because the producer-shareholders traditionally drew their benefits mainly out of the milk price rather than from dividends, and were always slow to provide new share capital.

This rationalisation programme, together with a general recovery in national milk volume, had almost immediate impact. In 1975 the company made a trading profit net of interest of almost £2m. The ratio of shareholders' interest to total borrowings improved from 25 per cent in 1975 to 63 per cent in 1976. Company turnover in 1976 was £55m on total assets of £19m, up from £26m on assets of £23m just two years before. The company itself described the turnaround as 'dramatic' and declared that 1976 might 'come to be regarded as a landmark' in its history (Annual Report 1976). The board was strengthened by the appointment of two prominent businessmen, the first ever outside directors. There also emerged a new watchdog group of young farmer-shareholders who styled themselves the 'Study Group'. They were 'enthusiastic but not popular enough to get on the board'. They 'were a most unlikely bunch' and 'the one thing they had in common was that they were interested in figures'. Though the board 'resented them' Lenihan 'had to try to work with them', and they became 'the bane' of managers' lives.

The crisis period saw the rise in influence of the Finance Department. Tony Curtin had joined Golden Vale as Chief Accountant in 1972. He became Financial Controller in 1975. It was Curtin who 'diagnosed the (liquidity) problem straight away' and played a key role in its resolution. As one senior executive recalled:

> During the rationalisation and refinancing period the refinancing package was largely done by Curtin and his star began to rise. At that stage the 'ism' that was in was rigid financial controls and the accountant was God. The 'ism' before that was technical people – today probably the 'ism' is marketing. The turnaround was quite dramatic. Curtin got enormous credit for that.

In 1978 Tony Curtin was appointed Assistant Chief Executive. He later succeeded Lenihan as Chief Executive.

The late 1970s witnessed the fall from grace of Engineering, once the jewel in the Golden Vale crown. The financial crisis, and the introduction of new controls and systems to resolve it, began to expose some problems in this business activity. Prior to then the division had become very powerful and autonomous under the aggressive and cavalier leadership of Denis Murphy. A senior manager gave this graphic account:

> My perception was that Engineering was driving the business I would guess from about 1968 to about 1972 and the power did not begin to wane until 1974. The personality associated with that was Denis Murphy. (In 1974) Engineering was still going great guns and had a high profile to the extent that they bought a site out at Kanturk so that they would not be fettered by strikes in here – they were doing a kind of UDI thing on us. Yet by the end of 1975 and the beginning of 1976 it became

apparent that they nearly had us broke. . . .

Engineering was told to conserve its resources and we were told to feck off – they would not be fettered by our bankruptcy but in fact Engineering was guzzling a lot of working capital.

From very modest beginnings this division had risen to become the major indigenous engineering activity in the Irish dairy sector and had played a significant role in its physical development throughout the 1960s and 1970s. It had also diversified into serving the UK dairy industry as well as securing contracts in the Irish brewing, soft drinks and chemicals sectors. Though 'technologically it was a superb outfit' it had grown arrogant with success. There was 'no control' or 'no reporting of Engineering'. Murphy was 'very aggressive and strong at protecting his own group's autonomy'. The farmers were 'very critical of it' because they saw it as 'siphoning off funds from the milk division which was theirs'. When the major markets of the division began to decline it had few outside supporters to help it revive its fortunes. Tony Curtin, in particular, 'became very worried about Engineering in Lenihan's last years' and 'very critical of the lack of control'. In 1977 'the role and the scope' of the division was more 'clearly defined' and the management structure 'reorganised' (Annual Report 1977). Engineering was reined in and Murphy resigned.

The 1974 slump in national milk production was a temporary setback. The industry recovered quickly and continued to expand for the rest of the decade. Once Golden Vale had implemented its rationalisation programme and strengthened its financial base it literally grew out of its problems with the growth in the industry. By 1978 it was a £90m company processing 94m gallons of milk. The O'Loughlin development strategy was a major success. The capital expansion programme, which had earlier extended the company to the point of near bankruptcy at the time, turned out to be an 'outstanding investment' in 1977 replacement cost terms as the company's own merchant bankers saw it. As a result of the dramatic recovery the company decided to discontinue the loan stock from the shareholders. This, according to the Company Secretary, was 'a strategically bad decision' because 'it stopped the idea that farmers should finance their own cooperative'. It 'perpetuated the idea' that the company 'could fund development with cash flow', and 'having put it in in the first place with great effort' the decision to discontinue it 'threw away the victory'.

The financial crisis left its mark on the attitude within the company to further investment. No major new projects were undertaken in the post-1975 period of Lenihan's tenure. Some insiders favoured an investment in a casein facility to increase the flexibility and responsiveness of the product mix, but as one supporter of this approach recalled:

From the mid-1970s experiences we were always on the defensive. Our farmers were restless and there was always a fraction on the board who were uncomfortable. A strategic investment was out of the question because (these people) would have gone banannas.

The company was to have ample reason later to regret the passing up of at least one major opportunity during this period. As one executive described it:

We were offered Limerick Dairies – a private liquid milk operator – (for £300,000). After the battering that we took in 1975/6 we were reluctant to buy it. We had the money but we did not have the bottle to do it. It would have been difficult with the board, and it was a scene that we knew nothing about. Lo and behold Kerry bought Limerick Dairies and then in quick succession bought Deal Dairies. This was the launching pad for Kerry to start poaching some of our milk suppliers. It was the advent of the change in the liquid milk scene that heralded the milk wars.

Mick Lenihan retired as Chief Executive of Golden Vale in 1980. He left the company with a trading cash flow of £6.2m and a debt to equity ratio of 80 per cent. However, by 1980, the signs of difficult times ahead were already visible. Milk supply had dropped back to 85m gallons from a 1978 peak of 94m. In his 1979 annual statement the Chairman told his shareholders that their company must 'face a period when increased benefits to suppliers may be influenced to a greater extent by their own and the Society's efforts, rather than by political decisions in Dublin or Brussels'. He saw 'challenging times ahead' facing 'not only Golden Vale but the entire Dairy Industry'.

THE CURTIN ERA 1980–85

Low growth and EEC surpluses

When Mick Lenihan departed in 1980 'in a blaze of glory' it was already clear that his successor, Tony Curtin, was going to face more difficult and challenging times. National milk production peaked at 864m gallons in 1979 and then dropped to 825m over the following two years. By 1982 it was once again growing towards the 1,000m level but by then it had become clear to all that the expansionary days in the industry were over. The sharp downturn in the early 1980s resulted from a combination of adverse weather conditions, the inflationary effects of the 1979 Oil Crisis on farm input costs and the decline in price supports for milk production under the Common Agricultural Policy. The first two of these factors were temporary. The third was more permanent and had serious implications for the industry's further development.

In the early 1980s the world market for dairy products was one of increasing supply and falling demand. Dairy production within the EEC went into serious and mounting surplus and reform of the Common Agricultural Policy became one of the Community's most pressing issues. The reduction of price supports was followed by quotas and cutbacks as the EEC tried to curtail its chronic over-production. In addition the Irish dairy industry faced the strategic need to reduce its over-dependence on commodities and to change its product profile towards more value-added, consumer-oriented, branded products. This was the environment that Tony Curtin faced as he assumed the leadership of Golden Vale.

Milk wars, Engineering and Castlemahon

In the new environment of the 1980s competition between the major cooperatives intensified. The industry had excess capacity and the capital intensive processors were operating close to their high break-even volumes. Their cash flow and profitability had become very sensitive to marginal gains or losses in milk supply and throughput. The long-standing industry norm of not competing for supply came under pressure. Supplier loyalty was weakened by the sharp drop in farm incomes from 104 per cent to 55 per cent of the average industrial wage over the 1979–81 period. The early 1980s saw the outbreak of a fresh wave of 'milk wars' between rival processors in neighbouring catchment areas.

Tony Curtin was only a matter of months in the job as Chief Executive of Golden Vale when his milk supply came under threat from the neighbouring Kerry Cooperative. Kerry served notice on the industry early on that it was taking a commercial approach to the milk supply question given the prevailing conditions. Over the 1980–85 period Golden Vale was to lose an estimated net 13m gallons in milk wars, primarily to Kerry. This loss represented a net reduction in annual profit of £1.3m in an inherently low margin business.

An opportunity was lost in early 1981 to end the milk wars before they had really begun in earnest. The boards and senior management of both Golden Vale and Kerry Cooperatives met in Limerick to try to resolve the situation. Kerry's purchase of Limerick Dairies had brought it into Golden Vale's catchment area and was the 'launching pad' for the milk war. Golden Vale agreed to purchase Limerick Dairies for just under £1m. This deal was described by Denis Brosnan, the Kerry boss, as 'the final permanent solution' to the milk war (*Irish Press* 22/2/81). However the deal subsequently fell through as a result of mutual mistrust and a 'total clash of personalities' between the two chief executives. Curtin 'took three months to assess it' because he 'was afraid that Brosnan was selling him a pig in a poke'. Brosnan got impatient with the delay and 'turned around and said he wasn't going to do it'. The two men never developed a personal rapport. The relationship between the two processors deteriorated after this episode and the milk war resumed.

In 1979 Golden Vale had already taken the prudent step of setting up a 'milk development fund' from current profits, designed to help support the incomes of its suppliers and protect its milk pool during the difficult early 1980s. Having invested £4.5m over 1979–83 for this purpose it was particularly frustrating for Golden Vale to see this effort seriously undermined by the concerted attacks on its milk supply. It is not surprising that the milk war gave rise to such bitterness within Golden Vale and that relationships with Kerry deteriorated in the way that they did.

Golden Vale's ability to ward off the aggressive attacks on its milk pool was weakened by a series of difficulties that put increasing strain on its financial reserves. Most of the larger processors entered the 1980s with plans for further development which had to be revised or abandoned. Golden Vale was no exception. As late as February 1979 it had been planning for a £25m expansion. Not only was this plan shelved in 1981 but the need to rationalise the milk assembly system became more urgent. This was a difficult task, involving a shift towards bulk collection and the politically sensitive consolidation of the branch creamery network. In 1981 the company made some progress in this area and reduced its workforce by 70 people. The cost of these redundancies drew down on reserves to the tune of £0.12m.

In 1981 and 1982 the company suffered trading losses on its engineering activity. Engineering's performance had been erratic since the mid-1970s. Curtin and his board took the difficult decision to close down the one-time star business in 1982 at a cost of £2.4m, bringing the activity's total drain on company resources to £4.2m over its final two years. Then in 1983, when its cash flow and financial position should have improved significantly, Golden Vale had to write off its investment in the acquisition of Castlemahon Poultry Products. Curtin had acquired Castlemahon as part of a move to diversify and reduce the company's dependence on the stagnant dairy industry.

The cumulative drain on resources from this succession of problems led to a growing erosion of supplier confidence in the company's stability and in its management. The debt to equity ratio had deteriorated to 120 per cent by 1983. Kerry Cooperative, which had stepped up hostilities in the milk war after the breakdown of the Limerick deal, took further advantage of Golden Vale's difficulties to make what many believed was a bold takeover bid and the milk wars came to be seen as a 'softening up process' for such a move. Curtin and his board decried the 'gross lies and malicious rumours' that were being spread in an 'attempt to undermine supplier confidence in their Society' and were emphatic that Golden Vale was 'not for takeover by Kerry, or anybody else' (*Irish Press* 29/9/83).

The company's bankers began to get worried about Golden Vale's financial position in early 1984. By the end of the year it reported a loss of almost £0.5m. By mid-1985 the milk war had reached alarming proportions. The *Irish Press* (10/4/85) reported that rapid expansion by Kerry had 'raised major fears that one of the 'Big Six' dairy coops may go under' and that there was 'strong speculation that the victim would inevitably be Golden Vale'. Less than two weeks later the Chairman of Golden Vale publicly charged that 'some societies seem to be hell-bent on the destruction of others' and asked 'do they want to destroy Golden Vale' and if so 'are we to believe that one group of farmers are actively trying to destroy the work of another, undermining their cooperative and ultimately their livelihood and that of their families?'.

Curtin introduced a new milk pricing structure in an attempt to stem the 'haemorrhage' of milk supply. The new pricing structure, however, had very limited impact. The unanticipated loss of revenue from this latest phase in the milk war forced Curtin and his team to speed up their rationalisation programme in order to improve profitablity. However, by the end of 1985 Golden Vale had lost close to 6m gallons in milk wars and reported a trading loss of £0.5m. Rationalisation reduced the workforce by 232 staff and put a further drain on reserves of £1.4m. The debt to equity ratio reached 149 per cent and the banks once more became concerned about the company's financial position. The loss of milk supply was depressing returns. This in turn was damaging the confidence of the remaining suppliers and leaving the company's milk pool more vulnerable to further erosion. It was now on a vicious cycle which had to be arrested quickly if the company was going to survive. When this cycle began to accelerate alarmingly in late 1985 Curtin's position came under pressure and he resigned.

Insiders readily acknowledged the great talents and abilities of Tony Curtin and his major role in the dramatic turnaround of the mid-1970s. However the situation that Golden Vale faced in the 1980s called for a different approach and different management skills at the top. 'Tony Curtin', as one senior manager recalled, 'was a very capable man, very hard-working'. He 'was faced with most of the internal rationalisation problems' but 'he did not understand the politics of farming' and was 'politically too straight, if anything'. His 'biggest problem was that he was not able to convince farmers that we were paying a good price for milk'. In the end it was the inability to retain the confidence of his suppliers that led to his resignation.

THE O'MAHONY ERA 1986–88, AND BEYOND

In 1986 Golden Vale hired Jim O'Mahony as Curtin's successor. O'Mahony was an experienced chief executive who had headed up Ireland's seventh largest dairy processor, North Connaught Farmers Cooperative, for many years. His father had been deeply involved in the dairy sector before him and he had strong roots in the industry. He was a dairy science graduate with an MBA, and had been a contemporary of Denis Brosnan (the Kerry Chief Executive) at university.

O'Mahony immediately identified the major challenges facing him at Golden Vale as the erosion of milk supplies, the high cost of milk assembly and the lack of farmer confidence. He arrived at Golden Vale in March 1986 just as 200 suppliers were about to transfer their 3.5m gallons of milk to Kerry. 'The new manager came in and was prepared to show strength straight away' as one insider recalled. 'He went out and met the farmers and convinced them that he was going to put things right and he won back farmers' confidence.' His message, as reported in the *Cork Examiner* (30/4/86) was 'give me one year to make Golden Vale's milk price one of the best in the land'. As a result he managed to retain 2.5m of the 3.5m gallons that was about to leave the cooperative. On the question of Kerry and Brosnan he said that his objective was 'to make as much money as possible for the farmers and Golden Vale'. He had 'no hang-ups about personalities or opinions' and believed that 'facts and figures dominate decisions' but he was 'not going to let him get any more milk'.

National milk production was down in 1986 to 985m gallons as a result of EEC cutbacks. The general decline along with some further milk losses to rivals left Golden Vale with a throughput of just 84m gallons in 1986, its lowest level for ten years. In spite of this Golden Vale was able to report retained profits of £1m and a debt equity ratio of just 89 per cent at the end of the year. The rationalisation carried out under Tony Curtin's leadership, and paid for during his tenure, contributed in no small way to the company's return to profitability. In addition, O'Mahony's own moves to stem the milk haemorrhage and further rationalise the milk assembly system were also key to this financial turnaround after four successive years of losses. Over the 1985–86 period the number of branches was reduced from 63 to 28 and the number of trading stores from 64 to 30.

Jim O'Mahony and Golden Vale 'hit back hard at Kerry Cooperative's attempts to 'poach' its milk suppliers' in December 1986 (Irish Times 3/3/87). In bringing the milk war to Kerry the company secured a net gain of 126 suppliers and 5.5m gallons. Through this latest skirmish O'Mahony had served notice to all and sundry that further attacks on his milk pool would be met with strong and swift retaliation. However, the personal animosity that had come to characterise the Curtin–Brosnan relationship was never developed in O'Mahony's case. Relations with Kerry in fact improved quite quickly. This was noted with some wonder in a *Business and Finance* feature (24/9/87) which recalled how 'these two were pirating each other's farmers goodo' up to the end of 1986 but how all that had 'changed since Jim O'Mahony arrived'. Whether this originated 'from O'Mahony's diplomacy or a change of heart by Denis Brosnan' was 'difficult to say' but the feature went on to report that 'the two organisations trade with each other now' and that 'Brosnan has also declared publicly that he does not intend to poach any more farmers'.

Over his first two years as leader Jim O'Mahony concentrated on reversing the decline in milk supply and improving the cost base of the company. Milk intake from the company's own suppliers stabilised at around 78m gallons. Over the 1986–87 period turnover grew by a modest 2 per cent to £135m but net profits improved by 140 per cent to nearly £5m. The fortunes of the company had been turned around and a platform established for its return to growth. During this period he also set about changing the internal structure and culture of the organisation. He retained two senior executives from the Curtin team, the Financial Controller and the Company Secretary, but made his own appointments to head the key areas of Production and Marketing. He made a strategic hire to head up his newly created Liquid Milk and Milk Assembly function and created a more visible strategic planning function which he placed under Marketing. He moved 'a lot more fire power' into the marketing area and brought in a 'live-in' process consultant to help him transform the internal culture of the organisation to rebuild confidence and move it towards being 'market-led' and 'market-driven'. The whole thrust of the first two years under O'Mahony was summed up by one senior executive:

> Basically the idea is to get ourselves more profitable by one means or another, and no big committments until we have built up a reserve. There won't be any great improvement in borrowings in 1987 because of our capital programme, but a significant improvement (is expected) in 1988 and 1989 if the Corporate Plan works.

Under EEC restrictions growth in national milk supply was ruled out for the foreseeable future. These restrictions forced major processors with growth ambitions to redefine their business missions and capital structures. Kerry and Avonmore led the way. They increased the scale of their operations through planned acquisition and diversification. They defined themselves more broadly as international food companies and restructured themselves into public limited companies to widen their access to capital for further development. By 1988 Golden Vale had established its own foundation for further development and was ready to follow the lead of the others. By 1990 it had regained much of its pre-eminence in the food sector which had been lost over the 1980–85 period. The business had grown to £210m in turnover and £12m in net profits. Its return to pre-eminence was marked by the achievement of the *Irish Times/PA Management Award* for 'contribution to the national good, achievement of outstanding results and generation of competitive advantage', the first company in the dairy sector to win it. In the same year it became a public limited company and seemed to be already embarked on a new phase in its history.

SUMMARY

In this and the previous four chapters we have presented the empirical data on which this multi-level study of context, leadership and strategy is based. In the remaining three chapters we go on to develop and examine the themes which emerge from our conceptual framework and empirical analysis and we synthesise the findings of our study.

8   Leaders – tenants of time and context

Our central theme in this study is the interaction of leaders and contexts in the formation of strategy. We have deliberately chosen to look at the effects of each of these variables separately in the first instance and then later to concentrate on their interaction. In this we are following an approach similar to that used by Allison (1971) in his classic study of the decision process in the Cuban Missile Crisis. We interpret our data from a mainly voluntarist perspective in this chapter in order to compare and categorise the contributions of the various leaders profiled in the study to the strategic development of their organisations. In the next chapter we will revisit our data from a more determinist viewpoint as we identify and examine the main contextual factors that shaped the strategies of our organisations. In the final chapter we will return to the theme of their interaction and synthesise the overall findings of the study.

When examined over time in full historical context we can see that the contributions of the leaders profiled in this study were clearly related to the historical challenges facing their organisations during their tenures at the top. They were truly *tenants of time and context*. We also see, however, the primary role that personal attributes and motivations played as each sought to leave his distinct imprint on the history of his organisation. In comparing and contrasting our leaders in terms of their historical challenges and personal attributes we have come to classify them into four distinct generic categories: *builders*, *revitalisers*, *turnarounders* and *inheritors* (Table 8.1).

BUILDERS – WALSH AND O'LOUGHLIN

Dr Tom Walsh of AFT and Dave O'Loughlin of Golden Vale were the builders of their respective organisations at the formative stage of development.

Table 8.1 Leadership roles (leaders as tenants of time and context)

Leaders	Primary role	Secondary role(s)*	Company
Walsh	Builder		AFT
O'Loughlin	Builder		Golden Vale
McCourt	Revitaliser		IDG
Costello	Revitaliser		CSET
O'Reilly	Turnarounder		CSET
O'Mahony	Turnarounder		Golden Vale
Ryan	Inheritor	Defender/Transformer	AFT
Burrows	Inheritor	Implementer/Defender	IDG
Daly	Inheritor	Stabiliser	CSET
Sheehy	Inheritor	Defender	CSET
Comerford	Inheritor	Transformer	CSET
Lenihan	Inheritor	Implementer	Golden Vale
Curtin	Inheritor	Defender	Golden Vale

* secondary roles played by inheritors

Dr Tom Walsh – AFT

The personal drive of AFT's first Director, Dr Tom Walsh, was a major, if not *the* major, factor in the organisation's early growth and development. The Doc was described as 'the driving force' by long-serving AFT executives. The view that AFT would 'never have been as big' as it became 'if it had not been for the Doc' was widely shared, and many insiders often asked themselves, looking back, 'who else could have done it?'. The Doc was clearly expansionist in outlook and temperament and 'had no conception of, and did not want discussed, when the end of the expansion of AFT was to be'.

Tom Walsh established AFT and expanded it quickly to over 700 staff after only three years, and to over 1,000 by the end of its first decade. The Institute was founded at the time when the First Programme for Economic Expansion was getting underway and this undoubtedly created a context for its rapid growth. However, the organisation had been born in controversy and powerful institutional interests, already active in the field of agricultural education and research, were jealously guarding their own domains. In the Doc's own words, AFT 'commenced quickly and this fact raised the ire of some people in the Department and in the Universities'.

Right from the start the Doc had to fight for his operational scope and a
person of lesser passion and conviction might have been forced to settle for
much less. The mission of the new Institute was 'to develop the agriculture
of the country'. The Doc was clear in his own mind that 'this did not just
mean farming' but 'included food' as well. It also 'brought in the socio-
economic structure' of agriculture and 'the behavioural sciences'. Many
other interests did not agree and wanted to restrict AFT's overall scope. As
the Doc saw it the most important decisions taken under his leadership were
'to develop the Institute as an institute and not just as a co-ordinating body',
to deal 'not just with farming but with the whole spectrum from soil to
table' and to 'have a rural economy division'. For the Doc 'operating the
autonomy of the Institute' was not a once-off issue over domain and scope
but 'a continual struggle day in, day out'.

In the face of such difficulties the Doc quickly managed to define the
major fields for research in the new Institute. He structured the initial
research programmes under the broad headings of Soils, Animal
Production, Plant Sciences and Crop Husbandry, Horticulture and Forestry,
and Rural Economy. He saw himself as building not just a research institute
but a national resource and he was determined to develop it to a level that
could make a real impact on Irish agriculture in the shortest possible time.
While he and his senior executives went out and acquired suitable lands and
buildings, in at least one case paying the deposit by personal cheque to
ensure that the right property was not lost, he had scores of his young Irish
scientists off taking higher degrees on Kellogg scholarships in US
universities. In this way he assembled the initial physical and human
resources for AFT with vision, opportunism and the minimum of
bureaucratic procedure.

In his own words 'the main thing was to get the work done' and he was
anxious to get the programme underway. As he saw it his 'main job was
building morale' through 'getting to know each person and their capacity'.
The 'big thing was the motivation of the staff' and letting them know that
while 'they might have thought they were small cogs' they 'had a national
job to do' and 'the work they were doing was important'. The fact that
many of his young pioneering scientists later left AFT to take up key
positions in the meat and dairy industries was a source of pride rather than
concern. He saw this as the natural consequence ot his vision of AFT as a
national resource providing 'a pool of scientifically trained manpower to
(the) country in a real sense' and offering a tangible return for the national
'intellectual investment' that AFT represented.

The Doc's approach to formal planning and organisation was an
extension of his basic pre-disposition to build and develop his scientific
base. Consistent with his passionate belief in the power of science and

empirical research he wanted to draw on the most up-to-date techniques of modern management. However, formal planning and management techniques did not sit easily with his very personal and dominating style of leadership. His 'Research for Agriculture 1970–75' corporate plan was by his own admission a propaganda device 'addressed at the government of the day to get more money' and he was disappointed with the result. The consultant-designed 1970 reorganisation gave him not only a new structural arrangement but also the new management supports of a Deputy Director, a central directorate and a consultative committee. The Doc was not cut out for these formal structures and planning mechanisms. He 'never believed that he needed all the planning paraphernalia' and remained convinced that 'research was managed best through the personal touch'. What he had really wanted from the reorganisation was to keep AFT from getting too institutionalised and losing its vitality. He was determined not to let it settle down 'into a mundane thing' because of his conviction that 'in any research organisation there has to be agitation or nothing will get done'.

The Doc was an inspirational leader who 'had a charisma of leadership where young scientists identified for themselves individually and collectively a mission in the revival of Irish agriculture'. However, he was a demanding boss and not easy to work for on a direct one to one basis. His lack of political sensitivity brought him into confrontation with some of his very best lieutenants and during the 1970 reorganisation led to the loss of one of the best of them, a man who in the Doc's own view 'had the attributes' to be a future leader of AFT. It also brought him into conflict with all of his research staff over the proposed amalgamation of AFT and the advisory services in 1977. The Doc lost credibility in both of these episodes and the second one marked the beginning of the end of his tenure at AFT. However, even those researchers that had led the revolt in 1977 never lost their affection and admiration for him and he remained a welcome visitor to AFT. He was widely recognised as the Institute's 'outstanding character' over its thirty year history as an independent entity.

Dave O'Loughlin – Golden Vale

Unlike the Doc, Dave O'Loughlin was not with his organisation from its foundation. Nevertheless, he is generally recognised as the great builder in Golden Vale's early history. Indeed he was brought into the company near the end of its first decade of operation because the board felt that the business was under-developed. O'Loughlin is widely credited with the main strategic developments that set the organisation on the road from being a small operation with a turnover of less than £1m in the mid-1950s to one of over £70m by the mid-1970s. He had a family background in the industry and was one of the first of a new breed of leader in Irish dairy processing, a professional manager by education and training, specifically geared for such a role.

O'Loughlin, like the Doc in AFT, was expansionary and opportunistic. He led the small federation into its first major diversification, engineering. There had been a small engineering activity at Golden Vale before his time but he developed it at a 'rate of knots'. He saw the potential in the sector's general physical development, and in the new regulations with regard to pasteurisation which greatly increased the industry's need for stainless steel fittings and equipment. Under his leadership Golden Vale Engineering became the pre-eminent engineering activity in the Irish dairy sector and developed the capability and confidence to win contracts from other sectors at home and the dairy industry abroad.

Golden Vale expanded under O'Loughlin throughout the 1960s. He built up the complex at Charleville and extended its capabilities to handle natural cheese. He diversified Golden Vale into the milk powder business and with his commitment to enterprise and development drew nine new members to the federation. As the decade progressed the company 'began to be noticed' by the other major processors, and 'more and more' as one senior industry figure recalled 'I perceived the growing influence of Dave O'Loughlin'. O'Loughlin's progressive outlook was reflected in his diversification into fat-filled milk, a technique he did not invent but was the first in the industry to see its real commercial potential. Based on this process he developed the Golden Maverick family of milk replacers that became brand leaders and company flagships. This new product base became the launching pad for the organisation's major capital expansion phase over the 1968–75 period. Finally he was one of the more far-sighted leaders in the industry who made the early moves on amalgamation at processor level during the structural transformation episode of 1958–74. Though, along with many in the sector, he was initially opposed to the Government's effort to rationalise the industry in this way he was quicker than most to see the inevitability of the move toward larger units and he positioned Golden Vale so that it would emerge from this process as one of the country's leading processors.

O'Loughlin was a bold and imaginative leader who had 'an extraordinary capacity to take risks' in his efforts to build his organisation to one of pre-eminence in its industry. His decision to commit Golden Vale to a major capital expansion programme in advance of amalgamation exposed the company to the possibility of severe over-capacity if it failed to achieve the level of consolidation anticipated. However this decision also pre-empted similar moves by other processors and ensured that Golden Vale would emerge as one of the main growth centres from the amalgamation process. The liquidity crisis of 1975 demonstrateJ just how risky this strategy was. Yet with a less imaginative and more cautious approach Golden Vale would not have emerged from the industry consolidation of the 1968–74 period as the second largest dairy processor in the country. O'Loughlin was a strong conviction leader like the Doc, who fully committed himself to his vision for Golden Vale. His painstaking efforts over three years to woo the targeted creamery societies into amalgamation, 'losing no opportunity to sell the benefits of amalgamation' and attending hundreds of meetings to convert opinion leaders and secure support, were testimony to this commitment.

In just fifteen years O'Loughlin built Golden Vale from a small federation of only minor significance into an industry leader. He is remembered as an entrepreneurial leader who dominated his board and his senior management team and 'stood way above the whole lot'. He was 'very much the boss', a 'forceful, driven risk-taker' whose 'basic strategic decisions were very right' and he, like the Doc in AFT, is remembered as the outstanding figure in his organisation's history.

REVITALISERS – COSTELLO AND McCOURT

General Costello of CSET and Kevin McCourt of IDG came to head up their respective organisations when the basic characters of these entities had been already established. The strategic task that each man faced was the challenge of revitalising his organisation and raising it to a new plane of development.

General Michael J. Costello – CSET

CSET was already in existence for over a decade when the General became its leader in 1945. The basic sugar activity was well-established and had proved its strategic value to the nation during the war years. However the industry emerged from the war in a state of 'exhaustion' and the General was brought in to revitalise it. He faced a situation where the fields had been over-tilled, the factories were in need of modernisation, the crop was threatened by various pests and diseases and the future growth of the industry was being held back by the labour intensity of the harvesting process and the growing shortage of farm labour. The country's leaders put their faith in the General as a man who not only possessed 'the ability and strength of character to shoulder a major industrial appointment, but who had proven his patriotism to the hilt'. Like Lemass, Costello had earlier been propelled into national prominence at a very young age because of the pressing needs of new nationhood.

General Costello clearly saw his task as developmental. He came to CSET not simply to head up a sugar processing company but to secure and revitalise an industry capable of providing both industrial and agricultural employment in rural areas. He was passionately committed to the development of Irish agriculture to its fullest potential for the social and economic benefit of the rural community itself and for the benefit of the nation at large. He took a special interest in the problems of small producers and continually exhorted them to consider new options, and to organise, to preserve the economic viability of their way of life. His guiding philosophy was his belief that 'the cooperative theories of Horace Plunkett' were 'superior to communism and capitalism' and the 'only workable alternative' for his beet growers and their communities (CSET 1986: 32).

His management style was that of the benevolent autocrat. He 'took the general's view' as he set about revitalising the industry by mobilising his 'civilian army' of CSET employees and beetgrowers and moulding them into an efficient machine. He recruited a number of ex-army officers to help him in this endeavour. He believed in consultation and in using people's talents to the full but he also took complete charge while he was at the top. He was a strict disciplinarian who was intolerant of sloppy or faint-hearted effort, yet he took a deep and abiding interest in the welfare of his employees and suppliers. He was a commanding figure in the sugar beet industry. He saw his task as one of winning over the hearts and minds of all connected with the sector, and of raising their sights and ambitions from 'the restricted economy and narrowed horizons' to which many of them 'had clung, in a changing world, almost since the time of their grandfathers' (Lynch 1986: 13–14).

His revitalisation efforts extended beyond the firm to the industry and the rural communities that depended on it. He attacked the problem with enormous energy and conviction on a broad front. He modernised the sugar-processing facilities. He brought the mechanical and chemical revolutions to Irish beet production through his initiatives on soil testing, lime quarrying, seed breeding, pest control and beet harvest mechanisation. He imported the best ideas from abroad and was not slow to innovate where these were inadequate for Irish conditions. Through all of these initiatives he brought the sugar beet industry up to the level of national self-sufficiency with sustained commitment over a fifteen-year period. He did this at a time when the prevailing mood across the nation was one of growing despondency as immigration reached alarming proportions and the country seemed incapable of generating a viable economy. At every turn he had to 'cope with the timid spirits who baulk at every obstacle' and could not 'bring themselves to believe in the ability of Irishmen to compete with men of other nations'. He brought modern organisation and management not only into the sugar processing activity but also into beet farming. He encouraged his suppliers to form small syndicates in order to achieve levels of mechanisation and specialisation efficiencies in the various production activities that would never have been possible with each producer acting alone.

The General responded to the national challenge posed by Lemass's programmes for economic development in a characteristically bold and imaginative way. The limited scope provided by the sugar business for export-led growth forced the General to look for other ways to use his resourceful company in the service of the nation. The strategic move into convenience food processing was a related diversification that was intended to leverage the company's 'knowledge and experience of handling farmers' produce over the years' and its 'intimate knowledge and understanding of the farming problems' of its '30,000 beet growers'. For all that it was still a venture that was not for the faint-hearted or small-minded. The General had to overcome the reservations of many who thought that his aim was so 'impossibly great' that 'their imaginations boggle(d)' at his vision to build an indigenous food industry to a scale that was to be 'larger than any industrial activity' then being 'carried on in Ireland'. The General was determined that his revitalised company should become a leading force in the revitalisation of the whole economy.

In its first few years the food project caught the imagination of the nation and was favourably received in Britain, the target market. The bold commitment to new products based on the first ever commercial application of accelerated freeze-drying technology proved to be the least hazardous part of the enterprise. The cost of establishing direct sales and distribution activities in the British market was grossly under-estimated as was the expense of winning market share from large entrenched competitors. The project turned out to have a much higher break-even level than expected and was taking longer than anticipated to reach a self-sustaining breakthrough. As time went on the price seemed higher and the rewards more uncertain. Belief in the viability of the project began to wither.

In November 1966, the General resigned from CSET, in controversial circumstances, after twenty-one years as the head of the company. He remained convinced of the wisdom of his strategy. Could self-sustaining scale have been reached at a reasonable cost to the company and the nation or was the strategy inherently flawed? The A. D. Little analysis of the time seemed to suggest that it was achievable but expensive and risky. Would it have been worth it? The General thought so. Reasonable people considered it debatable then and would still do so today. In the late 1960s Ireland's industrial policy took a distinct shift towards the inducement of direct inward investment in targeted high technology 'sunrise' industries like electronics and pharmaceuticals. This shift in policy staked the nation's money 'on the hare of foreign enterprise rather than on the tortise of native industry' and 'the approach produced quick but not lasting results'. In the late 1980s national strategy returned to emphasise indigenous industry in general, and food processing in particular. The current intention is to encourage the development of at least ten £1b-plus indigenous companies by the year 2000, many of them in the food sector. History may yet come to judge the failure to back the General's vision on the food project as a major missed opportunity.

Kevin McCourt – IDG

The modern history of the Irish distilling industry began with the 1966 merger of Power, Jameson and Cork Distillers. However the hiring of Kevin McCourt was crucial in making this merger work. It was he who 'forced the families to agree' to the downstream operation of the merger and he is remembered as 'the man for the time'. McCourt, with the strong support of his Chairman Frank O'Reilly, introduced modernity in marketing, technology and management into these traditional family baronies and forged them into an effective organic unit. He was the leader who, in accelerating the transition of Irish distilling from family capitalism to managerial capitalism, helped to revitalise the industry and change its outlook.

He came to IDG with impressive credentials as a professional manager and a career Chief Executive. He had spent the early part of his career in the tobacco industry and had held the Chief Executive position at Hunter Douglas and at Radio Telefis Eireann. He is remembered in IDG as a 'strong authoritarian' leader who 'brought through very difficult decisions' in his determination to modernise the company and make it competitive nationally and internationally. The broad strategic thrust for the company was already taking shape prior to his arrival. The logic of the merger was to secure the cost base of the operations and the profit base of the home market as the platform for export-led growth.

Right from the start McCourt faced formidable problems in making the merger work. He was confronted with three former companies whose traditions and operating systems were widely different. Even more daunting were the deep divisions that still remained at board level about just how far the process of integration should go. He was confronted with an inefficient configuration of ageing and inflexible distilling facilities and an inward-looking and production-dominated industry with a tradition that held the historical formulation of the products as sacred. Finally he faced a distribution system which gave the company little control over the consistency of its product and kept it too far removed from its consumer base.

He showed strength early on with his decision to take more control over distribution in the face of the 'vitriolic response' of the blenders and wholesalers that had long been integral to the industry structure. The process of forging the three family companies into an effective unitary organisation took longer. He began by merging the operations of marketing and finance, under newly hired professionals, in the face of three sales organisations with a long tradition of competing against one another and three financial systems that were unbelievably different. At board level Norbert Murphy, the strong independent-minded leader of Cork Distillers, remained a major obstacle to integration for many years. He was prepared for some joint-effort on export marketing but otherwise appeared to want the merger 'to go away'. However, he 'had not bargained for Kevin McCourt' and 'did not see a unitary hierarchy developing as quickly as it did'. The decision to consolidate distilling operations in one central complex was a crucial step in taking the process of integration to the point of no return. The involvement of A. D. Little consultants in the decision process helped 'to take the personal politics out of the situation' and the choice of Midleton in Cork as the location 'cured (Murphy's) opposition a bit'.

McCourt was an important transitional figure in the history of IDG and the distilling industry. Under his leadership the company began to overcome its reluctance to experiment with the distilling and blending processes in order to produce a wider range of end products to cater for a diversity of consumer tastes and preferences. This willingness to 'interfere' with the product would have been almost heretical to previous generations of distillers yet it was a crucial break with the past if the company was to be really serious about pursuing export-led growth. The decision to consolidate distilling operations was an even more dramatic break with tradition with 'absolutely far-reaching' implications, and there were easier options that might have been chosen. The decision meant the strategic withdrawal from locations with centuries-old distilling traditions. There were also very real fears that the distinctive images of the industry's traditional flagship brands might be compromised if they were all perceived to be coming from the same modern 'just-flick-a-switch' distillery. Confidence in McCourt 'was a major element' in allaying these fears. The strategic acquisition of Bushmills, which gave the company full control over the production and marketing of Irish whiskey as a generic product, was another break with the past and led to the consolidation of the Irish distilling industry across the political economies of Northern and Southern Ireland.

In sum the changes brought about in the Irish distilling industry during McCourt's ten years as leader were dramatic. Three disparate family firms, each with its own centuries-old traditions, were well down the road in being moulded into one of Ireland's largest corporations. The traditional structure of the company's domestic market had been dramatically changed. Centuries-old distilleries had been closed down with many traditional skills consigned to history. One of the world's most modern distilling complexes had been built and new skills developed to manage it. The production and marketing of Irish whiskey as a generic product had been totally consolidated. The company and the industry had become synonymous and had been transformed from production-dominated to market-led.

Over the ten years, while this transformation was taking place, group turnover had doubled and profits more than trebled. Total case sales had grown by 290 per cent, home sales by 195 per cent and exports by 552 per cent. Exports had risen from 27 per cent to 47 per cent of total volume. The main elements of the post-merger strategy were in place and working. The one major objective not yet reached by the time McCourt retired was the achievement of a self-sustaining breakthrough in the strategic US market. This turned out to be more difficult than the industry leaders had expected.

TURNAROUNDERS – O'REILLY AND O'MAHONY

Tony O'Reilly of CSET and Jim O'Mahony of Golden Vale were each hired in to achieve turnaround. O'Reilly's challenge at CSET was to turn around the performance of the company's troubled diversification while O'Mahony was called upon to turn around the fortunes of the company itself. In each case the principals involved believed that nothing less than a dramatic change in leadership was required to begin the turnaround process and to enhance the likelihood of its success.

A. J. (Tony) O'Reilly – CSET

Tony O'Reilly was hired into CSET in late 1966 to turn around the food project. He served the company as Managing Director for less than three years. Though his tenure at the top was short it was also dramatic and his legacy cast a long shadow.

O'Reilly was the hand-picked choice of the government of the day to replace the General and bring the food project to commercial viability. He was barely 30 years of age when he was chosen to succeed the man who had towered over the company and the industry for over twenty years. Yet he had already established himself as the leading light of a new breed of professional manager then emerging in Irish society. He had achieved a high national profile as a talented and competitive international rugby player and was the marketing whiz-kid most closely associated with the successful launch of the 'kerrygold' generic brand for Irish dairy products on the UK market. He was the archetype of the new national hero emerging from Lemass's economic revolution. He was on personal terms with Jack Lynch, Lemass's successor, and with many of the Lynch cabinet. He was a new breed of industrial leader for a new breed of national politician. In time he was to become perhaps the most successful career professional ever to come from the ranks of Irish management and the first ever non-family Chairman and Chief Executive Officer of the Heinz Corporation in its 117-year history.

Tony O'Reilly's appointment was clearly meant to signal a change in strategy and style. His imposition on the organisation with no prior consultation was public evidence of the growing impatience within government circles with the company's management of the food project. For some of the brash young ministers in the Lynch Government the General was already 'yesterday's man'. He had been successful in revitalising a protected industry but they believed that the food project needed the leadership of someone with more commercial acumen and proven marketing skills. O'Reilly seemed to be uniquely qualified to turn it around. He had shown his marketing flair on the target UK food market with the 'kerrygold' launch and few other Irishmen of his generation could demonstrate comparable success. The manner of his appointment stunned the company but it was national news and greeted with a high degree of expectation as an imaginative choice.

The task facing Tony O'Reilly was a major challenge. The losses on the food project were mounting and the timeframe within which he was expected to make an impact was short. Added to this was the resistance that he faced within CSET from the long-serving executives who had built the sugar business. O'Reilly concentrated on the food business and hired in new skills and talents to help him turn it around. He was content in the short term to let the sugar business take care of itself. He went with the joint-venture option recommended in the A. D. Little report that had been commissioned before his arrival. He eliminated the company's direct sales and marketing operation in the UK which had been an integral and expensive element of the General's strategy. The much-publicised joint-venture arrangement that he negotiated with the Heinz Corporation to replace it was the kind of bold and imaginative move that his admirers had expected and it enhanced his image as a marketing genius. The young brash 'David' had persuaded one of the food industry's 'Goliaths' to become directly involved. The Heinz association gave Erin Foods new prestige within the company and in the wider Irish community.

O'Reilly made considerable progress in bringing the food project to commercial viability with this new approach, almost tripling the sales volume and more than doubling the acreage sown by his suppliers over the 1966–69 period. By the time of his unexpected departure the food project had almost reached break-even on a cash flow basis and the company was overall showing an after-tax profit for the first time in four years. He had brought a new 'buzz' to CSET, but just as his turnaround strategy appeared to be working he left suddenly to take up a senior position with the Heinz Corporation in the United Kingdom. His move to Heinz came as a massive shock to company and government alike. It was an outcome of the joint-venture strategy that no one had anticipated. His departure marked the beginning of the end of the great food strategy dream at CSET. Insiders believe that the commitment of Heinz to the joint-venture weakened when O'Reilly was no longer there to drive it from the CSET side. It was left to leaders of lower profile and lesser talent than the General and O'Reilly to manage the slow painful task of reducing the scale and scope of the food business and extricating the company from many of the commitments in specialised assets and employment that were made during the project's heyday.

While he was the Managing Director the food business dominated the company's strategy and the 'food people took over the company'. O'Reilly had imported a new breed of executive and a foreign, and challenging, culture into the company but then left before this new culture had fully taken root. After his departure the ascendency of food ceased, and following a period of drift and uncertainty the sugar division once more gained the upper hand. The food business was consigned to diminishing importance.

Jim O'Mahony – Golden Vale

Like Tony O'Reilly in CSET, Jim O'Mahony was brought into Golden Vale to turn a critical situation around. In O'Mahony's case the company was caught in a vicious cycle which somehow had to be broken. Golden Vale was losing milk supply at 'haemorrhage' levels to neighbouring processors. The milk loss was depressing profits. This was eroding supplier confidence and leading to yet further losses. The company was losing its pre-eminence in the dairy industry, having slipped from number two to number six over the 1977–85 period, and was in very real danger of going under. The early 1980s had been a difficult period for all milk processors but Golden Vale had weathered it worse than most. O'Mahony's predecessor was a hard-working executive with a financial background. He had carried through some very difficult rationalisation measures. However he was rapidly losing the confidence of his suppliers and he had failed to sort out the deteriorating relationship with the neighbouring Kerry organisation to which he was losing a lot of his milk.

Golden Vale turned to an outsider to sort out the situation. O'Mahony's arrival was clearly meant to signal dramatic change. He came with impressive credentials. He had been the successful Chief Executive of the country's seventh largest processor, North Connaught Farmers, for thirteen years. He was a dairy scientist by profession and a contemporary of the Kerry chief at university. The challenge awaiting him at Golden Vale was daunting and success was far from guaranteed. He risked much of the reputation that he had already acquired in the industry, as well as his professional security, if he failed to turn around the situation. A man with less confidence in his own ability or less stomach for the challenge might easily have opted to stay where he was with little risk to his stature and reputation.

His ability to make an immediate impact on sorting out the erosion of supplier confidence and the relationship with the Kerry organisation was crucial to the successful turnaround that he accomplished at Golden Vale. He needed to 'show strength straight away' in both of these areas and could not afford to appear tentative or cautious in any way. He went out and met with his farmer-suppliers individually and in groups and 'convinced them that he was going to put things right'. His public appeal to them to give him 'a year to make Golden Vale's milk price one of the best in the land' bought him time and stemmed the milk loss. He bolstered up his image with his suppliers by bringing the milk war to Kerry and winning back a substantial portion of the lost gallonage. At the same time he let Denis Brosnan of Kerry know that while he was determined not to 'let him get any more milk' he had 'no hang-ups with personalities' and was not going to let personal politics damage the commercial interest of his company. With this overall approach he was able to bring about an end to the milk war within two years and actually see trading links develop between the former antagonists.

O'Mahony's skills in the 'politics of farming' were crucial in the initial phase of the turnaround. While his early moves were aimed at breaking the vicious cycle of milk loss and restoring supplier confidence his contribution to Golden Vale up to the end of the 1980s went way beyond that. He led the company back to growth and established a sound basis for its further development. In his first two years he concentrated on stemming the decline and improving earnings. There was little revenue increase. He recognised that the milk wars were the symptom of an industry which had to adjust to dramatic change in its overall context. Having bought time he used it to begin the process of transforming the company to a more commercial, market-driven organisation. This process involved a number of initiatives which were firsts of their kind in this very traditional of traditional industries. The most obvious example was the change process that he designed and implemented with the help of a live-in consultant to generate widespread understanding of the new business realities, build commercial skills and restore morale. The company that he led into the 1990s was once more a significant and self-confident player in the Irish food processing sector, a company that was ready to make the transition to public limited company status and to pursue growth through strategically planned diversification.

INHERITORS – RYAN, BURROWS, DALY, SHEEHY, COMERFORD, LENIHAN AND CURTIN

The six chief executives that we have looked at up to now were each brought into their respective organisations to take on a specific strategic challenge. Two were essentially builders of fledgling organisations, two were revitalisers of existing organisations that were ready for a new phase of development, and two were brought in to turn around organisations that were in difficulties.

The seven remaining chief executives that featured in this study were essentially insiders whose succession signalled continuity rather than change. They each inherited an organisation that was already past its formative period. They were expected to consolidate and build on the progress already made rather than to make any dramatically new strategic departures. As a result it is harder to link their personal contributions to substantial and highly visible strategic achievement than is the case for the builders, revitalisers and turnarounders. Their achievements as leaders are inevitably linked with their inheritances and all have had to live with the long shadows cast by higher profile predecessors. Yet some of them did emerge in their own right as leaders who initiated major strategic changes as their organisations came to face new contexts and issues during their tenure at the top. For the remainder their main contributions have been to see through to full effect the strategies that they had inherited. The inheritor can be one of the most difficult leadership roles to play as is shown in the following analysis. It is often under-rated by those outside the organisation who equate strategic leadership almost solely with the successful management of highly visible strategic challenges.

Dr Pierce Ryan – AFT

The Doc's successor, Pierce Ryan, was leader of AFT from 1979 until it ceased to be an independent entity in 1987. He had been the Deputy

Director for eight years but because of Walsh's dominant style he was very limited in what he had been able to achieve in this position. His succession was widely welcomed within the Institute. While a difference in leadership style was expected, his appointment as Director was generally taken to signal strategic continuity rather than change, developing on the sound base that had already been established. Few had foreseen that Ryan and AFT would have to face the most revolutionary changes in the structure and context of agricultural production since the organisation was founded. These changes, together with the mounting crisis in the state of the Irish public finances, came to pose fundamental questions about AFT's future role and operation. While the Doc will always be remembered as the leader who built AFT into an important national resource, Pierce Ryan will be remembered as the one who had to transform the organisation in difficult circumstances in order to realign it with the new priorities of the 1980s.

The situation that he faced quite early on in his tenure at the top was 'an absolutely new ballgame' in Irish and EEC agriculture with 'enormous implications for research'. He had to manage dramatic change in a number of directions at once. He had to get his staff to accept that fundamental changes were needed in the research programme. At the same time he had to bring about a major realignment of resources in a context where his room for manoeuvre was severely curtailed by declining budgets. He had to save his organisation from internal atrophy while at the same time trying to preserve its standing in the community. He had to do this at a time when the external pressures on AFT to demonstrate its continuing value to the economy had never been greater and in an environment for Irish agriculture which had never been more threatening or uncertain.

Many within AFT who worked with them both believed that Ryan was much more suited to the strategic task of transforming his organisation under such circumstances than the Doc would have been. With his expansionist nature and his driving, directive, style of leadership the Doc would have found the circumstances and challenges of the 1980s extremely frustrating. In contrast the demands of the situation were seen to be more suited to the patient, persistent, high-involvement style of Pierce Ryan. While the Doc's passion for AFT and its mission was inspirational and infectious, and he was an outstanding motivator of his professional staff in general, he was ironically not a great team builder with his own direct reports. He could be difficult to deal with at an inter-personal level. Ryan's was a more attractive persona which lent itself to easier relationships at all levels. While he did not have the passion or expansive outlook of the Doc he was 'equally committed to the advances that science and technology could make' and had a 'more balanced view of where AFT should be going'. Whereas the Doc's expansionism tended to 'threaten' a lot of other organisations 'by claiming their territories', Pierce Ryan had an easier acceptance of the limited role of AFT within the wider system at sector and national levels. Under Ryan's leadership relations with the other organisations, including the Department of Agriculture, were much smoother than in the Doc's time.

Ryan was a team-oriented leader, whose inclination was towards a 'more collegiate approach', a 'systems man', a 'logician and a diplomat'. He was willing to share power in a very substantial way, enlarging the office of director to include three deputy directors each of whom had a job of substance, status and clout. Under his leadership the central directorate, which included the research centre directors as well as the office of the director, became a more participative body with a more substantial influence on the direction and operation of the Institute than in the past. The review process that he implemented in the early 1980s was very different from that carried out over a decade earlier. It was designed to harness the involvement of all of the professional staff in the identification of the Institute's shifting priorities and was used by Ryan in the strategic management of AFT. At an inter-personal level he was able to effect the significant staff changes with little of the political fallout that had marked some of the Doc's attempts in this area. He saw his Council as a resource to be harnessed and its public support was an important factor in helping him to set up a dedicated food research centre in the mid-1980s in the face of potential opposition from other public bodies that considered this area as their domain.

It was a tribute to Pierce Ryan's own unique leadership skill that he was entrusted with the politically sensitive task of managing the merger of AFT and the advisory services and of forging Teagasc, the new organisation, into a vibrant resource to Irish agriculture with a unified sense of purpose.

Richard Burrows – IDG

The succession of Richard Burrows, like that of Pierce Ryan, was also a signal for continuity rather than for major change. Burrows came to Irish Distillers through the company's acquisition of Bushmills, where he had been Managing Director. His appointment at just 31 years of age was itself an indicator of the degree to which his predecessor Kevin McCourt had succeeded in modernising the company and breaking through its traditional conservatism. Within IDG Burrows was seen as the man that 'had brought the twentieth century into Bushmills'. He was 'clearly being groomed for succession' a full year before McCourt's contract was due to expire and his succession to the leadership was uncontentious and undramatic.

Richard Burrows inherited a strategy with three important elements: the rationalisation and modernisation of the Group's operations to improve its cost competitiveness nationally and internationally; the domination of the home market and the development of its full potential in order to provide a solid profit base; and export-led growth on the US market fuelled by this profit base where every 1 per cent gain in market share would have enormous impact on the expansion of the company.

The first two of these elements were well-advanced when Burrows took over. McCourt had modernised the company, rationalised its operations, made it more market-oriented, secured generic control over Irish whiskey and transformed the three former family companies into an effective corporate entity of scale and substance. On the export front case sales to the US market had expanded five-fold from 50,000 to 250,000 cases under McCourt's leadership. This was still just 18 per cent of the company's total volume. The really significant breakthrough was still to come and this was the strategic challenge that faced Richard Burrows as he took over as leader of IDG. The year 1979 marked the nadir of the McCourt era with historic highs in volume sales on both the domestic and export fronts. Both distilleries were operating at full capacity and Burrows was planning a £30m expansion in operations to provide for a targeted 50 per cent growth in volume by 1984. Most of this growth was expected to come from exports, particularly to the US. In the early 1980s the environment that faced Burrows and his company then changed dramatically. The new leader and his company found themselves unexpectedly on the defensive for most of the decade culminating in the takeover battle of 1988. Richard Burrows' tenure as the last leader of IDG as an independent entity will be remembered for his performance as defender of his company's interests under difficult trading conditions and later under takeover threat.

Just as Burrows was poised to accelerate the attack on the export front his domestic profit base, the main platform for this assault, came under severe threat. The combination of general recession in world trade and steep increases in excise duty from a government under growing fiscal pressure led to a sharp fall in volume and profit on the home market. In spite of this setback the company managed to retain Stock Market confidence because of the slow but steady gains that it continued to make on the export front. Burrows' decision to acquire BWG for its cash and carry business marked a turning point in the company's relations with the Stock Market. It was done to consolidate the home base but was seen as a defensive investment in a stagnant economy. The market began to lose its faith in the will and ability of the company to make a real breakthrough on the export front using the success of Bailey's Irish Cream as a benchmark for what should be possible in spite of the general trading climate. For most of the period from this acquisition in 1984 to the takeover in 1988 the company's share, for long a leading stock, continued to under-perform the market, keeping Burrows' and his board under constant pressure.

Within this pressure cauldron Richard Burrows led his company through some radical changes to improve its prospects and bolster confidence. On the export front he over-hauled the US marketing strategy that he had inherited to make it more focused, using the two-brand approach that had proved more successful for him in the United Kingdom and in other major European markets. With the full backing of his Chairman he also set about dramatically improving the earnings quality of the company through a further £12m rationalisation of transport and operations. These moves did much to restore the confidence of the company's major institutional investors. Ironically the same moves also helped to increase the attractivenes of the company as a takeover target. To a market which for many years had believed that IDG was nowhere close to exploiting the full commercial potential of its effective monopoly of Irish whiskey, the prospect of a takeover seemed to be much less a matter of whether than when.

When the bid finally came in May 1988 Burrows confounded supporters and critics alike by the determination and skill that he showed during the ensuing takeover battle. He was always considered within IDG as a strong leader who enjoyed the confidence of his staff and board alike, whatever the perception of the external critics and doubters. His gritty defence of his company's basic integrity as an organic unit during the takeover process will always be seen as one of his finest hours as leader of IDG, whatever the future may bring. His brave attempt to ward off the hostile bid alone, and when this failed, his skill in securing and succeeding with a competing friendly bid from Pernod Ricard, won him the admiration of supporters and critics alike. In the aftermath of the takeover the new parent continued to demonstrate its confidence in Burrows, his company and the future of Irish whiskey by preserving IDG as an autonomous business unit within the corporate structure. This would not have happened had the hostile bid not been successfully defeated.

Daly, Sheehy and Comerford – CSET

The General's immediate successor, Bart Daly, was one of the pioneers of the sugar industry and had given good service to the company for over thirty years. He was one of the six young Irish chemistry graduates that had been handpicked at the company's foundation in 1934 to learn the technology abroad. Daly and his colleagues enabled the company to eliminate its dependence on foreign technologists within five years of its operation.

He was seen by insiders as 'very much a traditional sugar man'. Within three months of his appointment he found his position undermined without warning by the dramatic appointment of Tony O'Reilly as Managing Director. Daly was understandably 'appalled' by this decision and the insensitive way in which it had been imposed on him and his board by the politicians. However, he decided to bear with the new arrangement. He retained his title as General Manager of CSET. O'Reilly concentrated his talent and energy on the food business and left Daly to manage the sugar operation. When O'Reilly departed just as suddenly and dramatically as he had arrived the CSET board simply reverted back to the previous arrangement with Daly once more head of the company.

Daly is generally perceived to have left a comparatively light footprint as leader on the sands of CSET's history. When he assumed the leadership for the second time he inherited a situation where the morale of the company had been severely undermined by the dramatic events of the 1966–69 period from the General's resignation to O'Reilly's departure to the Heinz Corporation. Very senior executives, particularly in the sugar business, had become 'very disillusioned' by the 'direction in which they had been pushed' by the Government. The Government itself had become disillusioned by the sudden departure of its 'golden boy' and had backed away, leaving the company to choose its own successor and sort out its future. The company itself had two businesses with very different ideologies, cultures and types of personnel. Daly was just five years away from retirement when he faced this difficult situation.

In the wake of O'Reilly's departure the board's decision to revert back to Daly was a cautious one and his tenure at the top was largely seen to reflect this conservatism and desire for a period of calm and consolidation. He basically 'maintained the status quo' and 'did not initiate' any major strategic departure during his five years at the top. In a relatively featureless tenure he 'kept the company ticking over' with no significant 'investment or innovation'. Though EEC entry took place during his time at the helm its full implications for the future competitiveness of the sugar business were not really taken on board until after he retired. In short he was a long serving sugar executive who had already made his most significant contribution to the development of the company before his time as leader.

The careers of CSET's two remaining leaders, Maurice Sheehy and Chris Comerford, were inextricably linked and can be fully appreciated only in the light of the divisive succession contest that was bitterly fought out between them following Daly's retirement. Not only did this contest split the company and the board down the middle into rival camps but the decision process itself was highly political and controversial. Sheehy was the more senior of the two in age and position but Comerford was seen as an ambitious and energetic young executive on the move. The legacy of this contest was to dog Sheehy's tenure as leader and form a difficult part of his inheritance that was only partly of his own making. In fact, in an effort to try to heal the wounds and mollify Comerford the board had him appointed as Sheehy's Deputy Chief Executive in charge of the sugar business. Both men felt encumbered by this 'awkward' arrangement for most of Sheehy's time at the top. It was eventually resolved when Comerford was later persuaded to take on a strategic planning role.

Three major strategic initiatives dominated the Sheehy and Comerford periods up to CSET's eventual privatisation. These were the major reinvestment programme in the core sugar activity, the substantial improvement in the company's capital structure through increased state equity, and the rationalisation of the company's main operations to a two-plant configuration.

Maurice Sheehy and his Chairman Denis Coakley are credited within CSET with having assessed the full implications of EEC membership for the company's future and with carrying out the modernisation of the sugar processing capacity. During the 1960s there had been little reinvestment in the sugar business. In fact it had been harvested to provide the funds to fuel the growth of the food business and its assets had become old and run down in the process. Entry into the EEC saw the sugar business faced with real competition for the first time. Community prices were pegged to the cost structure of the European beet processing industry and CSET found itself having to get its cost structure into line with the best in the EEC.

While Daly had already started the process of modernising the sugar processing activity before he retired his approach had been small-scale and cautious. Sheehy and his Chairman made their own first hand assessment of what was needed by studying directly the way in which the industry was developing throughout the EEC and recognised that a bolder and more extensive approach was needed. Their determination to press ahead with a major modernisation programme was a brave strategy considering the obstacles that they faced in implementing it. It meant committing £90m to an activity with limited growth potential in a company with total net assets of just £20m, an equity base of just £6m and a funds flow of less than £2m per annum. To add to their difficulties they were unable to get the State to increase its equity and had to be satisfied with 'letters of comfort' that would state-guarantee debt finance for the project. That they went ahead with their strategy in the face of these obstacles is a tribute to the tenacity and commercial bravery of both men. They refused to retreat into a more cautious and piece-meal approach because of their conviction that the future of their industry was at stake and that half-measures would not suffice.

Maurice Sheehy is remembered within CSET primarily for his leadership of the company's reinvestment strategy. As one senior executive put it if CSET had had 'a different type of man' at the helm in the mid-1970s 'we might not have had a sugar company' a decade later. Because their destinies as leaders were so inter-twined it was not surprising that many insiders tended to describe the leadership of Sheehy and Comerford in terms of contrasts with each other. Both were long-serving sugar executives. Sheehy was 'more of a Costello-type thinker' than his rival though he 'trimm(ed) his aspirations to the realities of his time'. Commerford, in contrast, had 'a totally commercial' outlook and approach to CSET. Sheehy was more political both internally and in his relationship with government and the civil service. He 'always tested the waters everywhere before going ahead' with any major initiative. Comerford, on the other hand, tended to 'tackle the problems more directly and deal with the reactions as they (arose)'. Maurice Sheehy is also remembered as a leader that fostered closer relationships between management and the board than his predecessors. His partnerships with his Chairmen, Denis Coakley and James Fitzpatrick, proved to be very productive. Sheehy 'was not a Costello or an O'Reilly' who could operate the company and the industry 'like the Portugal of Salazar or the Spain of Franco'. He 'was a team man' who 'humanised the board–management relationship' and while he 'wasn't really skilled in how to develop the team' he 'did it as best he could'.

While the strategic moves on securing more equity from the State and the rationalisation of CSET's primary activities around a two-plant configuration began to take shape under his leadership these moves were even more closely associated with his successor, first as head of the strategic planning function and later as leader in his own right. Sheehy was a transitional figure in CSET's history. He was the last chief executive with some major remnant of the developmental ideology that so characterised the General's tenure at the top. The food project, particularly after Tony O'Reilly's arrival, posed new questions about the fundamental mission of the company. From that time onwards the company began to see itself more and more as a commercial organisation and less as an instrument for economic and social development. The tension between Sheehy and Comerford was also a tension between the developmental and commercial ideologies. The full transition to commercial ideology was completed later under Comerford's leadership.

When Comerford succeeded his former rival in 1985 there was no divisive contest and he was able to begin his tenure as leader with a unified board. He had already played a major role, as Deputy Chief Executive and later as head of planning, in the main strategic thrusts of the Sheehy era. Through his own forcefulness and dynamism he won the right to bring his group's work directly to the board. His group's efforts were pivotal in securing the support of the Joint Committee of the Oireachtais for more equity and the freedom to operate the business on a more commercial basis. Comerford inherited a company that was just getting back into shape. Its capital structure had been strengthened and the first moves on rationalising the operation from a four-to a two-plant configuration had been made. The company was just barely back in profit.

The hallmark of Comerford's tenure at the top was the full and speedy transition of the company 'from any lingering notion' that it was a 'public service' to its eventual privatisation in April 1991, an event that probably made the General turn in his grave. He went through the company 'like a tornado'. The final moves on the Tuam closure had yet to be made, five years on from the announcement of the plan. Comerford closed it within a year of taking over. This was an important bridgehead in his drive for full commercialisation of the company's operations. After this closure the primacy of commercial viability as the key objective became more widely accepted throughout the political system. It enabled him to close the Thurles plant within a further two years in spite of a pre-election pledge from the incoming Minister for Agriculture to his constituents to keep it open.

These rationalisation moves made a dramatic improvement to the company's profit base and under Comerford it became once again ready and confident to grow and diversify. By 1990 his company was generating £20m in profit, up over ten-fold since he became leader. He had expanded the company considerably through acquisition and reduced its dependence on the profitable but static sugar business to under 50 per cent of turnover. He had paved the way for the successful privatisation of the company, the first in the Irish semi-state sector. This was the pinnacle of his achievement. Chris Comerford's controversial resignation undoubtedly tarnished his company's image, though not in any irreparable way. On the plus side he left behind a solid record of achievement and a company in strong commercial shape, a valuable inheritance for those who were to follow him.

From 1972 to 1987 the overall strategic thrust pursued by CSET under the leadership of three successive chief executives had two main elements. The first was the modernisation and rationalisation of the core business to make it internationally competitive within the EEC. The second element was the rationalisation and strategic refocusing of the food activity. This overall strategic thrust was begun rather tentatively under Daly, was boldly accelerated under Sheehy, and rounded off with crisp directness under Comerford. In the process the company was transformed from a developmental to a commercial organisation. Though there was a large degree of strategic continuity over the tenures of these three leaders the changes in mission, outlook and prospects of the company over their collective time at the top were quite dramatic.

Lenihan and Curtin – Golden Vale

When Mick Lenihan became leader of Golden Vale in 1972 he was not the obvious successor to O'Loughlin. The company, in difficult circumstances, spent some six to eight months searching for a new chief executive before he was chosen for the position. He had been the successful manager of one of the largest creameries in the federation. He was 'not really as technically strong' as O'Loughlin, nor was he as forceful or dynamic a personality. He was not seen as a strategist or a builder in the O'Loughlin mould but at the time of his succession the company already had big plans in place for its further development and needed someone with the operating ability to implement them. The choice of Lenihan was therefore seen as a conservative one which signalled continuity rather than change. Lenihan 'looked at his whole function as carrying out O'Loughlin's plan'.

Lenihan's style of leadership was more political than that of his predecessor, both with his management team and with his milk suppliers. The process by which he was selected was in itself political with the twelve original members of the federation jockeying for control. While the net was cast fairly widely the short-list was reduced to three candidates, all creamery managers in the federation. After years of being dominated, and somewhat over-awed, by O'Loughlin, the owners of Golden Vale, the federated creameries, went for 'one of their own'. Lenihan inherited a senior management team that was 'articulate' and 'aggressive' in the O'Loughlin mould and tended to see him as 'an outsider'. He was political in his management of this team and operated a largely hands-off style which 'allowed for a good deal of autonomy'. In sum he was seen as a shrewd political operator and a 'survivor' who was not as able as his predecessor but 'probably more astute'.

Mick Lenihan's main strengths were his credibility with his federated creamery managers and his sound intuitive grasp of the politics of dairy farming. His main contribution during his tenure was his role in bringing the amalgamation process to conclusion. He was a local man and a former creamery manager who could empathise successfully with the target societies and their management. He 'knew how to allay their fears' as he worked out many of the deals with them 'on his personal touch, over pints'. In this way he was able to move the final stage of the process along more quickly and smoothly than his predecessor might have done. However, some insiders believe that had O'Loughlin survived the company would not have lost as many of the targeted societies as eventually happened because 'Lenihan did not carry the clout that O'Loughlin did'.

The financial crisis of 1975 was Lenihan's biggest test and almost cost him his job. It arose from four developments, three of which he had inherited as part of the O'Loughlin strategy, and the fourth which was external to the organisation. The first three were the large pre-emptive capacity expansion programme, the funding of this programme by bank overdraft, and the shortfall in the milk pool that resulted from the failure of all of the targeted societies to amalgamate. The fourth was the unexpected setback in the expansion of the national milk supply that followed directly from the 1973 oil crisis. His inability to prevent the situation reaching crisis proportions was due in part to the hands-off management approach that he had adopted. However, most insiders recognised that the real problems that led to the crisis were more deeply rooted and they did not hold him directly responsible for them. The poor capital structure was a direct result of the long-standing reluctance of farmer-shareholders to increase their equity in line with the company's expansion. Moreover little progress had been attempted on downstream rationalisation, following the amalgamations, because of the political sensitivity of the process. There remained, however, a perception within Golden Vale that O'Loughlin would 'have been able to cope' with the 'problems likely to arise' with his strategy and 'would have been able to see them coming better than anyone else'. To that extent Lenihan's credibility as leader did suffer internally by comparison.

The farmer-shareholders were not so understanding and attempted to have Lenihan removed. If Mick Lenihan was unlucky in the situation that he had inherited he was fortunate in having 'the outstanding Chairman' in Golden Vale's history, Martin Flanagan, to prevent him from being unfairly scape-goated for the crisis. It was Flanagan that provided the strong hand at the tiller at this critical time and under whose leadership Lenihan and his management developed and implemented the recovery plan. The O'Loughlin blueprint proved itself to have been essentially sound in all of its major elements, once the necessary remedial action was taken on the company's cost and capital structure. By 1978 even the pre-emptive capacity expansion, which had brought the company close to bankruptcy, proved to be the bargain of the decade in terms of the then current replacement costs.

When Mick Lenihan retired from Golden Vale in 1980 he left behind him a profitable company and one that had grown by one-third in real terms over the 1975–79 period. Once the company strengthened its financial structure it literally grew out of trouble with the recovery in the industry. The company's growth during this period was largely attributed to the implementation of the O'Loughlin blueprint. Lenihan is remembered as 'an interim pope'. He was 'already past his prime' when he became leader of Golden Vale and his best years in the industry, as the successful manager of the Shandrum Cooperative Creamery, were already behind him. He was an able operator and an effective implementer but there was little in the way of 'new ideas and innovation' during his time as leader. After the financial crisis of 1975 his approach became even more conservative and the company's approach to new strategic departures was 'always on the defensive'. He was content to let the basic business grow with the 'natural' expansion in the industry and he took few risks from that time until his retirement in 1980.

Curtin, his successor, joined Golden Vale as Chief Accountant in 1972. He came to prominence within the company during the financial crisis in the mid-1970s. He was first to highlight the critical situation within the company and played a major role in its resolution. The finance function emerged from the crisis with more power than before within Golden Vale. Curtin was appointed Assistant Chief Executive in 1978, as Lenihan was winding down towards retirement.

It was Tony Curtin's destiny to inherit the leadership of Golden Vale at a time when the environment of the industry changed dramatically from conditions of growth and benignness to those of retrenchment and intensifying competition. Moreover, in spite of his having been Assistant Chief Executive there was internal competition for the leadership on Lenihan's retirement. Curtin never fully succeeded in mending the traces with his rivals for the job. This residue from the succession contest was unhelpful to him in his efforts to lead Golden Vale through the harsh environment that confronted it in the early 1980s and that ultimately led to his resignation in 1985.

Golden Vale's difficulties in the Curtin era began outside the organisation with the outbreak of the milk wars. The sharp fall in national milk production and in farm-incomes, following the 1979 Oil Crisis, weakened the long-standing industry tradition of not competing for supply. At least three elements of Curtin's inheritance from the Lenihan era undermined his capacity to protect his milk pool. His predecessor's reluctance to purchase Limerick Dairies in the late 1970s allowed Kerry Cooperative to acquire a 'launching-pad' in Golden Vale's traditional catchment area. Furthermore, during the milk war itself Curtin was hampered in his attempts to protect his profits and bolster supplier confidence by the erratic performance of the engineering activity. Engineering had already reached its zenith in the mid-1970s and had begun to decline rapidly after 1975. During his last years Lenihan had taken a very tolerant view of Engineering's erratic performance, in deference to its once prestigious place in Golden Vale's history, because the company overall was doing well. It was Curtin's misfortune that the company did not rationalise this activity when the problems were first recognised and the liquidation costs could have been more easily borne. Finally Golden Vale's financial position in the early 1980s would have been considerably stronger if Lenihan had been more willing to confront the politically sensitive downstream rationalisation of the overall branch network.

However, not all of Curtin's problems can be attributed to his inheritance or to the tough new environmental challenges that the industry faced over the 1980–85 period. He missed a vital opportunity to nip the milk war in the bud when Kerry offered to sell him Limerick Dairies for £1m. His inability to develop a personal understanding with Denis Brosnan, the Kerry chief, led to the deal falling through and an escalation of the hostilities. From this point on, until his resignation, relations between Golden Vale and the Kerry organisation steadily deteriorated. Curtin's own ill-advised acquisition of Castlemahon Poultry Products only added to his difficulties. This costly write-off depressed profits when he could least afford it and further eroded supplier confidence.

The progressive erosion of supplier confidence was the problem that dogged his tenure as leader and ultimately led to his resignation. In the end he ran out of time in his efforts to break the vicious cycle of milk loss that threatened the company's future. Curtin's last contribution as leader was a very significant one. With the problems of Engineering and Castlemahon behind him, he embarked on a tough rationalisation and modernisation programme in difficult circumstances which considerably strengthened the company's profit base. Unfortunately, in the end, the beneficial effects of this determined effort came too late to secure his future with the company.

Tony Curtin's experience at Golden Vale illustrates the vicissitudes of the leadership position. He was the first chief executive of the company, and one of the first in the industry, to have reached the top without a background in dairy science. He was an accountant and was perceived as more 'analytical' than 'intuitive'. He was publicly acknowledged to have played a pivotal role in Golden Vale's rapid recovery in the mid-1970s, when the critical issues were financial. Curtin was an energetic and able leader who was prepared to implement the tough rationalisation decisions that were largely avoided during the Lenihan era when the environmental pressures on the dairy processors were relatively benign. He left the company in a more healthy operational state than he had inherited it, and his successor became the main beneficiary of his efforts in this respect.

However, the dramatic change in the situation that Golden Vale faced in the 1980–85 period demanded strength in areas where Curtin's own abilities were more limited. Though his problems were compounded by difficulties inherited from his predecessor, it was his own inability to deal with the politics of maintaining supplier confidence, and with the related politics of the milk wars with Kerry, that ultimately undermined his position. Strengths in supplier and inter-firm relationships had become strategically critical in the context of the time. Curtin is remembered in Golden Vale as a 'very capable' and 'hard-working' executive who 'was politically too straight if anything' and who, when the situation acutely required it, just 'did not understand the politics of farming' well enough at the time.

LEADERSHIP AND STRATEGY FORMATION

In this chapter we examined the role of leadership in strategy formation and classified our leaders as builders, revitalisers, turnarounders and inheritors. Of course this classification did not come only from the personal attributes and pre-dispositions of the leaders in question. It also came from the challenges presented by history and context during their tenures at the top. Its implications for future research will be examined later. In the next chapter we turn to context and how it affected the strategic development of our four organisations.

9 Contextual factors and strategy formation

In the previous chapter the process of strategy formation was analysed from an action perspective in terms of the different roles played by the leaders. However, one of our underlying themes is that most studies of leadership and strategy tend to be over-voluntarist and to under-play the role of context. To gain more insight into the causal texture of context we concentrate in this chapter on isolating and examining the main contextual factors that influenced the development of our four organisations. In the final chapter we will examine the interaction of leadership and context in the formation of strategy and synthesise the findings of our study.

The situational context of any organisation is a complex web of political, economic, technological, social and cultural features as reflected in the national context and case narratives. Five contextual factors appear to have had the most influence on the shaping of strategy in the organisations featured here. We have classified them as *technology*, including production economics and asset specialisation; *industry structure*, nationally and internationally; the *international trading environment*; *national public policy*; and *social and cultural transformation* (Figure 9.1). We now examine how these factors were derived from the data and what effect they had on the strategic development of the organisations in our study.

TECHNOLOGY

Technology shaped strategy in the organisations and industries under study in a number of ways. The most dramatic examples were where breakthrough was involved. The development of the mechanical cream separator in the dairy industry prompted its transition from a farm-based to a creamery-based structure. Had beet processing technology not been developed the Irish sugar industry would have been merely a refining activity with little role to play in the process of national industrial development. On the negative side the rejection by the distilling industry of

Figure 9.1 Contextual factors and strategy formation

the path-breaking column-still effectively ceded the emerging mass market to blended Scotch and consigned Irish whiskey to a premium niche which greatly constrained its export potential.

Our study also showed how the development of organisations and industries can be enabled by technological breakthroughs, or constrained by the lack of them, at earlier stages in the production chain. The advent of the mechanical and chemical revolutions to Irish dairy and sugar-beet farming played very significant roles in the expansion of both industries from the late 1940s onwards. Indeed the General's strategy for the expansion of Irish sugar processing throughout the 1950s was explicitly focused on accelerating the expansion of the supply side. On the other hand the failure of the dairy industry to develop or adopt dairy productions systems designed to smooth out the severe seasonality in the national milk production has so far restricted the product-market scope of the processing sector to largely storable dairy products like butter, cheese, milk powder and the like. In contrast to the sugar and dairy sectors the distilling industry, which uses a relatively small proportion of national barley production, has been much less influenced or constrained by technological developments on its supply side.

Technology as a contextual factor also featured in other ways. The distilling, sugar and dairy industries all showed trends over time towards higher levels of concentration as continuing improvements in processing technologies created further economies of scale. Developments in refrigeration techniques led to major changes in the economics of milk assembly and this made feasible even higher levels of processing economies in the dairy sector. The trend towards configurations with fewer and larger processing centres in dairying and distilling allowed for more flexible multi-product operations that were more responsive to varying market conditions. Moreover the availability of new technology made major diversification possible, into fat-filled milk for Golden Vale and into convenience food processing for CSET.

Finally the cases showed how the concentration of capacity in specific technologies often involves a major commitment of resources to specialised activities. Such commitments become major contingencies for future strategy formation. The investments by Irish Distillers in the Midleton distillery complex, CSET in its specialised sugar factories, and Golden Vale in its Charleville dairy processing complex are among the most obvious examples from the data. Less obvious but equally important was AFT's commitment to the scientific specialisation of its research staff. This commitment was a major contingency in the strategic management of AFT in the difficult 1980s.

INDUSTRY STRUCTURE

Industry structure, in the Scherer (1970) and Porter (1980) use of the concept, includes the basic conditions of supply–demand, market structure and the relative concentrations of suppliers, competitors and buyers. It was also an important contextual factor influencing the strategies of the organisations under study.

Galbraith (1963: 45–46) noted a typical pattern in many US industries in which 'a point of stability is reached with a handful of massive survivors and, usually, a fringe of smaller hangers-on'. He argued that this tendency was 'deeply organic'. It arose from the development of structural biases over time that favoured incumbents and deterred new entrants rather than from 'some individual's imperial design'. This same tendency has been noticeable in the development of Irish industries, including those featured in this study, but often to a point of stability with just one large survivor. This is a reflection of the particular structural implications of operating in a small, open domestic economy.

Irish organisations have a small domestic market. Even in cases where an industry is dominated by one company this large survivor tends to outgrow the domestic market at a low level of turnover in international terms. For example, in the early 1980s Irish Distillers had an 80 per cent share of the domestic market. Yet this level of sales represented only a fraction of 1 per cent of the global total and less than 1 per cent of the US market by volume. Irish industries have rarely been able to support more than a few companies of international scale and signifance and more often than not, as in the distilling industry, only one. Prior to the 1966 merger domestic competition in Irish distilling was seen to be dissipating resources and none of the major companies was coming close to international scale. The merger allowed not only for greater concentration of capital but also for the concerted marketing of Irish whiskey as a distinctive generic product in the international arena where the industry's main growth potential lay.

The same broad strategic considerations were involved in the progressive concentration that has taken place in the dairy industry over the years. From the late 1970s onwards the industry typically exported around 80 per cent of its annual production, yet it still accounted for less than 3 per cent of world output and faced strong international competition. The first major concentration in the industry took place in the export marketing area with the establishment of An Bord Bainne in 1962. This enabled the dairy sector to concentrate much of its marketing resources behind the generic 'kerrygold' brand overseas. The concern to strengthen the industry domestically so that it might become more competitive internationally was the common theme behind the major waves of rationalisation that took place in the late 1920s, the 1959–74 period and in the late 1980s.

Industry structural considerations were also to the fore in the development of the sugar industry. CSET was set up as a state monopoly for pragmatic reasons. From the outset concentration of capital and domestic market power were seen as the structural prerequisites for the successful development of an indigenous sugar industry. This industry enjoys no comparative advantage in international terms, in contrast to the low cost advantage of Irish dairying or the generic distinctiveness of Irish distilling. Consequently most of its output goes to the domestic market. In fact the industry itself is multi-domestic rather than global. Less than 15 per cent of world output is disposed of in the free market. Sugar is typical of those agricultural commodities which are characterised by largely inelastic demand and the inability of the market mechanism to control supply

(Heilbroner and Thurow 1975). Without the price support mechanism the supply–demand pattern would tend to oscillate between glut and scarcity giving rise to serious instability in farm incomes and downstream processing that would ramify throughout the rest of the domestic economy.

Even the strategic development of AFT has been tied inextricably to the structure of the industry that it served. Agricultural production is by its nature difficult to concentrate and farming as an industry is highly fragmented. Its basic structure provides little scope or incentive for the producers to develop their own R&D activities. Few ever reach a scale that could support it on their own and it would be difficult to prevent the benefits from any such research from leaking out to the rest of the sector. For reasons such as these many Western governments have taken a direct role in the organisation and funding of research agencies to support the technical development of local agricultural production (Galbraith 1963). AFT, therefore, got its very *raison d'être* from the underlying economic structure of the industry that it supports. Furthermore, the major changes in AFT's research programme from production to process, government-funded to user-funded and basic to contract research all reflected how the organisation's strategic emphasis had to change over time with changes in the underlying economic structure of Irish agriculture.

The development of all four organisations was also influenced by developments in the industry structure internationally. The major capital investments by IDG in the Midleton distillery, Golden Vale in its Charleville complex, and CSET in its modernisation and rationalisation programme, were all made with reference to what was happening in their respective industries internationally. The initial mission and structure for AFT owed much to the US and Dutch models for similar institutions and the 1971 reorganisation drew heavily on the Canadian experience. All of the organisations constantly monitored their performance and impact using international benchmarks drawn from industry-wide contacts and published data. CSET assembled annual campaign statistics on productivity in other countries through the European Sugar Manufacturers Association. IDG, AFT and Golden Vale regularly carried out similar comparisons of their international standings and acted accordingly.

Vertical relationships in the industry structure have also been a significant influence on strategy. Supply relationships have been particularly significant in the dairy and sugar industries. Securing beet supply was the major thrust of the General's strategy in CSET over the 1945–59 period. He invested heavily in the expansion of acreage and in the improvement of crop husbandry and quality. Under constant threat of competition from alternative uses for land CSET always had to ensure that the production of sugar from beet continued to be a profitable proposition for the supplier as well as for the company. In the dairy industry the amalgamation blueprint of the 1968–74 period was an attempt to chart the orderly expansion of the whole industry through an agreed allocation of the milk supply. So critical has this relationship been that it was the industry norm not to compete for supply. On the few occasions when this norm was breached the ensuing milk wars created major instability and uncertainty, as was evident in the Golden Vale case over the 1980–85 period. Producers and processors cooperate in the development of their industry but compete on the sharing of the spoils through the establishment of milk and beet prices. This political dynamic could itself become a critical strategic contingency as the Golden Vale case so poignantly illustrated.

For Irish Distillers and An Foras Taluntais the relationships further forward in the industry were the most significant. IDG made two major and controversial strategic moves during its recent history to gain more control over distribution. It weathered the 'vitriolic' opposition of the traditional wholesalers and bonders in its move to gain more control over the quality of the product reaching the consumer and the 'torrent' of criticism from media analysts which greeted its move to gain more control over the growing cash and carry distribution channel. In AFT's case the relationship with its main 'distributors', the advisory service, was strategically significant. So significant was it in fact that two major efforts were made at national level to bring both under the one management, the second of which heralded the end of AFT's existence as an independent entity.

Finally, the strategies of the organisations in the study have been significantly influenced by basic changes in supply–demand patterns and by the development of substitutes. In the 1980s the distilling, dairying and sugar industries experienced substantial shifts in demand because of the growing concern among consumers generally about health and diet. This has forced the dairy industry in particular to be more consumer and less commodity oriented. On the substitutes side the development of low cost non-grass feeding systems threatened the natural comparative advantage of Irish dairy farming. Likewise the trend towards artificial low calorific sweeteners undermined the structural link between the sugar industry and its major customers the soft-drink producers. The consumer trends away from hard liquor and brown spirits forced IDG to revise its ambitions and strategy for the US market. At the more global level the slow decline in spirits consumption led to increasing consolidation in the industry internationally and was a major consideration in the takeover battle for Irish Distillers and its eventual acquisition by Pernod Ricard.

Supply–demand and substitute considerations have operated more indirectly in AFT's case but have been important none the less. The major review processes of the late 1960s were attempts to measure the impact and relevance of the organisation's research efforts in the absence of clear measures of demand and satisfaction. Later on the decline in state funding forced the organisation to meet more of its gross expenditure from user-funded research which indirectly changed its mission and strategic emphasis. Finally the dramatic decline in the demand for production research due to commodity surpluses in the EEC forced the organisation to change its emphasis towards process research. However, with the increasing concentration of capital in the dairy industry, many of the larger processors began to develop their own in-house R&D, a trend which had potentially major implications for the future role of state-funded research in Irish agriculture.

THE INTERNATIONAL TRADING ENVIRONMENT

Strategy formation in the organisations under study was also affected by elements in their situational context analytically separable from their technologies and industry structures. If the world was truly a single market economy then technology and industry structure would be the salient contextual elements in the formation of strategy. The fact that world trading patterns are affected by political as well as economic considerations made it meaningful to make the distinction earlier between industry structure domestically and internationally. It also suggests that the changing structure and 'rules of the game' of the international trading environment, and the domestic public policies of major trading partners, can have a marked effect on the development of trading organisations in a small open economy like Ireland's, as the following analysis of the data in this study tends to show.

International conflicts

The influence of the international trading environment was sometimes seen at its most dramatic during periods of major international conflict. The first structural rationalisation of the dairy industry was directly connected with the disruption in trading patterns brought about by the First World War and its aftermath. The post-war boom was short lived for this industry with its relatively inelastic demand and quickly turned into crisis as prices collapsed in the early 1920s. Only the direct intervention by a very reluctant government in 1927 prevented severe over-capacity and unbridled competition from doing untold damage to the industry and the cooperative movement. The disruption caused by the Second World War affected the industry's growth more than its stability. War-time scarcities, price controls, product rationing and compulsory tillage all tended to retard its development and delayed its eventual take-off for nearly a decade.

The advent of the Second World War accelerated the development of the sugar industry but strained it to near breaking point. It brought forward in time the withdrawal of the European technologists supporting the start-up and forced it to rely on indigenous management and skills much sooner than expected. CSET responded to the challenge, and the industry proved its strategic value to the country by being able to supply the home market to its pre-war levels throughout the period of the conflict. However, the hostilities did lead to severe difficulties with vital shortages of grease, oil, formalin, beet knives, beet seeds and fertilisers. The industry emerged from the war years in a state of exhaustion and 'was not in a very coherent state' by the time the war was over.

The structure of international trade

The structure of the international trading arena like that of many industries has tended to be dominated by a small number of major economic powers. The other trading nations, like Ireland, have had to learn to survive under the 'umbrella' of these leading players with relatively little influence over the prevailing patterns and structural evolution of world trade. These patterns and structures, and the economic ideologies of the major players that determine them, have gone through a number of significant changes since the end of the First World War. The changes which had the most impact on the organisations and industries featured here were the protectionism and isolationism of the inter-war years, the formation and development of the European Economic Community and the general trade liberalisation and boom of the 1950–74 period, the emergence of OPEC as an economic power and the redistribution of world income, and the neo-classicalism of the 1980s.

Protectionism and isolationism

The general protectionism and isolationism that characterised the inter-war period had its roots in the decline of free trade as the sovereign economic principle, the unwillingness of the United States to assume leadership in international economic affairs, and the Great Depression. Throughout the nineteenth century Great Britain was the world's leading economic power and its strongest advocate of free trade 'not only as part of an economic doctrine' but 'almost as part of a moral law' (Keynes 1933: 177). However, the development by the United States and Germany of strong industrial bases behind the shelter of selected protection called into question the universal efficacy of the free trade principle in the early twentieth century. When the United States emerged from the First World War as the world's strongest economy American opinion was split between those favouring it taking a leading role in trade liberalisation and those preferring a more isolationist and protectionist approach (Nye and Morpugo 1965).

The 1929 crash and the Great Depression that followed led to widening of support for isolationism and protectionism not only in America but throughout the trading world. Leading intellectuals like Keynes (1933: 186) supported this 'movement towards greater national self-sufficiency and economic isolation' as allowing each nation to make its 'own favourite experiments towards the ideal social republic of the future' as 'free as possible of interference from economic changes elsewhere'. International trade became more restricted during this period and its volume fell considerably. The use of the tariff extended to political issues, as the destructive economic war between Ireland and Britain in the mid-1930s so painfully illustrated.

For the Irish whiskey industry the inter-war years offered little scope for development, and in fact the industry saw its exports collapse from over 1m gallons to just 0.1m over the 1925–45 period. Prohibition, and later rising tariffs, effectively closed off the United States market, and the economic war with Britain, along with the general effects of depression and later on of wartime disruption, saw Irish whiskey's once pre-eminent position on the British market erode to insignificance. The industry concentrated almost entirely on the domestic market during the 1930s and 1940s and remained fragmented, inward-looking and inefficient behind the Irish tariff wall. These inter-war years were also difficult for the dairy industry. The *ad valorem* duty of 40 per cent on Irish imports into Britain at the height of the economic war had a major impact on the dairy sector which was almost totally dependent on this key export market. Between the go–stop conditions in the British market in the 1920s, the protectionism and economic war of the 1930s and the international conflict of the 1940s, the industry found little scope for development in the core activities of processing and production. In contrast, the Irish sugar industry was nurtured through its infancy during the 1930s under a measure of protection. The dominant economic ideology of the time provided strong support for this type of strategy at this stage in the country's economic development.

International trade liberalisation, expansion and the EEC

The aftermath of the Second World War brought very significant changes to the structure and pattern of world trade. This time the United States, as the leading economic power, played a more active role. The 'spectacularly successful' Marshall Aid Plan 'pumped desperately needed resources into the European economy and accelerated post-war recovery' (Livingstone

1966: 105). America's role in the reconstruction of the Japanese industrial and economic base was just as impressive. Within Europe itself a new order of cooperation emerged leading to the formation in 1958 of the European Economic Community involving France, Germany, Belgium, the Netherlands, Luxembourg and Italy. Britain, Ireland and Denmark joined the Community in 1972. In this new era of liberalisation the overall volume of international trade grew by nearly 500 per cent over the 1950–73 period in sharp contrast to the almost total stagnation (1 per cent growth over 1928–37) of the protectionist era (Sodersten 1980). Along with this massive expansion came a similar increase in the level of economic inter-dependency among trading nations. In the United States President Kennedy pressed Congress for the establishment of closer trading links with the newly formed EEC through a general reduction of trade barriers, arguing that 'the two great Atlantic markets' would 'either grow together or grow apart' (Schlesinger 1965: 721).

The European recovery plan, the general liberalisation and expansion in international trade and the evolution of the European Economic Community had major implications for all of the organisations in the study. The setting up of An Foras Taluntais was a Marshall Aid initiative to begin with. Furthermore the provision of start-up finance under this programme was very instrumental in allowing the first director to establish the basic mission and character of the Institute with minimum interference from the state bureaucracy and other vested interests during AFT's formative first decade. Later EEC entry came to provide AFT with a new source of funding and a renewed sense of mission as it sought, and was sought, for Community-sponsored research projects. This was particularly valuable to the organisation, coming at a time when state support for agricultural research began to decline.

Ireland's entry into the EEC was an important development for all of the organisations and industries featured in this study. It exposed the sugar industry for the first time to the 'cold winds of competition'. While sugar remained a protected industry even after EEC entry the rules of the game for CSET were dramatically changed. The company had to maintain beet prices high enough to keep growers in the industry while keeping sugar prices low enough to be competitive with imports from other EEC countries. Both requirements brought new pressures on margins and forced CSET to undertake a £90m modernisation programme to bring the competitiveness of the core business to European levels. The prospect of greater competition from EEC imports was also a major stimulus to the 1966 merger in the distilling industry and to its modernisation programme of the early 1970s. IDG did not really concentrate on developing the EEC market until the US market began to stagnate and decline in the 1980s. EEC entry had more immediate impact on the domestic market where the general rise in farm incomes stimulated demand. The down-side was that this diverted momentum away from the export effort, which was much more crucial to the company's longer-run growth prospects.

Post-war recovery and EEC entry brought unprecedented growth to Irish dairying and a major change in the industry's structure. The amalgamation process, which largely determined the basic structure and pattern of the industry from the mid-1970s onwards, was initiated in the context of impending EEC entry to ensure that the industry would be competitive under more liberal trading conditions. National milk output recovered dramatically from the stagnation of the inter-war years. It grew from 130m to 864m gallons over the 1945–79 period, first in response to general post-war recovery and later to the price support incentives of the EEC's Common Agricultural Policy. In the decade after EEC entry Irish dairy exports grew by 250 per cent and diversified greatly, as the share destined for the British market fell from four-fifths to one-third. On the down-side the industry, under EEC incentives, developed an over-reliance on commodities at the expense of branded consumer products. This became a serious structural problem in the 1980s.

The international oil cartel – OPEC

The oil crisis of 1973, which saw the price of crude oil increase sharply by 350 per cent, dramatically underlined how much the international trading economy had grown dependent on OPEC-controlled oil reserves. The resultant transfer of £100b per annum away from the advanced industrial economies into OPEC showed how sophisticated these oil producing countries had become in exploiting their new economic power. The severe inflationary pressures that were unleashed by the oil shock throughout the trading world led to the sharp setback in the expansion of Irish national milk supply in 1974, which was a major factor contributing to Golden Vale's liquidity crisis of the period. The same pressures threw the nation's finances into disarray and led directly to the shift in emphasis within AFT towards more self-funded expansion. Both CSET and Irish Distillers found themselves having to embark on major capital development programmes during this time of rampant inflation which added considerably to the costs and risks associated with them. The Midleton project at IDG, for example, out-turned at four times the original estimate. Both companies experienced unprecedented pressures on their margins.

The neo-classical 1980s

The short sharp recession induced by the 1973 Oil Crisis was followed by a fragile recovery as many countries reflated and general expansion in the international trading arena continued until the end of the decade. The second oil crisis, in 1979, set in train a process of major structural transformation in the world economy that continued throughout the 1980s, the seeds of which had already been sown over the previous two decades.

As the volume of world trade and output expanded greatly over the 1960–79 period the international economy became more integrated and diversified. By 1980 this structure consisted of a number of distinct groupings, the Advanced Capitalist Countries (ACCs), the Eastern Bloc Countries, the Oil Producers, the Newly Industrialising Countries (NICs) and the Less Developed Countries (LDCs). The Eastern Bloc countries played little part in the international economy. The ACCs continued to dominate but the influence of OPEC and the NICs was on the increase. The NICs were fast becoming 'the terrain on which competition between the advanced countries was fought out' (Armstrong *et al*. 1984: 358). Within the ACCs the balance was shifting. Japan's aggressive export surge in steel, cars and consumer electronics was fuelled in no small measure by its desire to create a massive dollar surplus to insulate its oil-dependent economy against further sharp rises in oil prices. Over the 1960s–80s America's share of world manufacturing output fell from 40 per cent to 29 per cent as those of Germany and Japan, taken together, rose from 15 per cent to near parity with the leader at 28 per cent (Dicken 1986). By the early 1980s dominance of the international arena by any one economic power was no longer possible and the coordination of world trade had become more difficult (Thurow 1987). In addition, the growing influence of the transnational corporation on the distribution of capital formation and employment in the global economy was reducing the scope for national governments to manage the process of economic development.

The relative decline of the United States and Great Britain as industrial powers forced both countries to fundamentally reassess their own national economic policies. New leaders came to power with new agendas based on the espousal of neo-classical economic doctrines. At the heart of Thatcherism and Reaganomics were the convictions that control of inflation rather than full employment should be the primary goal and that the market mechanism should be allowed to regulate as far as possible the economic activity of the country. Fundamental structural changes were needed to restore international competitiveness. Future economic growth would depend on putting the incentive for enterprise back into these economies through control of inflation and reductions in personal taxation. This required a substantial reduction in the role of the State in the provision of goods and services and the early return of many state enterprises to private ownership. In line with this rise in neo-classicalism both the United

States and Britain refused to reflate their economies with traditional Keynesian style interventions in the aftermath of the 1979 Oil Crisis. As a result of all of these developments the international trading arena in general, and the Western industrialised economies in particular, entered an era of recession, prolonged low growth and economic uncertainty at the beginning of the 1980s.

The onset of recession and prolonged low growth in the international arena sharply affected the prospects of the Irish economy and the organisations featured in this study. For Irish Distillers 1979 was a watershed. Sales and profits reached record levels on both the domestic and export fronts. The company had plans for capacity expansion and felt confident that it was finally poised to make a substantial breakthrough on the US market. Within two years the outlook had dramatically changed. The onset of the low-growth 1980s saw the domestic market contract due to falling disposable incomes and sharp increases in excise duties as the government scrambled to protect its revenues. Recession and declining disposable incomes in the US and other key overseas markets slowed down the company's export-led growth. Declining demand in the global market also motivated the larger international spirits producers to seek marginal revenues wherever possible and the company saw the domestic market come under intensified competitive pressure from imports. The shelving of the capacity expansion plans, the defensive acquisition of BWG, the radical revision of the US marketing strategy and the rationalisation of the company's operations were all influenced by the overall change in the international trading environment that characterised this period.

As the Irish dairy industry entered the 1980s all of the major processors had plans for further capacity expansion. National milk supply had yet to reach the 1,000m gallon mark and the widespread belief within the industry was that there was still much scope for further development. In the immediate aftermath of the 1979 Oil Crisis national milk production suffered a sharp setback. Capacity expansion plans were shelved and as processors scrambed to maintain volume a fresh wave of milk wars broke out that brought Golden Vale to the brink of disaster. The situation for the industry and all of the processors was made more difficult by developments in the EEC and in the larger international arena. The general recession brought with it a slump in world demand and the EEC started to experience mounting surpluses of dairy commodities. This put enormous strain on the Community's budget at a time when all of its major trading economies were in recession and attitudes to the Common Agricultural Policy hardened. Over the 1980–85 period the dairy industry experienced a reduction in price supports, followed by the imposition of quotas and cutbacks. These measures signalled the effective capping of the Irish dairy industry at the

1,000m gallon mark for some time ahead. All of the leading processors found themselves having to fundamentally reassess the future of their businesses in light of this development.

CSET's strategic thrust towards a two-plant configuration and AFT's major reorientation from a production to a process research emphasis were both directly influenced by the dramatic changes taking place in the structure of the international market for agricultural commodities and in the EEC's Common Agricultural Policy. However, for these two state-owned organisations it was the general change in attitudes throughout the international trading arena to direct state involvement in the economy that had the biggest impact in this period. As the influence of Thatcherism and Reaganomics spread to the Irish scene support for the full commercialisation of public enterprise and for the rationalisation of the state bureaucracy became more widespread. This paved the way for the most radical changes in the history of both organisations, the amalgamation of AFT with the advisory services in 1988 and the privatisation of CSET a few years later.

NATIONAL PUBLIC POLICY

National public policy as an important contextual influence sometimes mediated the effects of the international trading arena on the industries and organisations featured here, as in the aftermath of the oil crises, and was at other times derivative as in the protectionist and Thatcherite eras. However, we have also seen positive national leadership deliberately harnessing the natural forces in the international arena to the process of national economic development. In short, national public policy has independently, both directly and indirectly, affected the formation of strategy in the organisations under study. It is its more active, direct role that is examined in this section.

Ireland 1921 – from a provincial to a national economy

Securing independence in 1921 was the major watershed in modern Irish history. The alternative would have been to have remained in some form or another a regional province of the United Kingdom. The separatist argument was that the welfare of the Irish people politically, economically and socially would be better served through self-government. Assessing the degree to which this assumption has been justified by subsequent history is outside the scope of this study and the interested reader is referred to Lee (1989) for a recent provocative analysis of the country's performance since independence. What we can safely assert here is that the change in status from province to nation-state was of fundamental contextual significance for the development of the industries and organisations in this study, for good or ill, from that time onwards.

To begin with the change in the structure and scope of the national economy from United Kingdom to Irish dimensions made public policy of more immediate relevance to Irish industries and organisations. Secondly, the 'Irishness' of Irish organisations took on a new distinctiveness and strength of association in the context of an independent national economic structure. It is unlikely that the developmental roles of the Irish sugar industry or of AFT would have been so focused and energised by economic nationalism had they been just extensions of Britain's sugar-beet industry or agricultural infrastructure respectively. It seems improbable that the generic competition between Irish and Scotch, and the concentration of capital along national lines, would have remained so sharply delineated within a United Kingdom national context. It is almost certain that the cooperative movement would not have been so dominant in Irish dairying nor would the industry have had such strategic signifance for public policy within a British context. While we can only speculate on what might have happened had Ireland remained in the United Kingdom, we can be more positive in analysing how national public policy influenced the development of the industries and organisations in this study in the period since independence.

Early self-government – *laissez-faire*

The first Irish administration concentrated on the orderly assumption and development of the institutions of government and on the establishment of public order. However, even this most *laissez-faire* of Irish governments had some direct and far-reaching effects on the development of the distilling and dairy industries. In 1926 the distilling industry secured from it a measure which extended the compulsory bonding period for all whiskies from three to five years. This move penalised the imported Scotch blends on the domestic market which gained little in product quality from the extra period in bond. However, the same move later placed Irish whiskey at a competitive disadvantage on the US market, which unintendedly encouraged the distilling industry to become more inward-looking and conservative in relation to export development. In 1927 this administration, with much reluctance, made the crucial intervention in the Irish dairy sector which helped to save the industry and preserve the pre-eminence of the cooperative movement in its organisation and management. It provided only minor help to the fledging sugar industry as it struggled to survive in the early 1930s.

Economic self-sufficiency and state enterprise

The 1932 Fianna Fail administration came to power with a very definite interventionist strategy based on economic nationalism and self-sufficiency. The general tendency towards protectionism and isolationism then taking place in the wider international arena served to make this policy easier to defend and legitimise within the Irish national context.

It was under this self-sufficiency strategy that the state-owned enterprise emerged to become a major element of the national economy and a key instrument in industrial development. Nearly twenty such bodies were set up over the 1932–48 period for pragmatic rather than ideological reasons and CSET was one of the earliest and most prominent. Sean Lemass founded it not only to rescue a failing enterprise but to develop a major national agri-industry 'at a cost to the community of an extra halfpenny a pound of sugar'. These early state-owned enterprises, like CSET, were to play a pioneering role in the country's overall industrialisation, introducing into Ireland 'modernity in mechanisation and in management methods, in industrial environment and in the training of staff' (Andrews 1959: 299). CSET was a direct product of the economic self-sufficiency policy and one of its major successes. Bringing the industry up to the level of national self-sufficiency was the primary thrust of its strategy up to the late 1950s.

The fortunes of the dairy and distilling industries were more mixed during this phase in national policy. Both were heavily dependent on the British export market. The overtly political use of protectionism by Ireland and Britain in the 1932–38 economic war deepened the general effects of the Great Depression on both industries. The Government tried to soften the blow on dairying with price supports for exports. There was little help forthcoming for the distilling industry and the economic war was one of the factors that led to the almost total collapse of Irish whiskey exports during this period. Later, during the wartime stringencies of the 1939–45 period, the Government, under its self-sufficiency strategy, imposed restrictions on whiskey exports in order to conserve supplies for the home market and preserve excise revenue levels. This led to a further weakening of the industry's export position at a time when the Scotch industry was becoming well poised for post-war take-off. The implementation of a national policy of compulsory tillage during the war years, again in line with self-sufficiency, diverted resources away from the export-oriented dairy industry. Industry growth remained static for most of the 1930s and 1940s.

Sean Lemass, economic expansion and entry to EEC

The basic character and structure of the modern Irish economy was formed under the self-sufficiency policy. However, by the late 1950s this isolationist and inward-looking national economic strategy was seen to be failing to deliver a viable economy in the post-war situation. Emigration had reached alarming levels and throughout the country the prevailing mood was one of despondency and loss of confidence in the ability of the country's leaders to control its economic destiny. Sean Lemass, one of the architects of the self-sufficiency policy, was the political leader that officially abandoned it and set about generating a resurgence of will throughout the country with a dramatically new approach. His programmes for economic expansion were based on the French model of national indicative planning and were designed to take more direct control of the whole process of economic development at national level. The strategy emphasised export-led growth and opened out the economy to new ideas, new skills and new capital. In garnering support for this new approach he publicly challenged the post-revolutionary generation of Irishmen with the historic task of securing the economic viability of the State.

This was the era of Ireland Inc. under Lemass's corporate style of national economic management. Many state organisations were directly mobilised, and many non-state enterprises nudged, cajoled, induced and otherwise pressured into support for the national economic development effort. The industries and organisations featured in this study were no exceptions. AFT's main growth phase took place under this national strategy. It was established during the first of these programmes and was directly involved in the process through which the second programme came to be formulated. The Institute got its one and only multi-year budget, to support the planned development of its research programme, during the 1963–66 period. As one long serving senior researcher recalled 'there was great growth and buoyancy associated with the Programme for Economic Expansion'. The 'rising tide was raising all boats' and 'it raised our boat'.

By the end of the 1950s Ireland was already self-sufficient in sugar and CSET was ready for diversification. It was willing and anxious to respond to the new national strategy and play a full role in Lemass's effort to expand the economy through export-led growth. The company considered it 'our duty in the national interest to utilise our special knowledge and our very considerable technological resources to exploit the vast opportunities of economic expansion offered by the convenience food business' (Annual Report 1964: 8). Its response was daring and imaginative and drew public tributes from Lemass himself, who personally performed the opening ceremony at the world's first commercial AFD (Accelerated Freeze-Drying) food processing operation in Mallow. This food project was one of the major dramas in CSET's history. The company saw the project as having the potential to develop a national food processing enterprise larger than any industrial activity at that time carried on in the country. Whether it should have been modified sooner or stuck with longer, when breakthrough on the British market proved more difficult and expensive than had been anticipated, remains debatable. By 1972, with Lemass and the General both long gone from the national stage, the great dream was essentially over. The experience, however, continued to leave its mark on CSET's development well into the future.

The Lemass-led drive for economic expansion played a direct role in the major rationalisation in the dairy industry over the 1958–74 period. Indeed the process was initiated at national level as part of the new economic strategy when Lemass commissioned a study of the industry to determine its readiness for Common Market entry. The Government also helped to sustain the momentum for rationalisation, in the face of much resistance and inertia at industry and firm levels, when Common Market entry was initially turned down in 1963. The 1958–74 amalgamation process had major implications for the future development of the industry as a whole and led to the emergence of Golden Vale as one of the leading processors. The Government also set up An Bord Bainne, the Irish Dairy Board, to concentrate the export marketing effort of the Irish dairy industry behind a generic brand, something that the industry itself had failed to accomplish on several occasions since the late 1920s. By 1961 the issue had become too important to the overall national interest to delay any longer and Lemass addressed it directly in typically pragmatic fashion through the mechanism of the state agency.

The national drive for economic expansion played a significant, if less direct, role in the major rationalisation that took place in the distilling industry in the mid-1960s. Distilling had emerged from the self-sufficiency period as an inefficient, fragmented, inward-looking and conservative industry with a self-satisfied dominance of the home market. It was stimulated and threatened by the new national emphasis on export-led growth and freer trade. This strategy intensified public attention on the dismal post-war export performance of the industry relative to its Scottish counterpart. The primary positive rationale for the 1966 merger was to bring about a greater concentration of skills, capital and organisation in the industry. This was clearly intended to strengthen its competitiveness and to develop it through export-led growth in tune with the prevailing mood at national level. There were also real fears, in this more liberal trading context, that one of the major British brewing concerns might enter the industry through acquisition of the financially weakest player, with uncertain consequences. The merger was justified to the shareholders and the public in terms that closely resonated with national policy as the chairman explained that the three 'long-established and famous companies' had 'united in a spirit of partnership to enable our industry to make its maximum contribution to economic development in Ireland by utilising all our resources to the fullest extent' (Annual Report 1966: 14).

Ireland's eventual accession to the European Economic Community in 1972 was a logical and positive extension of the dramatic change in public policy that had taken place since 1958. The effects of entry on the development of the industries and organisations featured in this study have already been examined earlier in this chapter.

Public debt and fiscal rectitude

Entry into the EEC allowed Ireland's economic expansion to continue through to the end of the 1970s. In 1977 the incoming government tried to inject a Keynesian-type demand stimulus into the economy, using public borrowings to accelerate its recovery from the recessionary effects of the first oil crisis. This strategy gambled on continued economic growth in the international trading arena and on the willingness of Irish workers to accept wage increases that were lower than those operating in competitor countries. Both bets lost and Ireland entered the recessionary 1980s with a high level of public debt and with little room for manoeuvre in fiscal policy.

The public sector expanded and diversified greatly as the economy experienced a sustained level of unprecedented growth for most of the 1960s and 1970s. Many state agencies had been created or revitalised to help support the economic expansion programmes. Economic development had also brought vast improvements in education, health and social welfare which had greatly extended the demand on the public purse. Added to all of this was the enormous increase in security expenditure that became necessary as the Northern Ireland troubles developed and deepened throughout the 1970s. All in all over the 1958–78 period public sector current spending had risen from 24 per cent to 42 per cent of GNP. As the recession of the early 1980s deepened the weight of this public expenditure and the rising debt-servicing commitments became a growing burden on a contracting private sector. This burden became the single biggest obstacle to national economic recovery. A succession of politically weak administrations could only tackle the problem piecemeal over most of the 1980s, with much pain and little impact. In 1987 the political system finally produced an incoming administration with the political will and popular support for more radical reform of the public sector and stabilisation of the national debt, which had burgeoned from 29 per cent to 70 per cent of GNP over the 1976–85 period.

For all of the industries and organisations featured in this study the 1980s was a period of great change. Much of this was due to the dramatic changes that were taking place in the international trading arena during this time. However, in the Irish context the State's deepening fiscal crisis and the public policies that were pursued to address it directly affected the development of all of the organisations in this study, especially AFT and CSET.

As the problem with the public finances deepened over the 1980s AFT saw its grant-in-aid from the State become progressively tighter in real terms. Yet the Institute was left to its own devices to determine how to operate within this declining situation. Progressive fiscal constraint by the Government pushed AFT indirectly towards the increasing commercialisation of its services. This in turn led to a distinct shift in the basic focus of the organisation, though its statutory mission had never been altered, and to a gathering crisis of confidence within. Many insiders interpreted the reduction in state funding as a decline in political and public support for the Institute, concluding that either 'there were no votes' in supporting AFT 'or they do not see us as contributing'. Many were further concerned that the forced emphasis on problem solving, short-term, fee earning projects meant that 'in the long run' the Institute 'would lose its scientific base'.

For AFT the 1980s was a decade of major transformation, carried out in very difficult circumstances. It faced the task of realigning its primary research emphasis away from production towards process research, in line with the 'revolutionary' changes that were then taking place in the structure of agriculture at national and EEC levels. The tightening fiscal constraints left it with little organisational slack within which to effect a smooth and gradual reorientation. Furthermore the Institute had to transform itself within a funding context that had become more critical of its continuing value to the economy, as evidenced by the *Sunday Independent*'s inclusion of it in its list of state agencies that 'test the taxpayer's patience' and the public disparagement of its efforts in food research by the Chief Executive of Kerry Cooperative. Whatever their objective merits these criticisms sent shock waves through the organisation and increased the pressure for transformation and reform. As the decade progressed the public policy of fiscal rectitude helped accelerate the transformation in AFT, first through the impact of the Cashman Study of 1985 and finally through the merger with the advisory services in 1988 under the Programme for National Recovery.

The losses posted by CSET in the difficult trading conditions of the early 1980s brought the sugar company back to the centre of government attention after nearly a decade at arm's length. Many within the company resented the losses and began to seek greater freedom to manage it on a commercial basis. Over the 1980s CSET made the final transition from a developmental agency to a commercial company. The State's financial difficulties and the growing support for fiscal rectitude and public sector reform were crucial elements in the transition. The Report of the Joint Committee of the Oireachtais and the 'mind-set' change within the civil service were also key, and reflected the growing support for change within the wider political system. The company's decision to close the uneconomic Tuam operation became the final battle-ground in the struggle between the receding developmental and the ascending commercial ideologies, as political vacillation dragged out the process for almost five years. In the end not only was the battle won but also largely the war. By 1985 the commercialisation of state enterprise became official government policy. The final step to privatisation, when it came in 1991, was a relatively tame and uncontroversial affair.

The State had long been a major stakeholder in Irish distilling because of the importance of excise revenues to the public finances. Its fiscal difficulties led to higher levels of general taxation which removed spending power from the economy and in itself depressed the domestic demand for the industry's products. The sharp increases in excise duties of more than 200 per cent between 1979 and 1983 dramatically heightened the effect. Domestic sales fell by 27 per cent in volume terms over the 1981–83 period and the company had little doubt that the 'excessively high rate of duty' was 'the main cause of the sharp decline' (Annual Report 1982: 6). These developments diverted the company's attention back onto the domestic market and were an important consideration in the company's much criticised £16m acquisition of BWG, at a time when the Stock Market was looking for an imaginative move on the export front. The decline in Stock Market confidence that followed on from this acquisition was the beginning of the process which led to the IDG's own takeover four years later. Finally, and briefly, turning to the dairy sector, it was largely the case that 'the Common Agricultural Policy and its fiscal difficulties had more effect on the industry than the Government and its fiscal difficulties' during the 1980s, as one insider acutely observed.

SOCIAL AND CULTURAL TRANSFORMATION

At certain times the influence of our fifth factor, social and cultural transformation, mediated or was mediated by one or more of the other four. Yet the data reveal it to have been an important contextual influence on the development of our four organisations in its own right. Social and cultural transformation is ongoing. Usually it is a gradual and evolutionary process. Then again it can sometimes be dramatic, as in the 1960s, which in Ireland was 'one of those periods when a society swings on its axis to face a new direction' (Lee 1979b: 166). The effects of this contextual influence on the organisations under study are now examined.

Traditionalism to empiricism

One of the major transformations that took place in Irish society during the 1960s was the decline in traditionalism and the emergence of a new emphasis on information and empiricism that permeated all aspects of Irish life.

The drive for economic expansion put a new premium on the use of empirical research and analysis as the basis for public decision making in the development of the economy. De Valera could lead a less educated Irish populace through the power of his personality and could determine public policy by 'looking into his own heart'. Lemass did not have, or want, this luxury. The analysis on which the First Programme for Economic Expansion was based was outward looking. It recognised the role that research and education had played in the development of more advanced economies, and public investment in these areas was seen as productive and essential for economic take-off. Within the education system there was a shift in emphasis towards science and technology. On the wider front the advent of television helped to open up the whole culture to new facts and new influences, and the Second Vatican Council invited wider participation by the laity in Church affairs and encouraged more dialogue and debate.

This transformation in Irish society was reflected in the development of the organisations in the study, in a variety of ways. It seems certain that the original configuration of CSET's sugar operations would have been very different had the decision been made in the more empirical context that characterised the 1960s. Tuam would almost surely have been excluded on economic grounds alone. As it was the decision, according to the company's historian, went to the local lobbying committees 'with the biggest political clout'. Traditional Catholic social thinking, with its doctrinaire wariness of any extension of the state apparatus, was a major influence in delaying the start up of AFT and restricting its eventual form and scope. In contrast there was no such opposition to the rapid growth of the Institute in the post-Vatican II period when the Catholic social movement 'appeared increasingly concerned with empirical investigation of the actual needs of Irish people' instead of 'promoting a ready corpus of doctrine' as in the past (Whyte 1980: 332). Likewise, the threat of state intervention used by the Lemass Government to pressure the Cooperative Movement into organising the rationalisation of the dairy industry would not have had the same credibility or effect if it had been contemplated while traditional Catholic social thinking was at its nadir in Irish social life.

The new empiricism that characterised the Ireland of the 1960s was also reflected in developments taking place within the organisations in the study. The youthful AFT, for example, was a product of the times. It was peopled largely by a young cohort of agricultural science graduates fired up with a strong mission to bring science to the land. The Institute's early effort and impact were supported by, and contributed to, the growth of empiricism in Irish life. In a society that was undergoing a transition from tradition to modernity, Irish agriculture was undergoing its own transition from a tradition-based to a knowledge-based industry. AFT, and indeed CSET and Golden Vale, were all important agencies in this transition, contributing to it and being in turn transformed by it.

The impact of this cultural shift from traditionalism to empiricism was manifest right across the economic structure. It was a time when many Irish organisations considered new ideas and new departures from their traditional fields and modes of operation. CSET's imaginative diversification into convenience food processing, based on the first commercial application of a totally new technology, was evidence of the growing belief in the power of ideas and in the capability of a more scientifically literate rising generation of Irishmen to harness them. Around the same time a younger, more empirical, generation of leaders in the distilling industry showed a greater willingness than their forebears to experiment with the centuries-old distilling process to produce a line of whiskies, still distinctly Irish, yet tailored to the taste and colour requirements of the overseas markets. The commissioning of the world's most modern distillery complex also reflected a triumph of empiricism over tradition in this most conservative of industries.

Finally, the series of studies of the dairy sector carried out as part of the Lemass strategy for economic development was the most comprehensive empirical examination of the industry ever carried out up to that time. It set in motion the process that ultimately led to radical change in the structure of the industry. This change in turn helped to hasten the decline of traditionalism throughout the sector because of its enormous social as well as economic impact.

The rise in careerism

One of the most significant of the changes taking place during the transitionary 1960s was in the leadership of Irish society in all spheres. This was a period of rising careerism, managerialism and professionalism. The extension of organisation throughout the fabric of society was a product of, and a further stimulus to, this change. In the political sphere the revolutionary generation had grown old in power without any significant renewal until the 1950s. Lemass accelerated the renewal process when he became Taoiseach. He used his junior ministries to prune and develop young talent. He was an ideal transitionary figure. As a former freedom fighter he managed to harness the revolutionary spirit to the 'historic challenge' of the 1960s, the task of securing the economic viability of the country.

Under his leadership a new kind of hero or economic patriot, the professional manager, began to rise in stature. The men who rose to govern the country in the post-Lemass era had come to power because they were men of ambition rather than of destiny and had chosen politics as a career. The economic expansion drive had created the need for an expanding cadre of managers right throughout the public and private sectors. It was a period marked by a dramatic growth in the provision of management education through the Irish Management Institute, the universities and in-company training and development. As the 1960s progressed the values of managerialism and careerism began to pervade more and more of Irish economic, social and cultural life.

This transition to careerism and managerialism was most obviously reflected in this study in CSET when Tony O'Reilly was chosen to succeed the General. This leadership change was a microcosm of the wider transition happening throughout Irish society at this time. The General epitomised the national hero of the revolutionary generation, O'Reilly that of the post-revolutionary era. The General was one of those young army men who had proved their patriotism to the hilt and on whom Lemass and his colleagues relied to help pick the economy up by its bootstraps. He was handpicked to shoulder a major industrial appointment at a time when in 'a small society with no inherent momentum of its own' Lemass believed that 'the initiative, or lack of it, of a handful of individuals could make or mar important institutions for a generation' (Lee 1979a: 24). The General saw his role as not just commercial but developmental in a very basic sense. He was passionately committed to the development of Irish agriculture and to maintaining the viability of the rural way of life. He took a special interest in the problems of the small producers and continually exhorted them to be forward-looking, confident in their own ability and potential, and self-reliant. He railed against 'the timid spirits who baulk at every obstacle and cannot bring themselves to believe in the ability of Irishmen to compete with men of other nations' in his great, and possibly fatally flawed, crusade to build a national food processing industry.

To the post-revolutionary generation of Irish political leaders such deep-rooted passion and conviction, however forceful, were not enough to make the food project successful, particularly in the face of international competitors with superior professional commercial skills. They preferred to put their faith in a man whose basic character and national pride had been tested in the green jersey of the Irish rugby team rather than the green jacket of revolutionary combat. Tony O'Reilly had already seen the limitations of passion and conviction in the face of superior professional skills in sport and in business life. He came to CSET, fresh from his successful launch of 'kerrygold' in Britain, with a proven track record as a professional marketer. The transition from the General to O'Reilly at CSET was a reflection of the passing of the era of traditional leadership in Irish organisational life and the arrival of the professional era. O'Reilly's arrival brought the seeding of a new counter-culture to CSET, the commercial ideology, which within two decades had grown to replace developmentalism as the dominant ideology guiding the company's future strategy.

This type of leadership transition at CSET from nation-builder to professional manager was played out right across the national canvas. The General was one of a generation of leaders that was driven by values forged during the revolutionary times and that in peace time had turned its nationalistic passion and leadership talents to the practical patriotism of laying down the economic infrastructure of the new state. Such men, like the long-time 'Dean' of the industry Eamonn Roche of Mitchelstown, and Captain David Barry who founded Golden Vale, were also among the early builders in the dairy processing sector. In AFT the Doc was also part of the revolutionary generation, having been reared at the height of the War of Independence in a strong republican household. The transition from the Doc to Pierce Ryan was also that of traditional nation-builder to more modern professional manager. Even in the proprietary distilling sector, where former revolutionaries found little scope to apply their leadership talents, the industry began to undergo the change from family to managerial capitalism during this general transitionary period in Irish life.

Transformation in social structure

The 1960s and 1970s were decades of major transition in the Irish social and economic structure. During this period the country became increasingly urbanised. In 1971 over half the population lived in towns of over fifteen hundred people, up from less than one third in 1926. The country was also becoming more industrialised. Industry's share of GDP rose from 28 per cent to 38 per cent while that of agriculture declined from 22 per cent to 15 per cent over the 1961–78 period, and there were corresponding changes in the relative levels of employment in both sectors. Within the workplace the number of workers classified as employees was increasing and there was a shift away from unskilled to professional and semi-skilled categories. The general educational level rose right across the spectrum. In 1979 more than 85 per cent of 15 year olds were still at school, up from less than 50 per cent just two decades earlier, and progression to third level had increased by nearly two thirds over the same period.

Finally, all of these structural changes were accompanied by the growth of direct state involvement in the social and economic spheres. In the 1960–80 period the overall numbers employed in the public service increased from 182,000 to 295,000. In addition, over forty new state agencies had been formed with responsibilities ranging from the export marketing of dairy products to the improvement of public health. All in all the social and economic structure of the country had become more diversified and differentiated, both horizontally and vertically. Irish society had become less rural, less homogenised and more cosmopolitan in outlook and values.

This transformation in the national social and economic structure affected the organisations in this study. Indeed they were often agents of this transformation as well as being influenced by it. In the dairy industry the amalgamation process of the 1958 to 1974 period was a transformative process which was both enabled and constrained by the pace of change throughout the country as a whole. This process meant the break-up of the parish structure and the end of the kind of close professional and personal relationships that dairy farmers traditionally enjoyed with their local creamery managers. These creamery managers had long been among the most important social figures in traditional rural Ireland and the economic vitality of local parishes often depended on their enterprise or lack of it. The farmers, for their part, had come to see their local creamery as a place where they had personal influence and stature. The transformation of the industry structure to larger, more regional, processing centres was little short of social revolution and it is not surprising that it took sixteen years to implement fully. The younger generation of farmers and creamery managers generally welcomed the business and professional opportunities that the larger processing units promised. The older farmers and creamery managers resisted the passing of a traditional way of life that had contributed so much to their social status and sense of personal worth.

AFT and CSET, as development agencies, were actively involved in the country's transformation to a modern, urban, industrialised society. AFT was aware from the very beginning that its mission would have wider implications for the economic and social transformation of Irish agriculture and the communities that depended on it. That is why the Doc insisted on the inclusion of a Rural Economy Division in his initial structure. He knew that his Institute was involved in a 'mini revolution' in the 'farm economy' where 'rural people' would 'no longer work in isolation but as an integral part of the whole national endeavour' (Walsh 1980: 8). He saw AFT as an active agent in the creation of 'the farmer of tomorrow', who would be engaged in 'a business-like agriculture' as 'technically demanding as any other productive activity' (Walsh 1984: 21). CSET, for its part, was one of the first agencies to bring the systems and structure of modern management into the rural heartlands and to bring new wage labour and new industrial occupations into the economic and social structures of the regions in which it operated. CSET was also active in creating the farmer of tomorrow by bringing the mechanical and chemical revolutions, and the techniques of industrial engineering and specialisation, into Irish tillage farming.

Finally the history of Irish distilling in the two decades that followed the merger was one of internal social transformation, and itself an integral element of the change in the wider national context. Distilling was one of the oldest and most traditional industries in a country which even up to the mid-1960s still had relatively little industrial tradition. Making the merger work involved the forging of three very disparate family capitalist traditions into a modern unitary managerial culture. Traditional class, religious and regional differences in the wider national context had long before sedimented into these disparate cultures and had to be dissolved in the common solvent of wider social and cultural change. Power, for example, had been predominantly Catholic, and Jameson, Protestant. Power had drawn general workers from the regions, Jameson from Dublin's inner city. Jameson had a tradition of hiring British army veterans as first line supervisors, Power tended to promote theirs from within the company. In contrast to both, Cork Distillers long considered supervision a white-collar position, reflecting strong regional class attitudes, and hired their supervisors accordingly. The post-merger modernisation of the company involved the buying out of centuries-old trades like coopering and the importation of more modern technical and professional skills. Over two decades, through the processes of change and attrition, the proportion of personnel within the company hired after the merger had reached nearly 80 per cent. The company's own transformation had drawn on the forces for modernisation and change in the wider context and in turn had helped to reinforce them.

Powerful interest groups and weak bonding agents

In the 1980s the difficulties that a succession of governments had in dealing with the need for fiscal rectitude and public sector rationalisation were in no small way the consequences of the social transformation that had been taking place since the beginning of the economic expansion drive. The growth and proliferation of vested interests within the diversifying economic structure and the progressive weakening of the traditional bonding agents in Irish society were particularly significant.

The process of economic expansion gave rise to new occupational diversity in Irish society. For example AFT, as it grew, developed different categories of staff, professional researchers, technicians, general farm workers and administrators, each with its own linkages to similar occupational groupings in the wider social context. Similar diversity emerged within the other organisations in the study as they developed and modernised over time. The process of economic development more generally was accompanied by the expansion of the public sector and the enlargement of the State's position as an employer, making it increasingly difficult for national policy makers to mediate between the unions and the employers over wealth distribution. Moreover, the same process led to an expansion in the level of state spending on social welfare, health and education which came to be seen as a basic right no longer contingent on overall economic performance. Finally it resulted in an expanded and diverse range of state agencies which in time developed vested interests in their own perpetuation.

When the economy entered the low growth 1980s these diversified vocational and sectional interests all fought to maintain their economic positions. National leaders, in their attempts to restore order to the public finances and lay the basis for economic recovery, found it difficult to confront these interests and mobilise the national will because of the progressive dilution of the traditional bonding agents of nationalism and Catholicism. In the more empirical and contingent Ireland of the 1980s there were fewer absolute ideals to draw upon. Nationalism as a unifying force and common passion had been on the decline since the late 1950s. The passing of the revolutionary generation had its effect, so also did the rise in senseless violence in the name of nationalism in Northern Ireland. As a result it was not easy for the political leaders of the 1980s to link nationalism to economic sacrifice as de Valera was able to do during the 1930s and 1940s or to use it as a motive force for national enterprise as Lemass did in the early 1960s.

The cultural bonding power of the Republic's traditional Catholic ethos (in the sense of a shared system of Christian values rather than in any narrow sectarian dogmatic sense) had also been considerably weakened over the 1960s and 1970s. In the post-Vatican II period the Church became less authoritarian and more empirical. In addition, economic development and the advances in telecommunications brought in their wake the spread of materialism, secularism and pluralism throughout Irish society. The demise of the Church's secular leadership had left the Ireland of the 1980s in a situation where there was 'no large group of people in the society' who had 'the trust of the population and can get its cooperation for medium- or long-term goals' (Garvin 1982: 32). The country had entered the 1980s with a 'peculiarly weak sense of identity by European criteria' (Lee 1982: 13).

The weakening of these cultural bonds and the development of strong structurally-embedded sectional interests were together major factors in prolonging the public fiscal difficulties throughout the 1980s and in delaying the process of economic recovery. This in turn had strategic implications for the industries and organisations in this study which were fully examined earlier in the chapter.

CONTEXT AND STRATEGY FORMATION

In this chapter we identified and analysed the five most salient contextual factors that influenced the formation of strategy in the four organisations under study. The approach we took of examining the influence of leadership and context separately up to this point was useful in helping us to gain insight into the most important dimensions of these two variables as they were manifest in the case histories presented here. This of course has been an analytical convenience since the data clearly indicate a deep level of inter-play between both leadership and context in the formation of strategy. We are now nicely set up to analyse this interaction in our final chapter.

10 Synthesis and conclusions

INTRODUCTION

This book has been a study of leadership, context and history and of their interaction in the formation of organisational strategy. As we noted in Chapter 2, a more traditional way of accounting for the leader/strategy linkages would have been to concentrate on the person, the role and the psychological characteristics of key players such as O'Reilly, Walsh and O'Loughlin. Yet the data indicate the strong influences of context and history, each of which plays an important part in both leadership action (i.e. constrains or facilitates what leaders do) and in the selection and retention of individual leaders themselves at different points in the life-cycle of each organisation. In other words we see both the artistic and the instrumental sides of leadership in action. To paraphrase a well-known aphorism of Karl Marx we see our leaders making strategy but not always in circumstances of their own choosing and we also see them as historical instruments of strategic change. In the previous two chapters we deliberately looked at leadership and context and their influence on strategy formation separately, suspending the question of where the balance of influence lies between them, in order to gain more insight into the historical character of leadership and into the contextual factors that shape strategy. In this chapter we try to assess the balance of influence generally between leadership and context in the formation of strategy and to synthesise the findings from the cases.

CONTEXT AND STRATEGY

Much of the literature in organisational studies tends to reveal very little about the causal texture of context. Yet it is important for us to know how, and in what way, context influences strategy if we are to achieve the kind of understanding of the interaction of leadership and context in the formation of strategy that was a primary objective of this study. In situational-contingency approaches, for example, the causal texture of the environment is most often reduced to uni-dimensional surrogate measures of uncertainty and complexity, in spite of the key influence that the environment is assumed to have on organisational actions and outcomes in such theories (see Crozier and Friedberg 1980; Pfeffer 1982 for critiques of this reductionism). At the other extreme some of the deeply contextual studies of context-strategy interaction, like that of Pettigrew (1985), have succeeded in painting a descriptive tapestry of context but have not attempted to isolate its most salient elements (and were not designed to do so).

The long historical view that we have taken in our study helped us to take a middle ground. We managed to explore the context-strategy interaction in some rich descriptive detail but we were also able to identify and examine the five most salient contextual factors that shaped the strategies of our four organistions. In contrast to Porter's (1980: 3) view that *industry structure* is 'the key aspect of a firm's environment' in the shaping of organisational strategy, we found that factors such as *technology, international trading environment, public policy* and *social and cultural transformation* were also crucial in our cases. Our findings suggest that the relative importance of these factors may well differ from sample to sample and from country to country, which may explain our departure from Porter and provide some extension to his analysis. In Figure 10.1 we illustrate the relationship between three of our five factors. The predominance of industry structure in Porter's view is understandable when seen in the context of the United States up to the early 1980s. Industry leaders in the US, as the world's dominant economy, were more often than not also the leading players in the industry internationally. The organisations in our study were typically large players, indeed sometimes dominant players, in the domestic economy but much smaller players in their industries internationally. Thus the immediacy of national context (economic, political and social) was found to have a much more potent influence on organisational strategy than the classic Porter analysis would suggest. Now that many leading US companies have formidable global rivals in the 1990s it does not surprise us, from our analysis, to find that many US economic commentators are calling for a more targeted national industrial policy to help American companies compete with leading players from Japan and Germany (which have much closer government–industry strategic linkages). National context and public policy are now important contextual influences on the strategies of organisations in even the world's leading (though no longer dominant) economic power, as Porter's (1990) more recent work clearly reflects.

The way in which context affects strategy is something which is rarely

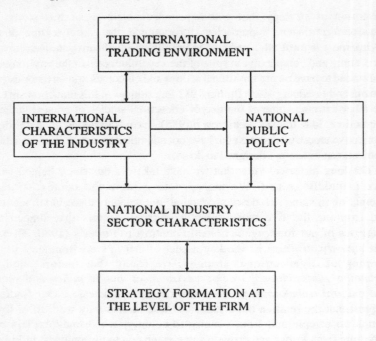

Figure 10.1 Multiple levels of analysis of context
Note The directional relationships in this figure apply to the case of the Small Open Economy – uni-directional arrows are used where one direction in the inter-relationship is considered to predominate.

examined in organisation studies. It is sometimes implied and more often simply not addressed at all. It is, as Pfeffer and Salancik (1978: 226) so aptly pointed out, 'as if a Mr Environment came into the organisation, giving orders to change organisational structures and activities'. Our study reveals something of the variety of ways in which context influences strategy and the variety of types of process involved (see Table 10.1 for a summary). Our cases reveal five modes of influence and three types of process by which context shaped strategy in the four organisations. Firstly we see many examples of the organisations *selecting* their contexts and reselecting them over time. For example when we look at CSET choosing to enter the convenience food industry in the 1960s or Golden Vale divesting itself of its engineering activity in the early 1980s we see both companies reshaping the pattern of their relationships with their situational contexts and redefining the scope of potential contextual influence over their future strategies. We also see our organisations *anticipate* various developments in their contexts and reshape their strategies accordingly as, for example, when Golden Vale commits itself to a major capacity expansion programme in anticipation of substantial growth in the national milk supply in the late 1960s, or indeed when the same company sets up a milk development fund to protect its milk supply as the industry enters a serious slowdown at the beginning of the 1980s.

We see the influence of context on strategy also *felt* more directly by our organisations as certain contextual pressures infuse into their activities. The most obvious example is the spiralling cost inflation that follows on from both oil crises in the 1970s which induces various rationalisation and cost reduction responses. At other times we see contextual influence being more *directive* as when the Government curtails the export of Irish whiskey during the war years or when national policy makers put direct pressure on the dairy industry to consolidate and rationalise during the 1960s. Perhaps the most interesting, and least well recognised and understood, mode is when we see the influence of context being *internalised* in the organisations through the development of norms, values, beliefs and shared ideologies with their industries and wider social contexts. We see this, for example, in the norm developed in the dairy industry that processors do not compete for suppliers and indeed in the consternation within that industry in general, and in Golden Vale in particular, when the Kerry Group no longer accepts this constraint in the early 1980s. We also see it in the resistance of the Irish and Scottish pot-stillers to the new blended whiskey product that led to the whiskey wars of the late nineteenth century. We see it, yet again, in the bold and imaginative responses of the General and the Doc to the patriotic challenge offered by Lemass to the 1960s generation of Irish industrial leaders to help him modernise and expand the national economy.

We see these various modes of contextual influence shape the strategies of our organisations through a variety of processes. There are clearly *social-psychological* processes of cognition and shared perception involved in the selection and anticipation modes as our organisations enact (Weick 1977) or selectively attend to particular elements of their overall environments through their planning processes. We also see processes of social exchange in the select, directive and felt modes of influence. One of the most developed social-exchange theories in the organisational analysis and strategy fields is the power–dependence paradigm (Emerson 1962; Thompson 1967; Pfeffer and Salancik 1978; Porter 1980). We see this power-dependence motor at work for example in the case of Irish Distillers where the three traditional rivals are induced into merger at least partly to increase their power over the industry and ward off the very real threat of entry presented by major British brewing interests. We also see the Irish Distiller Group bypass the wholesale trade in the late 1960s, and enter the cash and carry business in the early 1980s, to reduce its dependence on distributors and increase its influence with the consumer. Organisational responses based on power-dependence considerations tend to be aimed at the avoidance of uncertainty and the reduction of dependence.

Again perhaps the most interesting, and least well-understood, type of context–organisation interaction that we see in our cases is the one of *cultural* (or ideological) *transmission* most evident in the internalised mode. Actions by organisations aimed primarily at uncertainty avoidance and the reduction of dependence are largely conservative and defensive by nature. Theories of organisational action that are primarily dependent on the avoidance of uncertainty and the reduction of dependence are inadequate in helping us to understand the processes of growth, innovation and entrepreneurial risk-taking. As Schumpeter (1934) has argued the processes of growth and innovation are distinct from stability seeking or equilibrium seeking economic behaviours. The cultural mode of analysis seems to us, from our cases, to be a vital element in explaining innovation and growth in organisations. Through this mode of cultural transmission we see context in a new way, not just in terms of external impersonal forces to be reacted to or exploited, but also as a more active agency which can stimulate innovation, growth and risk seeking strategies in organisations. We see the organisations of the General and the Doc stimulated and energised by the 'national challenge' of the 1960s. However we also see this cultural transmission at work in forming the very values and deep motivational springs of such leaders and in this way influencing their whole strategic postures and outlooks, a point to which we will want to return later. Finally we see this mode of cultural transmission being actively used by national policy makers, along with economic and political (social-exchange) influences, in their stimulation of strategic and structural change in the dairy industry over the 1958–74 period (see Leavy 1991b for a more extensive analysis of the role of cultural transmission in this change process).

Table 10.1 How context influences strategy

Modes of influence	Types of process
1 SELECTED- context	A SOCIAL - PSYCHOLOGICAL
2 ANTICIPATED- context	
3 FELT- context	B SOCIAL - EXCHANGE
4 DIRECTIVE- context	
5 INTERNALISED- context	C CULTURAL TRANSMISSION

LEADERSHIP AND CONTEXT

For those readers who prefer to locate their analyses of leadership around the characteristics and actions of the individual manager, this book may possibly be somewhat of a disappointment. Although individuals have surfaced and figured large on the organisational stages described in the study, they have not always been the leading players. Indeed, some have had to wait until later 'acts' of the play, as it were, to enter our conscious-ness and emerge in the guise of the more traditional, individualistic, view of the leader. While leadership has been a central theme of this research the insights that we have gained into this important phenomenon have been achieved largely by deliberately not studying leaders directly as individuals and not centring our research primarily on their own personal attributes and styles, and their own reported experiences and philosophies of leadership. We have indeed sought such insights where available but our primary perspective has been to study them as historical figures in the context in which they have emerged, submerged and re-emerged.

Czarniawska-Joerges and Wolff (1991: 542) have questioned the value of any research on leadership which is overly pre-occupied with the personal attributes and personas of individuals and argued that 'such an egocentric representation can be sustained' only as a result of 'isolation from the political, social and economic context of organizing'. Our data support the view that isolating context from the analysis would give a very partial and inaccurate view of leaders and the process of leadership. We might be tempted with 'charismatic' individuals such as O'Reilly or Walsh to attribute primacy to their actions via such traits. Yet a deeper look reveals the influence of context in shaping both individual and organisational action. A central question of interest to all who are interested in the interaction of leaders and contexts is where does the balance lie? Where is the locus of influence over the organisation's strategy and destiny. Is it primarily with the leader as an individual 'shaker and mover' or is context the ultimate arbiter?

Clearly, the cases in this book revolve around both context and individual leaders. Tables 10.2 to 10.5 summarise the data for each of the four organisations in terms of the study's overall framework and the categories which were derived in the previous two chapters. On close examination these figures show the balance of influence over strategy formation changing from organisation to context and back again in historic cycles. To some extent these cycles are reflections of distinct phase changes taking place in the wider context of all of our organisations. For example, we see the post-1979 period presenting all four organisations with a more constraining and defining context than in the previous two decades. We see, for example, Walsh, McCourt, Costello and O'Loughlin enjoy far greater scope for autonomous action with few of the sharply defined economic imperatives that face their successors Ryan, Burrows, Sheehy and Curtin. There is clear evidence in the cases of leadership activity tending to become more reactive and defensive in the post-1979 era.

While it seems from the data that some contexts are more constraining and defining than others we also see that some leaders and their organisations seem better able to transcend the influence of context and retain their scope for action than their counterparts elsewhere. We see this most clearly in the dairy industry. During the 1979–86 period when all of the major processors face unprecedented constraints on growth and pressures on margins we see Golden Vale drop from number two to the bottom of the big six and being kept on the defensive and driven by context for most of this period. In stark contrast we see the Kerry Group, facing the same overall contextual pressures, successfully pursue an aggressive growth strategy (under the imaginative leadership of Denis Brosnan) which catapults it from number six to industry leader over the same period. Indeed we see Kerry approaching the challenges of the period by breaking out from the industry norms that traditionally restrained competition for milk supply and by widening the scope of its business to reduce its dependence on the mature Irish dairy sector.

The industry environment is clearly not an unfailing pre-determinant of organisational strategy even at its most bounding and constraining. There is still scope for autonomous action. Partially it appears, at least from the example just discussed, that this is a result of the individual attributes of the organisational leader. Imaginative and ambitious leaders like Brosnan clearly have the ability to 'play with the requirements and constraints imposed by the environment and even manipulate them in (their) turn' as Crozier and Friedberg (1980: 76) have so aptly described it. Our perspective on leaders as tenants of time and context and our classification of them as Builders, Revitalisers, Turnarounders and Inheritors does indeed support this view – but only so far. Such classifications are meaningful only in the context of *organisational history*. For example, Tom Walsh of AFT was the builder of that organisation. When he was appointed this was the clear task to be accomplished. In addition he was fortunate to be favoured by a supportive environment for the growth and expansion of his organisation since investment in research was then high on the agenda of the government of the day. Yet all our respondents agree that the Doc would have been a builder irrespective of context. We see him in the case as a man with charisma and a vision, capable of lifting the sights of the young scientists that he drew to his cause and firing them up with a deep sense of national mission.

Table 10.2 Changing locus of influence over strategy at AFT

Strategy formation episodes	Situational context						Organisation			Primary locus of influence
	Technology	Industry structure	Intl. trading environment	National public policy	Social & cultural transformation		Organisational leader(s)	Organisational history	
1 AFT gestation and foundation 1948–58		Under-developed and too fragmented to do own R&D.	Keynesianism. Marshall Plan for European Recovery.	Self-sufficiency. Sluggish post-war recovery.	Traditionalism. Catholic social thinking. Inward-looking. Residue of fatalism.				
2 Early rapid growth 1958–68	Ongoing rapid developments in agricultural production sciences and technologies.	Expansion in agricultural production. Transition from tradition-based to knowledge-based industry. Growing demand for research and advice.	Expansion and liberalisation. Formation of EEC.	Lemass injects fresh hope & confidence with new outward-looking national economic programmes. Investment in research.	Ireland in transition. Empiricism, careerism and materialism on the rise. Social structure elaborating and differentiating.		Tom Walsh (the 'Doc') – Builder.	Controversy over establishment and scope.	INT*
3 Review and reorganisation 1968–73								Rapid growth phase over. AFT a significant national resource.	INT/EXT
4 Expansion through user-funding 1973–80.		Diversifying industry and growing user sophistication.	Oil crises and inflation.	Expansion within EEC. Agri-sector to pay towards development of AFT.	New skills, new demands and new ambitions in rural Ireland. 'Farmer of tomorrow'.			Organisation settled in too much. Re-organisation and controversy.	
5 Retrenchment and realignment 1980–87	Developments in processing technologies. 'New sciences' like bio-tech.	Retrenchment and new priorities. EEC restraints on production.	World recession. Neo-classical policies. EEC commodity surpluses.	Public financial stringency. Cashman study on AFT.	Emergence of strong sectional interests. Weakening cultural bonds.		Pierce Ryan – Inheritor, transformer.	Production-research dominance. Ageing specialist skills out of line with new priorities. History of growth.	EXT/int
6 Merger with ACOT and rationalisation				Public financial crisis. Programme for National Recovery.	Sense of national crisis mobilising support for radical change.				EXT

Legend for Tables 10.2–10.5
Locus of influence perceived to be:
INT = primarily internal
ext/INT = mainly external

EXT/INT = slightly external
INT/EXT = slightly internal

INT/ext = mainly internal
EXT = primarily external

Table 10.3 Changing locus of influence over strategy at IDG

Strategy formation episodes	Situational context					Organisation		Primary locus of influence
	Technology	Industry structure	Intl. trading environment	National public policy	Social & cultural transformation	Organisational leader(s)	Organisational history	
1 Transition to factory system 1770–1820		First phase of industry consolidation.	Laissez-faire, free trade.	Government excise policy raises effective minimum operating scale.	Traditionalism, Authoritarianism. Rural values, agriculture dominant. Mass of population at subsistence level.			EXT
2 Early concentration. Emergence of major centres 1820–60	Energy a primary input. Access to coal imports & water help determine location.	Concentration around east and south-east ports.	Growth in international trade. Early development of global whiskey market.	Laissez-faire policy – under United Kingdom Government.	Emergence of middle class to lead struggle for self-government. Living standards slowly rise in mainly rural economy as coops develop.	Power Jameson Murphy – Builders.	Family capitalism. Traditional, conservative product and production orientation.	INT
3 The emergence of blends. 'Whiskey war' 1860–1920	The Coffey-still, technological breakthrough. Development of blended product.	The whiskey war. Blends broaden market and become the volume segment.	Leading economies create the world's first mass markets for consumer goods like whiskey.					EXT/INT

Phase	Technology	Market	Political/Economic environment	Strategy	Economic/Social development	Personalities	Orientation	
4 Contraction of exports. Strong domestic focus 1920–58		Global market favours blends. Emergence of strong international competition.	Prohibition in US. Great Depression. Isolationism and protectionism.	Self-sufficiency. Economic war. War-time curbs on production and exports.	Economic development slow. Industrialisation process underway. Family capitalism.		Domestic orientation. Inward-looking.	EXT/int
5 Consolidation through merger 1958–66		Threat of entry of large British brewing companies.	Post-war trade liberalisation and expansion. Emergence of new large markets like EEC.	Economic expansion. Trade liberalisation. Free trade with UK.	Ireland in transition. Empiricism, careerism and materialism on the rise.	O'Reilly and other architects of the merger.	Transition to managerial capitalism. More market orientation, merging of three disparate cultures.	INT/EXT
6 Modernisation, domestic market dominance and export-led growth 1966–79	Technological developments offer greater flexibility and efficiency.	Wholesalers by-passed. All Irish whiskey under one organisation. Increasing competition from imports.	EEC entry. Oil crisis. Inflationary cost pressures.	Export-led growth. Further growth on EEC entry. Government discourages Seagrams takeover moves.	Agri-incomes rise to par with industry. Advent of domestic mass market and consumer society. Rising urbanism.	McCourt (and O'Reilly) – Revitalisers.	Replacement of traditional with modern skills.	INT
7 Consolidation of domestic position, rationalisation realignment and takeover defence 1980–88		Declining demand globally and domestically. Changing channels of distribution. Global consolidation by acquisitions.	Prolonged recession. Neo-classical economic policies. Single European Act and the single market.	Public fiscal stringency. Steep rise in excise, personal taxation. SEA commitment means no scope to stop takeover of 'national champion'.	Emergence of sectional interests. Weakened cultural bonds. Swing to right. More European in outlook.	Burrows – Inheritor and defender.	Defensive BWG acquisition. Problems with US marketing organisation. Revision of export strategy. Rationalisation.	EXT/int

Table 10.4 Changing locus of influence over strategy at CSET (strategy formation variables)

Strategy formation episodes	Situational context					Organisation		
	Technology	Industry structure	Intl. trading environment	National public policy	Social & cultural transformation	Organisational leader(s)	Organisational history	Primary locus of influence
1 Sugar industry – private enterprise phase 1926–33	Prior availability of beet sugar extraction technology.	Attempt at vertical integration from refining to production and processing.	*Laissez-faire*, free trade.	Independence. Free trade, *laissez-faire*.	Traditionalism, authoritarianism. Rural values, agriculture dominant. Revolutionary	Private entrepreneurs.	Failure of private enterprise project.	
2 CSET formation, early growth and development 1934–45	Beet processing not as economical as cane processing.	Protected state monopoly. Regional configuration. Free world market than 15% of total.	Isolationism, protectionism. War-time scarcities and stringencies.	Self-sufficiency. Protectionism. State-led industrial development under Lemass.	generation in leadership positions. Nationalism and Catholicism major cultural forces.	Connell and Hanrahan – administrators and custodians.	Politics of initial configuration. Civil service control.	INT (1934–39) EXT/int (1939–45)
3 CSET revitalisation, sugar business to self-sufficiency 1945–59	Mechanical and chemical revolutions to Irish beet production.	Domestic capacity expanded to meet national requirements.	Keynesianism. Post-war recovery and trade liberalisation. EEC formed.	The extension of industrial employment to regions. Sugar industry developmental.		General Costello – Revitaliser/developer.	Developmental ideology. Sugar dominance. Nation-building vision.	INT
4 CSET diversification into food processing 1960–72	Accelerated Freeze Dried technology (AFD).	Company now involved in two related activities but very different industries.	General expansion in world trade.	Lemass's dramatic new export-led growth strategy. His historical challenge to 1960s Ireland.	Ireland in transition. Empiricism, careerism and materialism on the rise. Post-revolution-generation in leadership positions. Agricultural incomes rise to parity with industry. More diversified society and economy.	O'Reilly – Turnarounder 1966–69.	Food dominance. New commercial culture influences. Sugar assets run down. Food project legacy and leadership dramas.	INT/EXT

Stage	Technology	Market	Economic context	Policy	Interests	Key actors	Outcome	EXT/INT
5 CSET rationalisation and modernisation (phase one) 1973–79	Technological refinements to improve throughput & efficiency.	CSET now part of the European industry. Winds of competition. Production quotas.	Oil crisis and cost inflation, but continued expansion in world trade.	EEC membership. Industrial policy shifts away from indigenous industries to hi-tech inward investment.		Daly – Inheritor, stabiliser, care-taker 1969–74. Sheehy (Coakley) – Inheritor(s), defender(s) 1974–79.	Return to sugar dominance. Uncommercial capital structure, high debt/interest.	EXT/int
6 CSET rationalisation and modernisation (phase two) 1980–87	Economics of processing in EEC conditions point to two-plant config.	New sugar substitutes. Decline in underlying demands. New pressures on margins.	Recession. Neo-classical economics. EEC budgetary problems.	Public fiscal stringency. SOEs under review. Commercial viability policy replaces developmental.	Emergence of strong sectional interests. Weakened cultural bonds. Greater public debate over 'value for money' of state enterprise. Gathering sense of crisis builds up acceptance for radical measures and support for privatisation of SOEs.	Sheehy (Fitzpatrick) – Inheritor(s), defender(s) 1980–84. Comerford (Cahill) – Inheritor(s) transformer(s) 1985–91.	Resentment at losses. Rise of commercial ideology. Tuam closure controversy.	EXT/int
7 CSET growth through acquisition and privatisation 1988–91	Static/even slow decline. Consolidations within EEC industry becoming more likely.	EEC 150% self-sufficient. SEA increasing intra-EEC competition.		Radical rationalisation of state sector.			Two plant confutation. Transition to commercial ideology complete. Privatisation.	INT/ext

Table 10.5 Changing locus of influence over strategy at Golden Vale (strategy formation variables)

| Strategy formation episodes | Situational context | | | | | Organisation | | Primary locus of influence |
	Technology	Industry structure	Intl. trading environment	National public policy	Social & cultural transformation	Organisational leader(s)	Organisational history	
1 Transition from cottage- to factory-based indus. 1889–1921	The mechanical cream separator.	Horace Plunkett and the Cooperative Movement.	*Laissez-faire*, free trade.	New Dept. of Agriculture & Technical Instruction.	Traditionalism. Authoritarianism. Rural values, parish structure.			
2 Early rationalisation. Industry saved and coop dominance secured 1921–27		Fragmented. Over supplied. Destructive competition. Leadership of Henry Kennedy.	Post-World War I depression in agriculture.	Government drive rationalisation through Dairy Disposal Co.	Independence. Revolutionary generation lead the country and the industry.			
3 Industry begins to consolidate. Overall growth rate slow 1928–47	Technology imported for processed cheese manufacture by Mitchelstown.	Growth in milk supply slow. Some consolidation. Diversification into agricultural trading.	Depression. Protectionism, isolationism 1932–38. War-time fragmentation. 1939–45.	Self-sufficiency. 'Economic war' with UK. Price supports. Compulsory tillage.				
4 Foundation of Golden Vale & early growth 1947–56	Processed cheese the initial product.	Federal movement by small processors to improve their power.	Keynesianism. European recovery. EEC formed. General liberalisation and expansion in world trade. Consolidation in the industry internationally. Emergence of large international producer trading blocks.			Capt. D. J. Barry – Statesman.		EXT/INT

Phase	Technology / Farm	Industry	Economic (global)	Economic (national)	Ireland / Social	Leadership	Strategy	INT/EXT
5 GV grows to major player status 1957–68	Mechanical & chemical revolutions on the farm.	Industry growth. Supply expands rapidly. Generic export marketing.		Economic expansion programmes. State central marketing agency 3 major studies. Sustained effort to rationalise the industry.	Ireland in transition. Empiricism career-ism, materialism and urbanism on the rise. Break up of the parish structure in dairying. Emergence of the farmer-businessman. Rise in agricultural employment. Town–country and farmer–wage earner tensions. Sectional interests and weakening of cultural bonds.	O'Loughlin – Builder 1956–71.	Engineering and fat-filled milk powder emphasis. Physical development. Amalgamation & associated politics. High D/E. Crisis. Recovery. Rise in finance/ systems. Fear of new initiatives. Production-led.	INT
6 Amalgamation GV no. 2 in industry 1968–74	Economies of scale. Process improvements & efficiencies.	Major rationalisation and consolidation.		EEC entry gives further growth impetus to the ind. Brussels becomes an important political centre for farmer lobbying.				INT/EXT 1968–74 (EXT in 1975)
7 Financial crisis, recovery & expansion 1975–79		Unexpected set-back in 1974. Then further growth to 1979.	Post-oil crisis cost inflation, but world trade growth continues.			Lenihan/ Flanagan – Inheritors 1972–79		INT 1976–79
8 Stagnation and decline to no 6 in the industry 1980–85		Setback in milk expansion. Milk wars. Global over-supply.	2nd oil crisis. Prolonged recession. EEC surpluses and budgetary pressures. Neo-classical economic ideology.		Decline in 'green' nationalism. More European in outlook – values.	Curtin – Inheritor 1980–85.	Milk wars. Rationalisation. Loss of supplier confidence. Sense of crisis.	EXT
9 Turnaround and realignment 1986–88 and beyond	Shift in emphasis towards new products and new food process technologies. In-house R&D.	Dairy industry static. New wave of consolidations. Entry of private interests. Major coops seek funds on S.Ex. & diversify.	SEA makes EEC market more competitive. Production cutbacks imposed by EEC. EEC & global over-supply. EEC industry consol. likely after 1992.			O'Mahony – Turnarounder 1986–91 and beyond.	Rationalisation. More market-led orientation. Return to growth. PLC status.	EXT/int 1986 INT/ext 1987–88 INT 1988–91 & beyond

Pierce Ryan, on the other hand, was an inheritor with a very different historic challenge in more difficult circumstances. During his tenure AFT remained on the defensive and his period as leader of AFT (as successor to Walsh) might seem to bear all the hallmarks of determinism with the context of the organisation very much in the driver's seat. However, this neat dualism is confounded by the skill that Ryan showed in managing retrenchment and transformation in very difficult budgetary circumstances (a situation that many insiders doubted the Doc would have relished or handled as well). It becomes even more confounded when we see the one leader, Richard Burrows, play two different roles in the distilling industry. He was a revitaliser at Bushmills before taking on the role of inheritor of the O'Reilly/McCourt strategic legacy at IDG. A future research agenda for examining the relationship between leadership and context in the formation of strategy would seem not only to be of necessity context-specific but also to be sensitive to multiple levels of analysis over the histories of organisations. But that is for the future and hopefully the patterns and the themes examined here will inform such an agenda.

Leadership – symbolic or substantive

One of the major debates in the leadership literature, relating directly to our locus of influence theme, is whether in fact the role of leaders in the shaping of organisational strategies is primarily substantive or symbolic. Pfeffer and Salancik (1978) in their examination of the external control of organisations argued that because of the way in which the contexts of organisations severely delimit their actions the role of leadership is largely symbolic and that this is an important aspect of leadership deserving of more empirical attention (a call that was responded to by much of the subsequent work on corporate culture). Our study clearly shows that situational context and organisational history do tend to determine and define to a significant degree the kind of historic challenges that are presented to leaders during their tenures at the top. However, our cases also show that to be given the historic opportunity to build is not to build (for example, two leaders of Golden Vale had the opportunity to be the builders of this organisation before Dave O'Loughlin came on the scene), to be given the opportunity to revitalise is not to revitalise, and so on. Leaders do appear to be very variable in their capacities to perform these historic tasks, and even in their abilities to recognise the true nature and full potential of their historic challenges and opportunities.

What is more interesting to us than the either/or question is what our study shows about how the symbolic and substantive elements of leadership interact to generate organisational actions and outcomes of strategic significance. This was most clearly seen in the area of leadership succession, particularly in the CSET and Golden Vale cases. The drama that surrounds the departure of the General and the arrival of O'Reilly strongly symbolises and serves to underline the expectation of a major change in strategy with respect to the troubled food project. It represents not just a change in leadership but a change in ideology from the developmental to the commercial. In a very real way O'Reilly's subsequent ability to bring about a substantive change towards a more commercial and marketing-oriented culture is facilitated by the heavy symbolism represented in the drama of the succession. Similar but perhaps even more revealing is the functionality of the symbolism that we see in the arrival of O'Mahony at Golden Vale in helping to create the conditions for a successful substantive turnaround. Ironically we also see much of the substance of the initial turnaround being achieved on the back of the tough rationalisation measures implemented by his predecessor before his departure. However, the case clearly shows that little short of the dramatic arrival of someone who can be credibily presented as a 'saviour' will be sufficent to break the vicious cycle (fuelled by declining supplier confidence) and create the breathing space that must be the starting point for any successful turnaround.

Inspirational and visionary leadership

Few issues have generated as much interest in the leadership literature over the last decade as the 'vision thing' (Kanter 1990:4). The perspective on leadership that we have developed here, with its long historical view, gives us some valuable insight into this important but often elusive phenomenon. Leadership, as our analysis clearly shows, is not just about having the right attributes or generic skills. It is also about the art of leading with a keen sense of current context and historic opportunity. It is only by refocusing onto the more expressive side of leadership (rooted in the interaction of leader, context and organisational history) that we can begin to get a better understanding of the wellsprings of strategic vision and inspirational leadership.

We see the leadership of the Doc and that of the General, for example, both characterised by vision and inspiration. When we examine this more closely we find that the twin deep-rooted passions that drove the Doc and helped him to raise the sights of his young scientists and inspire them were his nationalism and his belief in the power of science to solve the problems of Irish agriculture. We see him not just running a research organisation but building a nation's agriculture and securing its economic viability. His use of metaphors for Irish agriculure like the country's 'mine at the top of the land' indicate the breadth of his vision and his conviction that the revival of agriculture was the key to the revival of the whole economy. Likewise the visionary and inspirational leadership of the General is rooted in his own deep convictions. We see him not just running a sugar company but building a national food industry, bringing fresh hope and confidence to rural communities right around the country. His own upbringing in the rural heartlands of Tipperary, his nationalism and his belief in the cooperative ideology as the best principle on which to help build vibrant, self-reliant and viable rural communities are the driving passions of his leadership at CSET.

The cases of the Doc and the General strongly indicate that the wellsprings of true visionary and inspirational leadership are very deeply rooted in basic values which are developed over a long period in the leader's life. These values are very situational and connect the leader and his efforts in a specific time and place to his organisation and the society that it serves. This connectedness with deeper values and larger purposes seems to be at the heart of what distinguishes truly visionary and inspirational leadership and makes it special. The General and the Doc clearly have their counterparts in some of the world's great corporations (Edwin Land's passionate belief in the power of science to improve the human condition as the source of the inspiration and vision that built Polaroid comes immediately to mind). Such attributes cannot easily be taught. This we believe is why many of the current exhortations to company strategists to develop their capacities for visionary and inspirational leadership, as though these were largely generic skills, are somewhat wide of the mark. To a significant extent history (nature and nurture) chooses these leaders of vision who not only see possibilities that the rest of us with much narrower horizons have never dreamt of but who are also moved by strong and deep-seated passions to make those visions a reality. In so far as it can be consciously developed, however, the capacity for truly visionary and inspirational leadership will, it seems to us, be best enhanced by the kind of liberal education that helps leaders to explore their own deeply held values and beliefs and to connect with the sweep of human history and with their own cultures and contexts.

Our perspective on leaders as tenants of time and context also serves to avoid the danger of developing an overly heroic and somewhat mythological view of these rare and important individuals. All of the leaders featured in our cases are people of exceptional ability but even the most inspirational and talented of them are seen to have feet of clay. Visionary leadership is not always seen to be the undisputed virtue that those promoting the 'vision thing', like Bennis and Nanus (1985), might make it appear. Like most conviction leaders the Doc and the General tended to be directive and authoritarian in their overall leadership styles. We see the power of their convictions inspire their organisations but we also see the tenures of both of these leaders end in frustration and controversy and both men leave their organisations, still much admired but with their credibility dented. We see the visionary builder of Golden Vale almost drive his organisation to the brink of liquidation by his bold and imaginative but high risk approach to the capital development of his company. We see the heroes of one era lose their haloes in different historical circumstances in both Golden Vale and CSET. We see some succeed in circumstances where it would have been difficult to fail and others become ineffective in circumstances where it was difficult to succeed. We see leadership as an imput, a sort of human energy source, that sometimes get used up or consumed in the service of organisations. These are some of the downside and darker aspects of the leadership phenomenon that are also worthy of attention in any future research agenda in this perennially important area and that have only recently begun to be seriously discussed in the strategy field (Hambrick and Fukutomi 1991; Leavy 1992).

LOCUS OF INFLUENCE – PATTERNS AND THEMES

Perhaps, then, the key theme to emerge from the present study and foregoing analysis is that of historical perspective. Long time-frames of analysis lend a perspective to the potency and powerlessness of individual action. They also re-emphasise the role of strategic choice. Leaders might be tenants of time and context but are rarely reduced to purely passive agents. They often can and do make their organisations' histories though not always in circumstances of their own choosing. To summarise these points:

1 The strategies and development of all the sample organisations appear never at any stage wholly pre-determined by managerial action nor external events.
2 Any patterns and predictability which do emerge both in the strategies of organisations and the action of leaders are significant only with regard to historical context. Variation in context emerges as the dominant unit of analysis rather than individual or organisational strategies.
3 The data question the current pre-occupation with transformational leadership as the sole route to organisational success or survival (e.g. Block 1991; Nanus 1992; Harper 1992). Our findings reveal a variety of ways in which the leader-organisation-context interaction fits together. There appears no single best way to manage for long-term success.

We have seen the data reveal that the locus of influence over strategy formation varies over time between the organisation and its context, with some contexts being more structuring than others, but also with some leaders better able to manage the requirements of contexts than others. In this respect, the data lend longitudinal support to the strategic choice thesis presented by Child (1972). Beyond the strategic choice perspective, the data reveal the influence of organisational history as an important factor in strategic leadership. The strategic options open to leaders appear to be a product of previous constraints and opportunities fashioned either by earlier decisions of their predecessors or by previous decisions made by themselves. Leaders may have demonstrable levels of strategic choice but such choice is apparently bounded by the historical pattern of their organisations' development. Those authors who subscribe to the institutionalist perspective would acknowledge the potency of such strategic patterning (Meyer and Rowan 1977; Zucker 1988, for example). Yet, the prevailing determinism inherent in the institutionalist perspective is not wholly borne out. We also found that the autonomous actions of leaders often proved to be the decisive elements in determining the pace and direction of change despite apparently strong contextual constraints which exerted pressure for action in perhaps the opposite direction to that taken. We would include in this category, for example, such leaders as McCourt (IDG), Walsh (AFT), O'Loughlin and O'Mahony (Golden Vale) and O'Reilly (CSET).

Our perspective, therefore, attempts to bridge determinism and choice by setting the arguments for each in a temporal and historical perspective. The data indicate that this dualism inherent in much of the leadership literature (voluntaristic versus deterministic actions) is an over-simplified model when placed in the context of organisational history. A corollary of this finding from the data is that patterns and themes of organisational strategies are rarely predictable in advance. Strategy formation is the result of interactions between history, individuals and organisations and such patterning as it does exhibit flows 'from particular temporal conjunctions of material circumstances and human will' to quote from historian David Thompson (1966:16) rather than from any 'eternal causes' or towards any pre-determined or pre-patterned destinies. Unlike the biological metaphors which abound in the literature, the most famous being the organisational life cycle concept (Kimberley and Miles 1980), we ascribe neither linearity nor inevitability to the historical patterning of the development of organisations. Indeed we prefer to use the more existential and less determinist metaphor of organisational 'career' (a concept that we hope to develop further in later publications) rather than 'life-cycle' to represent the longer-term historical patterning of strategy formation in the relational model of process that we have developed to summarise our findings (see Figure 10.2).

Our relational model also facilitates comparison of the current findings with developments in the field of strategy and leadership. We find it

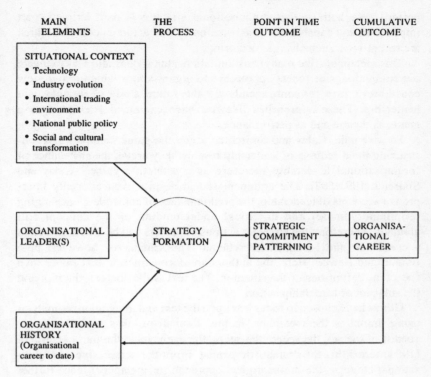

| MAIN ELEMENTS | THE PROCESS | POINT IN TIME OUTCOME | CUMULATIVE OUTCOME |

Figure 10.2 A relational model of strategy formation

fascinating that other scholars lend support to our frame of reference, in particular the development of an interpretive view of leadership within an overall strategic context. To employ a dramatic metaphor, we view the relationships between leaders and strategic contexts as the script, the play and the process of improvisation. Strategy does not happen synoptically without individual leadership nor does it wholly derive its character from empowered visionary leaders. There is a text, most probably written by someone other than the actor (the leader). It is this text which forms the guiding parameters for players. But there is a sub-text. Actors can choose to interpret the text both literally and dynamically in ways not intended by the original author. Literally, they can choose to interpret the words of the script in ways which emphasise some over others. Dynamically, actors can transcend the structural parameters of the play and in effect produce a new revised version perhaps radically different from the author's intention. Whether this process of transformation 'works' or not is largely a function of the context in which the play is performed (to whom and in what time period). We believe that organisational strategy is part scripted, part improvised and capable of transformation by key actors in contexts which are receptive to such changes occurring.

This metaphor (like many) has limitations, but it does allow us to locate our study alongside recent approaches to organisations which in our view constitute a firm research agenda for the future study of strategy and leadership. These approaches likewise have examined leadership as a game, as theatre and as performance.

For example, Calas and Smirchich argue the game metaphor. Deconstructing the discourse of leadership reveals, they argue, the sustenance of 'organisational leadership literature as a seductive game' (Calas and Smircich 1991:567). The argument is that despite even allegedly interpretive accounts of leadership, the predominance of embedded, unchanging (dominantly male) and uncritical understanding of the concept still abounds. Therefore, the strategic actions of leaders can be characterised in a consistent and recognisable schema. The schema is, however, both limited and flawed. Here, the authors are deconstructing text rather than speech as definitions of the situation. The text is the context, the plot and the sub-plot of leadership action.

Others have chosen to focus less upon the text and more upon an analysis using drama as the metaphor. In this, dramatism takes social action to consist of the act, the scene, the agent, the agency and the purpose. Burke (1984) terms this the dramatistic pentad. From the perspective of organisational strategy, the dramaturgical approach (or metaphor) lends further insight into the roles of leaders and the ontological status of organisation.

Mangham (1986) and Mangham and Overington (1987) developed Burke's original analysis to argue that executive action could best be understood as a set of roles played out much as in a theatre by individual actors. The 'play' and its interpretation are central to such a perspective. In addition, the dramaturgical perspective allows the observer of executive action (leadership) to de-mystify what is unfolding under the guise of autonomous action. Burke's work allows us to consider the 'taken for granted' nature of much action by organisational leaders. Much 'role' action is unconsciously played out on the organisational stage. Mangham and his colleagues sought to apply their perspective to organisational interventions (particularly under the rubric of change). From the perspective of the current analysis, they throw fresh light on the voluntarist–determinist debate outlined earlier.

In the extreme, the dramatist argument is that leaders have little or no 'true' voluntarist scope. Their actions and the roles they apparently choose to adopt are mostly pre-ordained in much the same way that a written play can be interpreted differently but that the pressure is for the written form to remain the same. It is an 'authorised' template for action. Empirical analysis indicates that this extreme position rarely occurs in so deterministic a fashion. For example, Bormann (1980) and Cragan and Shields (1981) have shown that managers inherit the outcomes of previous interactions between groups in the organisation. They thus inherit a 'fixed script' which includes indirect messages of past behaviours and norms. Yet, despite the strength of these messages, managers (leaders) can choose to reinterpret (rewrite) the script and escape from the historically generated parameters which set boundaries around autonomous action (Wilson *et al.* 1986).

Vaill (1989), too, argues that leaders' actions might be characterised best as a 'performing art'. There is always the play (or the 'content' of the action) but this content also has 'form' given to it by those actors who 'per-form' the part. In other words, leaders (indeed all managers) have the capacity to link form and content (what they do and how they do it) in a variety of ways. This kind of analysis is close to that described above. Yet Vaill (1989) goes further in extending the performing art metaphor. He argues that the linking of form and content is variable, but is not a completely autonomous action since there are 'artistic standards' which transcend and set parameters around actions. Thus, performing occurs in a wider context, tacitly understood by both players and audience alike. Vaill's metaphor provides one way of transcending the inherent dualism in the voluntarist–determinist debates by the introduction of context as a tacit but recognisable and powerful influence over action. No longer need the debate be couched in terms of either/or; the concepts of where and when are equally important.

The current study and the work of other scholars seem to be coalescing around the interfaces of organisational context and the individualistic and interpretive role of the leader. The impact of such debates and empirical findings should be of significant import to practitioners and scholars alike. The terrain also lends itself to consideration of future developments and we approach these in our concluding section.

CONCLUSIONS AND FUTURE RESEARCH AGENDA

This study has attempted to bridge and synthesise the relationships between context, leadership and strategy formation. To do this adequately has meant a great deal of discursive exploration into both national and economic contexts for the organisations in the study. Our deep contextual and historical approach has shown that these relationships are complex, multi-level and multi-lateral and will not easily yield their true nature to cross-sectional research. They can only be really understood in full historical perspective.

A second conclusion would be that, in the light of our findings, the simple linear chronology of organisations is also limited in its power to explain these context-history-leadership-strategy formation inter-relationships. Life cycles, for example, chart organisational history but do so in a rational, developmental way. As organisations get older, they become more formalised to the point where such formalisation becomes stifling and renewal or demise become the only strategic options. Our findings indicate that the impact of context is likely to be more potent than organisational age on factors such as change and turnaround.

The data reveal, however, that we would be wise as strategists not to base our analyses wholly at the organisational or contextual levels of analysis. There is strong evidence in all the case histories to support the more individualistic view of strategy which is 'crafted' (Mintzberg 1987) by specific individuals in specific ways. We would be confident that many of the leaders described in our study would have acted as they did irrespective of context (organisational or socio-political). It would appear that there are enduring and identifiable characteristics of leadership that emanate solely from individuals themselves.

This balance between individuals and contexts leads us into relatively untrodden intellectual terrain. Although many authors have alluded to the mixture of leadership vision, strategy content and the context in which this mix is crafted (Mintzberg and Waters 1985; Pettigrew and Whipp 1991; Bryman 1992; Whittington 1993), few have sought to combine empirically the elements of institutional and individual perspectives. Our study too goes only so far along this route yet it highlights (to us) the need for further research along a number of dimensions. Firstly, the pressing need for empirical data would seem to be very much aimed at the level of analysis of organisational governing bodies. These may be boards, trusts, stand-alone or inter-linked, but the key feature of all is that these are the forums for individual leaders to manage and create their own internal contexts. It is this context which may reveal further clues about the leadership-strategy formation linkage. The role of the board (or its equivalent) can be viewed as a smaller level of institutional analysis within the much wider contextual lens that we have adopted in this book. Our study alludes to this inner context, but more detailed data are needed if relationships between individual leaders and strategic outcomes are to be identified. It is through the social processes and mechanisms of corporate governing bodies that leaders themselves establish organisational direction by forming strategic choices amongst their peers. There is evidence that this process may well be linked to a wider context (see Judge and Zeithaml 1992 for example) whereby the degree of control exercised by the board increases as the wider context becomes more turbulent and unpredictable. However, much greater comparative data are required before we can be sure of the nature of the linkage between strategy and leaders via the boardroom.

A further area of investigation prompted by our research concerns the organisation as the unit of analysis rather than individuals or context. More precisely, the organisation as a focus of study through time would seem to be a logical area for further research. The results from the present study reveal a possible patterning of organisational development. Such a pattern may be discerned from the interaction of individual leaders with organisations over time. While there was no evidence whatsoever of pre-determination (of leaders' strategic actions), the data indicate strong evidence for constraint over the scope of strategic choice open to leaders as they accommodate strategic choices made by their predecessors, or even themselves at an earlier period. From the perspective of the organisation, the data reveal how some strategic issues span the biographies of two or more individual leaders. The question of organisational patterning thus becomes important in understanding the processes by which strategic decisions are made. Organisational patterning differs from pictures which can be built up by a historical analysis since the patterning logic of history rests on the temporal examination of sequence and consequence; the patterning logic of organisation lies in the production and reproduction of a social system through time.

Key to this organisational patterning are the notions of distinctive competences and cumulative experiences which shape and sculpt organisational action. Strategic commitments by organisations and their leaders are necessary to build and sustain such competences (like the career skills and choices of individuals – hence our preference for the 'career' metaphor in our relational model in Figure 10.2). Yet these strategic commitments are also, by their very nature, potential sources of rigidity and inflexibility in the future. They are not always easily reversed or transferred to other activities. From the present study it would appear that major patterning departures are not only difficult but also relatively rare and often risky (see the case of CSET and its diversification into convenience food processing in the 1960s – a major patterning or career departure which ended as an heroic failure).

The key issues which come out of the analysis are those of intersections both of strategic issues and of individual biographies. It is perhaps from a greater understanding of these intersections that future developments in the fields of leadership and strategy formation will come. The patterning of these intersections should be of fascination to scholars of process in organisations and, hopefully, will provide one significant basis for future empirical studies of the relationship between context, leadership and history and the process of strategy formation.

References

Abell, D. F. (1978) 'Strategic windows', *Journal of Marketing* July: 21–26.

Adorno, T. W. (1991) *The Culture Industry* (edited with, and introduction by, J. M. Bernstein), London: Routledge.

Aldrich, H. E. (1979) *Organizations and Environments*, Englewood Cliffs, NJ: Prentice-Hall.

Allison, G. T. (1971) *Essence of Decision*, Boston: Little Brown.

Andrews, C. S. (1959) 'Comments' (on S. F. Lemass 'The role of the state-sponsored bodies'), *Administration* 6, 4: 295–299.

Ansoff, H. I. (1987) *Corporate Strategy*, (revised) Harmondsworth: Penguin.

Ansoff, H. I. (1991) 'Critique of Henry Mintzberg's "The design school: reconsidering the basic premises of strategic management"', *Strategic Management Journal* 12: 449–461.

Armstrong, P., Glyn, A. and Harrison, J. (1984) *Capitalism since World War II*, London: Fontana.

Astley, W. G. (1985) 'The two ecologies: population and community perspectives on organisational evolution', *Administrative Science Quarterly* 30: 224–241.

Astley, W. G. and Van de Ven, A. H. (1983) 'Central perspectives and debates in organization theory', *Administrative Science Quarterly* 30: 245–273.

Bain, J. S. (1968) *Industrial Organization* (2nd edn), New York: Wiley.

Bennis, W. (1989) *On Becoming A Leader*, Reading, Mass.: Addison Wesley.

Bennis, W. and Nanus, B. (1985) *Leaders: The Strategies for Taking Charge*, New York: Harper & Row.

Berger, P. and Luckmann, T. (1966) *The Social Construction of Reality*, New York: Doubleday.

Blackwell, J. (1982) 'Government, economy and society' in F. Litton (ed.) *Unequal Achievement*, Dublin: IPA.

Block, P. (1991) *The Empowered Manager: Positive Political Skills at Work*, San Francisco: Jossey-Bass.

Bolger, P. (1977) *The Irish Cooperative Movement*, Dublin: IPA.

Bormann, E. G. (1980) *Communication Theory*, New York: Holt, Rinehart and Winston.

Bower, J. L. (1970) *Managing the Resource Allocation Process*, Homewood: Irwin.

Bower, J. L., Bartlett, C. A., Christensen, C. R., Pearson, A. E. and Andrews, K. R. (1991) *Business Policy: Text and Cases* (7th ed.), Homewood, Ill.: Irwin.

Bristow, J. (1982) 'State-sponsored bodies' in F. Litton (ed.) *Unequal Achievement*, Dublin: IPA.

Brophy, S. A. (1985) *The Strategic Management of Irish Enterprise 1934–84*, Dublin: Smurfit Publications.

Brown, T. (1985) *Ireland: A Social and Cultural History 1922–85*, London: Fontana.

Brunsson, N. (1982) 'The irrationality of action and action rationality: decisions, ideologies and organisational actions', *Journal of Management Studies* 19, 1: 29–44.

Bryman, A. (1986) *Leadership and Organizations*, London: Routledge.

Bryman, A. (1992) *Charisma and Leadership in Organizations*, London: Sage.

Buckland, P. (1981) *A History of Northern Ireland*, Dublin: Gill & Macmillan.

Burgleman, R. A. (1983) 'A model of the interaction of strategic behavior, corporate context, and the concept of strategy', *Academy of Management Review* 8, 1: 61–70.

Burke, K. (1984) *Permanence and Change: An Anatomy of Purpose* (3rd edn), Berkeley: University of California Press.

Burns, T. (1963) 'Industry in a new age', *New Society*, Jan 31st: 17–20.

Burns, T. and Stalker, G. M. (1961) *The Management of Innovation*, London: Tavistock.

Burrell, G. and Morgan, G. (1979) *Sociological Paradigms and Organizational Analysis*, London: Heinemann.

Byrne, J. J., Hennerty, A. J. and McKenna, R. (1963) *Report of the Survey Team on the Dairy Products Industry*, Dublin: Stationery Office

Calas, M. B. and Smircich, L. (1991) 'Voicing seduction to silence leadership', *Organization Studies* 12, 4: 567–602.

Caves, R. E. (1980) 'Industrial organization, corporate strategy and structure', *Journal of Economic Literature* XVIII: 64–92.

Chakravarthy, B. S and Doz, Y. (eds) (1992) 'Strategy process: managing corporate self-renewal', *Strategic Management Journal* (Special Issue) 13(S): 1–192.

Chandler, A. J. (1977) *The Visible Hand: The Managerial Revolution in American Business*, Cambridge Mass.: Harvard University Press.

Child, J. (1972) 'Organisational structure, environment and performance: the role of strategic choice', *Sociology* 6: 1–22.

Chubb, B. and Lynch, J. (1969) *Economic Development and Planning*, Dublin: IPA.

Clegg, S. (1975) *Power, Rule and Domination*, London: Routledge & Kegan Paul.

Cohan, A. S. (1972) *The Irish Political Elite*, Dublin: Gill & Macmillan.

Cook, H. L. and Sprague, G. W. (1968) *Irish Dairy Industry Organisation*, Dublin: Stationery Office.

Coolahan, J. (1984) 'Science and technology as elements of educational and socio-economic change in Ireland', *Administration* 32, 1: 89–99.

Coombes, D. (1983) 'Ireland's membership of the European Community: strange paradox or mere expediency' in D. Coombes (ed.) *Ireland and the European Communities*, Dublin: Gill & Macmillan.

Cragan, J. F. and Shields, D. C. (1981) *Applied Communications Research: A Dramatist Approach*, Prospect Heights, Ill.: Waveland Press.

Crozier, M. and Friedberg, E. (1980) *Actors and Systems*, Chicago: University of Chicago Press.

CSET (1986) 'The General and the poorer areas' in CSET (Company tribute to General Costello) *General Michael Joseph Costello 1904–1986*, Dublin: CSET.

Cyert, R. M. and March, J. G. (1963) *A Behavioral Theory of the Firm*, Englewood Cliffs, NJ: Prentice-Hall.

Cyert, R. M. and March, J. G. (1992) *A Behavioral Theory of the Firm* (2nd edn), Englewood Cliffs, NJ: Prentice-Hall.

Czarniawska-Joerges, B. and Wolff, R. (1991) 'Leaders on and off the organizational stage', *Organization Studies* 12, 4: 529–546.

Deming, W. E. (1986) *Out of the Crisis*, Cambridge, Mass.: MIT Center for Advanced Engineering Study.

Dicken, P. (1986) *Global Shift*, London: Harper & Row.

Di Maggio, P. and Powell, W. (1983) 'The iron cage revisited: institutional isomorphism and collective rationality in organizational fields', *American Sociology Review* 48: 147–160.

Dooney, S. (1976) *The Irish Civil Service*, Dublin: IPA.

Emerson, R. M. (1962) 'Power-dependence theory', *American Sociological Review* 27: 31–41.

Farrell, B. (1986) 'Politics and change' in K. A. Kennedy (ed.) *Ireland in Transition*, Cork: Mercier.

Fennell, D. (1986) 'Creating a new Irish identity', *Studies* 75: 392–400.

FitzGerald Government (1985) *Building On Reality*, Dublin: Stationery Office.

Flanagan, T. (1988) *Tenants of Time*, London: Bantam.

Fogarty, M. P. (1980) 'Trade unions and the future' in D. Nevin (ed.) *Trade Unions and Change in Irish Society*, Cork: Mercier.

Fombrun, C. and Shanley, M. (1990) 'What's in a name? Reputation building and corporate strategy', *Academy of Management Journal* 33, 2: 233–258.

Foy, M. (1976) *The Sugar Industry in Ireland*, Dublin: CSET

Foy, M. (1981) 'Tuam', *Biatas* XXXV: 161–174.

Foy, M. (1986). 'The General and the Sugar Company' in CSET (Company Tribute to General Costello) *General Michael Joseph Costello 1904–1986*, Dublin: CSET.

Foy, M. (1987) 'Mr. Denis Coakley', *Biatas* XL, 9: 405.

Galbraith, J. K. (1952) *American Capitalism: The Concept of Countervailing Power*, Boston: Houghton Mifflin.

Galbraith, J. K. (1963) *American Capitalism: The Concept of Countervailing Power*, Harmondsworth: Penguin.

Galbraith, J. K. (1984) *The Anatomy of Power*, London: Hamish Hamilton.

Garfinkel, H. (1967) *Studies in Ethnomethodology*, New York: Prentice-Hall.

Garvin, T. (1982) 'Change and the political system' in F. Litton (ed.) *Unequal Achievement*, Dublin: IPA.

Goffman, E. (1982) *The Presentation of Self in Everyday Life*, Harmondsworth: Penguin.

Gouldner, A. (1980) *The Two Marxisms*, London: Macmillan.

Granovetter, M. (1985) 'Economic action and social structure: the problem of embeddedness', *American Journal of Sociology* 91, 3: 481–510.

Greenwood, R. and Hinings, C. R. (1988) 'Organizational design types, tracks and the dynamics of strategic change', *Organization Studies* 9: 293–316.

Greiner, L. E. (1972) 'Evolution and revolution as organizations grow', *Harvard Business Review* 50, 4, July–August: 37–46.

Grinyer, P. H. and Spender, J. C. (1979) 'Recipies, crises and adaptation in mature businesses', *International Studies of Management and Organization* IX, 3: 113–133.

Hakansson, H. and Johanson, J. (1992) 'A model of industrial networks' in B. Axelson and G. Easton (eds) *Industrial Networks: A New View of Reality*, London: Routledge.

Hambrick, D. C. (ed.) (1989) 'Strategic leadership', *Strategic Management Journal* (Special Issue) 10(S): 1–172.

Hambrick, D. and Fukutomi, G. D. S. (1991) 'The seasons of a CEO's tenure', *Academy of Management Review* 16: 719–742.

Hamel, G. and Prahalad, C. K. (1989) 'Strategic intent', *Harvard Business Review* 67, May–June: 63–76.

Hannan, M. T. and Freeman, J. (1977) 'The population ecology of organisations', *American Journal of Sociology* 82, 5: 929–964.

Harper, S. C. (1992) 'The challenges facing CEOs: past, present and future', *The Executive* VI, 3: 7–25.

Heilbroner, R. L. and Thurow, L. C. (1975) *Understanding Microeconomics*, Englewood Cliffs, NJ: Prentice-Hall

Henderson, B. (1973) 'The experience curve revisited: the growth share matrix of the product portfolio', *Perspectives*, The Boston Consulting Group.

Hickson, D. J., Butler, R. J., Cray, D., Mallory, G. R. and Wilson, D. C. (1986) *Top Decisions: Strategic Decision Making in Organizations*, Oxford: Blackwell.

Higgins, T. (1973) 'ARMIS – a data system for research planning', *Administration* 21, 2: 182–189.

Hillery, B. (1980) 'Industrial relations: compromise and conflict', in D. Nevin (ed.) *Trade Unions and Change in Irish Society*, Cork: Mercier.

Hinings, C. R. and Greenwood, R. (1988) 'The normative prescription of organizations' in L. G. Zucker (ed.) *Institutional Patterns and Organizations: Culture and Environment*, Cambridge, MA.: Ballinger Publishing Company.

House, R. J. and Mitchell, T. R. (1974) 'Path-goal theory of leadership', *Journal of Contemporary Business*, Autumn: 81–97.

IAOS (1966) *Proposals for Re-Organisation in the Dairying Industry*, Dublin: IAOS.

IAOS (1972) *Proposals for Creamery Rationalisation*, Dublin: IAOS.

Isabella, L. A. (1990) 'Evolving interpretations as change unfolds: how managers construe key organizational events', *Academy of Management Journal* 33, 1: 7–41.

Johnson, G. (1992) 'Managing strategic change – strategy, culture and action', *Long Range Planning* 25, 1: 28–36.

Joint Committee of the Oireachtais. (1980) *Comhlucht Siuicre Eireann Teoranta*, Dublin: Stationery Office.

Judge, W. Q. (Jr) and Zeithaml, C. P. (1992) 'Institutional and strategic choice perspectives on board involvement in the strategic decision process', *Academy of Management Journal* 35, 4: 766–794.

Kanter, R. M. (1983) *The Change Masters*, New York: Simon & Schuster

Kanter, R. M. (1990) 'Values and economics' (editorial) *Harvard Business Review* 68, May–June: 4.

Katz, D. and Kahn, R. L. (1966) *The Social Psychology of Organisations*, New York: John Wiley.

Keat, R. and Abercrombie, N. (eds) (1990) *Enterprise Culture*, London: Routledge.

Kennedy, K. A. (1986) 'Industry: the revolution unfinished' in K. A. Kennedy (ed.) *Ireland in Transition*, Cork: Mercier.

Keynes, J. M. (1933) 'National self-sufficiency', *Studies* 22: 177–193.

Kimberley, J. R. and Miles, R. H. (eds) (1980) *The Organizational Life Cycle*, San Francisco: Jossey-Bass.

Knapp, J. G. (1964) *An Appraisement of Agricultural Cooperation in Ireland*, Dublin: Stationery Office.

Kotter, J. P. (1982) *The General Managers*, New York: Free Press.

Lawrence, P. R. and Lorsch, J. W. (1967) *Organization and Environment*, Boston: Harvard University Press.

Leavy, B. (1991a) 'Strategic leadership in a public sector organization: the Walsh and Ryan eras in An Foras Taluntais', *Administration* 39, 1: 17–41.

Leavy, B. (1991b) 'A process model of strategic change and industry evolution: the case of the Irish Dairy Industry 1958–74', *British Journal of Management* 2: 187–204.

Leavy, B. (1992) 'Strategic vision and inspirational leadership: two case studies' in H. E. Glass and M. A. Hovde (eds) *Handbook of Business Strategy* (1992/93 Yearbook), Boston: Warren Gorham Lamont.

Lee, J. (1979a) 'Sean Lemass' in J. Lee (ed.) *Ireland 1945–70*, Dublin: Gill and Macmillan.

Lee, J. (1979b) 'Continuity and change in Ireland 1945–70' in J. Lee (ed.) *Ireland 1945–70*, Dublin: Gill & Macmillan.

Lee, J. (1980) 'Workers and society since 1945' in D. Nevin (ed.) *Trade Unions and Change in Irish Society*, Cork: Mercier.

Lee, J. (1982) 'Society and culture' in F. Litton (ed.) *Unequal Achievement*, Dublin: IPA.

Lee, J. (1989) *Ireland 1912–1985*, Cambridge: Cambridge University Press.

Lee, J. and O'Tuathaigh, G. (1982) *The Age of de Valera*, Dublin: Ward River Press.

Lemass, S. F. (1959) 'The role of the state-sponsored bodies', *Administration* 6, 4: 277–295.

Likert, R. (1967) *The Human Organization*, New York: McGraw-Hill

Livingstone, J. M. (1966) *Britain and the World Economy*, Harmondsworth: Penguin

Lorsch, J. and MacIver, E. (1989) *Pawns or Potentates: The Reality of America's Corporate Boards*, Boston: Harvard Business School Press.

Lynch, P. (1986) 'The General and the farmer' in CSET (Company Tribute to General Costello) *General Michael Joseph Costello 1904–1986*, Dublin: CSET.

Lyons, F. S. L. (1973) *Ireland Since the Famine*, London: Fontana.

McAleese, D. (1986) 'Ireland in the world economy' in K. A. Kennedy (ed.) *Ireland in Transition*, Cork: Mercier.

McCarthy, C. (1973) *The Decade of Upheaval*, Dublin: IPA

McGuire, E. B. (1973) *Irish Whiskey*, Dublin: Gill & Macmillan.

McKiernan, P. (1992) *Strategies For Growth*, London: Routledge.

Magee, M. (1980) *1000 Years of Irish Whiskey*, Dublin: O'Brien Press.

Mangham, I. L. (1986) *Power and Performance in Organizations: An Exploration of Executive Process*, Oxford: Blackwell.

Mangham, I. L. and Overington, M. A. (1987) *Organizations as Theatre: A Social Psychology of Dramatic Appearances*, Chichester: Wiley.

Meenan, J. (1967) 'From free-trade to self-sufficiency' in F. McManus (ed.) *The Years of the Great Test 1926–39*, Cork: Mercier.

Meyer, J. W. and Rowan, B. (1977) 'Institutionalised organisations: formal structure as myth and ceremony', *American Journal of Sociology* 83: 340–363.

Miller, D. and Friesen, P. H. (1980) 'Momentum and revolution in organisational adaptation', *Academy of Management Journal* 23, 4: 591–614.

Mills, C. W. (1970) *The Sociological Imagination*, Harmondsworth: Penguin.

Mintzberg, H. (1978) 'Patterns in strategy formation', *Management Science* 24: 934–948.

Mintzberg, H. (1979) 'An emerging strategy of 'direct' research', *Administrative Science Quarterly* 24: 582–589.

Mintzberg, H. (1983) *Power In and Around Organizations*, Englewood Cliffs, NJ: Prentice-Hall.

Mintzberg, H. (1984) 'Power and organizational life cycles', *Academy of Management Review* April: 207–224.

Mintzberg, H. (1987) 'Crafting strategy', *Harvard Business Review* 65, July–August: 66–75.

Mintzberg, H. (1990) 'The design school: reconsidering the basic premises of strategic management', *Strategic Management Journal* 11: 171–195.

Mintzberg, H. (1991) 'Learning 1, Planning 0: reply to Igor Ansoff', *Strategic Management Journal* 12: 463–466.

Mintzberg, H. and Waters, J. A. (1985) 'Of strategies, deliberate and emergent', *Strategic Management Journal* 6: 257–272.

Montgomery, C. (ed.) (1988) 'Strategy content research', *Strategic Management Journal* (Special Issue) 9(S): 1–142.

Nanus, B. (1992) *Visionary Leadership: Creating a Compelling Sense of Direction for your Organization*, San Francisco: Jossey-Bass.

Neary, P. (1984) 'The failure of economic nationalism', *The Crane Bag* 8, 1: 68–77.

Norburn, D. (1984) 'The British boardroom: time for a revolution?', *Long Range Planning* 17, 5: 35–44.

Nowlan, K. B. (1967) 'President Cosgrave's last Administration' in F. McManus (ed.) *The Years of the Great test 1926–39*, Cork: Mercier.

Nye, R. B. and Morpurgo, J. E. (1965) *The Growth of the USA*, Harmondsworth: Penguin.

O'Brien, C. C. (1972) *States of Ireland*, New York: Pantheon Books.

O'Brien, G. (1962) 'The economic progress of Ireland', *Studies* 51: 9–26.

O'Malley, P. (1983) *The Uncivil Wars*, Belfast: Blackstaff.

Osborne, R. L. (1991) 'The dark side of the entrepreneur', *Long Range Planning* 24, 3: 26–31.

O'Sullivan, M. (1973) 'Policy for research and development', *Administration* 21, 2: 157–165.

Packenham, F. (1951) *Peace By Ordeal*, Cork: Mercier.

Pennings, J. M. (ed.) (1985) *Organisational Strategy and Change*, San Francisco: Jossey-Bass.

Perrow, C. (1970) *Organizational Analysis: A Sociological View*, Belmont, CA.: Wadsworth.

Pettigrew, A. M. (1979) 'On studying organisational cultures', *Administrative Science Quarterly* 24: 570–581.

Pettigrew, A. M. (1985) *The Awakening Giant*, Oxford: Blackwell.

Pettigrew, A. M. (1987) 'Researching strategic change', in A. M. Pettigrew (ed.) *The Management of Strategic Change*, Oxford: Blackwell.

Pettigrew, A. M (1990) 'Longitudinal field research on change: theory and practice', *Organisational Science* 1: 267–292.

Pettigrew, A. M. and Whipp, R. (1991) *Managing Change for Competitive Success*, Oxford: Blackwell.

Pfeffer, J. (1982) *Organizations and Organization Theory*, Boston: Pitman

Pfeffer, J. and Salancik, G. R. (1978) *The External Control of Organisations*, New York: Harper & Row.

Plunkett, H. C. (1904) *Ireland in the New Century*, London: John Murray

Porter, M. E. (1979) 'How competitive forces shape strategy', *Harvard Business Review* 57, March–April: 137–145.

Porter, M. E. (1980) *Competitive Strategy*, New York: Free Press.

Porter, M. E. (1981) 'The contributions of industrial organisation to strategic management', *Academy of Management Review* 6: 609–620.

Porter, M. E. (1985) *Competitive Advantage*, New York: Free Press.

Porter, M. E. (1990) *The Competitive Advantage of Nations*, New York: Free Press

Porter, M. E. (1991) 'Towards a dynamic theory of strategy', *Strategic Management Journal* 12: 95–117.

Pugh, D., Hickson, D. J. and Hinings, R. (1969) 'The context of organizational structures', *Administrative Science Quarterly* 14: 91–114.

Quinn, J. B. (1980) *Strategies for Change*, Homewood, Ill.: R. D. Irwin.

Romanelli, E. and Tushman, M. L. (1983) 'Executive leadership and organisational outcomes: an evolutionary perspective', Working Paper 508A: Columbia University.

Rottman, D. and O'Connell, P. (1982) 'The changing social structure of Ireland', in F. Litton (ed.) *Unequal Achievement*, Dublin: IPA.

Scherer, F. M. (1970) *Industrial Market Structure and Economic Performance*, Chicago: Rand McNally.

Schlesinger, A. M. (1965) *A Thousand Days – JFK in the White House*, London: Andre Deutsch.

Schneider, S. S. (ed.) (1991) 'Interpreting organizational leadership', *Organization Studies* (Special Issue) 12, 4: 489–632.

Schoeffler, S., Buzzell, R. D. and Heany, D. F. (1974) 'Impact of strategic planning on profit performance', *Harvard Business Review*, March–April: 137–145.

Schumpeter, J. A. (1934) *The Theory of Economic Development*, Oxford: Oxford University Press.

Sculley, J. (1987) Odyssey: Pepsi to Apple (with J. A. Byrne), London: Fontana.

Shaeffer, R. (1984) *Developing Strategic Leadership*, New York: The Conference Board (Report Number 847).

Shaw, F. (1972) 'The canon of Irish History – a challenge', *Studies* 61: 117– 153.

Sheehan, J. (1979) 'Education and society in Ireland, 1945–70' in J. Lee (ed.) *Ireland 1945–70*, Dublin: Gill & Macmillan.

Silverman, D. (1970) *The Theory of Organisations*, London: Heineman.

Sodersten, B. (1980) *International Economics* (2nd edn), London: Macmillan.

Staw, B. M. (1976) 'Knee-deep in the big muddy: a study of escalating commitment to a chosen course of action', *Organization Behaviour and Human Performance* 16: 27–44.

Stogdill, R. M. (1974) *Handbook of Leadership*, New York: Free Press.

Sudnow, D. (1967) *Passing On: The Psychology of Dying*, New York: Prentice-Hall.

Telesis Consultancy Group (1982) *A Review of Industrial Policy*, Dublin: NESC.

Thompson, D. (1966) *Europe Since Napoleon*, Harmondsworth: Penguin.

Thompson, J. D. (1967) *Organisations in Action*, New York: McGraw-Hill

Thurow, L. C. (1987) *The Zero-Sum Solution* (revised edn), Harmondsworth: Penguin.

Tobin, F. (1984) *The Best of Decades: (Ireland in the 1960's)*, Dublin: Gill & Macmillan.

Tushman, M. L. and Romanelli, E. (1983) 'Organizational evolution: a metamorphosis model of convergence and re-orientation', Working Paper, Graduate School of Business, Columbia University.

Useem, M. and McCormack, A. (1981) 'The dominant segment of the British business elite', *Sociology* 15: 381–406.

Vaill, P. B. (1989) *Managing as a Performing Art*, San Francisco: Jossey-Bass

Von Bertalanffy, L. (1950) 'The theory of open systems in physics and biology', *Science*, January 13th: 23–29.

Vroom, V. and Yetton, P. (1973) *Leadership and Decision Making*, Pittsburg: University of Pittsburg Press.

Walsh, B. (1979) 'Economic growth and development 1945–70' in J. Lee (ed.) *Ireland 1945–70*, Dublin: Gill & Macmillan.

Walsh, T. (1980) 'Rural development', *The Dr. Henry Kennedy Memorial Lecture*, Dublin: ICOS.

Walsh, T. (1981) 'Developing our disadvantaged rural areas', *The O'Dalaigh Lecture*, Dublin: ACOT.

Walsh, T. (1984) 'Developing national potential in the new era', *Series of Occasional Papers*, No. 1, Dublin: NCEA.

Weick, K. E. (1977) 'Enactment processes in organisations', in B. M. Staw and G. R. Salancik (eds) *New Directions in Organizational Behaviour*, New York: Wiley.

Whitaker, T. K. (1958) *Economic Development*, Dublin: Stationery Office.

Whittington, R. (1993) *What is Strategy – And Does It Matter?*, London: Routledge.

Whyte, J. H. (1980) *Church and State in Modern Ireland 1923–79* (2nd ed.), Dublin: Gill & Macmillan.

Williamson, O. E. (1975) *Markets and Hierarchies: Analysis and Antitrust Implications*, New York: Free Press.

Wilson, D. C. (1992) *A Strategy of Change*, London: Routledge

Wilson, D. C., Butler, R. J., Cray, D., Hickson, D. J. and Mallory, G. R. (1986) 'Breaking the bounds of organization in strategic decision making', *Human Relations* 39, 4: 309–331.

Woodward, J. (1965) *Industrial Organisation: Theory and Practice*, London: Oxford University Press.

Woodward, J. (1970) *Industrial Organisation: Behaviour and Control*, London: Oxford University Press.

Zaleznik, A. (1992) 'Managers and leaders: are they different?' (1977 classic with retrospective comment), *Harvard Business Review* 70, March–April: 126–135.

Zucker, L. G. (ed.) (1988) *Institutional Patterns and Organizations: Culture and Environment*, Cambridge, MA.: Ballinger Publishing Company.

Name index

Subject index